T0372504

Palgrave Studies in the History of Economic Thought

Series Editors
Avi J. Cohen
Department of Economics
York University & University of Toronto
Toronto, ON, Canada

G. C. Harcourt
School of Economics
University of New South Wales
Sydney, NSW, Australia

Peter Kriesler
School of Economics
University of New South Wales
Sydney, NSW, Australia

Jan Toporowski
Economics Department
SOAS University of London
London, UK

Palgrave Studies in the History of Economic Thought publishes contributions by leading scholars, illuminating key events, theories and individuals that have had a lasting impact on the development of modern-day economics. The topics covered include the development of economies, institutions and theories.

The series aims to highlight the academic importance of the history of economic thought, linking it with wider discussions within economics and society more generally. It contains a broad range of titles that illustrate the breath of discussions – from influential economists and schools of thought, through to historical and modern social trends and challenges – within the discipline.

All books in the series undergo a single-blind peer review at both the proposal and manuscript submission stages.

For further information on the series and to submit a proposal for consideration, please contact the Wyndham Hacket Pain (Economics Editor) wyndham.hacketpain@palgrave.com.

Pervez Tahir

Joan Robinson in Princely India

palgrave
macmillan

Pervez Tahir
Economics
Council of Social Sciences (COSS), Pakistan
Islamabad, Pakistan

ISSN 2662-6578   ISSN 2662-6586   (electronic)
Palgrave Studies in the History of Economic Thought
ISBN 978-3-031-10904-1   ISBN 978-3-031-10905-8   (eBook)
https://doi.org/10.1007/978-3-031-10905-8

Cover illustration: Joan Violet Robinson by Walter Bird bromide print, February 1959 ©
National Portrait Gallery, London

This Palgrave Macmillan imprint is published by the registered company Springer Nature
Switzerland AG.
The registered company address is: Gewerbestrasse 11, 6330 Cham, Switzerland

In the loving memory Geoff Harcourt, my mentor, who celebrated his 90th birthday on 27 June 2021 and left the world he struggled throughout his life to make 'a better place for ordinary men and women' and 'a more just and equitable society' on 7 December 2021. May he rest in eternal peace and may Joan and Wendy Harcourt have the patience to bear the irreparable loss. Tracy Mott, an inspiring teacher, passed away on 4 November 2021. The book is also dedicated to him.

PREFACE

It seems that the 'provocative'[1] Joan Robinson continues to provoke the practitioners of the dismal science even long after her death. The writing of this book is an example. On 29 January 29 2020, the Social Policy and Development Centre (SPDC), an independent thinktank, and the Department of Economics, University of Karachi, organized the launch ceremony of my book on Joan Robinson's writings on China[2] in Karachi, Pakistan. One of the panellists, Dr Arshad Zaman, a distinguished Pakistani economist, drew my attention to a statement made by Alec Cairncross in his biography of Sir Austin Robinson. Cairncross observed:

> The difficulty of establishing the authorship of particular passages is illustrated by the experience of the unfortunate student who submitted a PhD dissertation at Cambridge with the firm conviction that *The British Crown and the Indian States* was the work of Joan, not Austin, Robinson.[3]

The 'unfortunate student' was none other than this writer. In that fateful June of 1988, I submitted my dissertation for the degree of PhD in Economics at the Faculty of Economics and Politics, University of Cambridge. The dissertation dealt with the early contributions of Joan Robinson, Sir Austin Robinson's wife.[4] It contained four essays, two of these relating to her work while in the state of Gwalior in the Princely India towards the end of the 1920s. This work was published in the book[5] referred to by Cairncross. A revised dissertation was submitted in 1990 after dropping the two contested essays.[6] This book tells my side of the story in the light of information not available at the time.

I had never known Joan Robinson—not even from a distance. It gave me an advantage. My dissertation was not the artwork of a devotee. It could have been a grave disadvantage. That did not happen. With the late Geoff Harcourt as my supervisor, I could not have gone wrong on backgrounds, intellectual environments of idea formulation, nuances, prejudices and sensitivities. All this does not even begin to indicate how much the dissertation owed to him. He read each word, made stylistic improvements and weeded out the 'un-English' in my English and the nonsensical in my economics. Peter Nolan, my faculty advisor, acted as a development critic. Many of the arguments were drastically recast in the light of his valuable comments. I wish to sincerely thank him for his time and effort. I also thank the chairman of the committee, W.J. Macpherson, for his interest in the progress of my work.

Sukhamoy Chakravarty was especially kind. I had the opportunity to discuss my work with him whenever he was in Cambridge and the benefit of written comments on parts of the work when he was in Delhi. The dissertation involved some historical details and analysis, an area totally unknown to me. I am grateful to Gordon Johnson for going through the relevant parts at a very short notice and making invaluable comments.

I consider myself extremely fortunate in having been granted an interview by Lord Kahn to discuss Joan Robinson's life and work. Among other interviews, I must acknowledge my debt of gratitude to Gamni Correa, Ajit Singh and Ronald Berger.

The dissertation inevitably required a lot of correspondence. Space considerations force me to be selective. But I must put on record my deepest appreciation to Sol Adler, Robert Clower, T.N. Krishnan, Tracy Mott, K.N. Prasad, Carl Riskin, K.N. Raj, Juliet Schor and Michael Weinstein.

Thanks are due to the cooperative staff of the following Cambridge libraries: Marshall, University, Centre for South Asian Studies, Selwyn College, Social and Political Science, and History. I am indebted to King's College Library for permission to use its JVR Collection and especially for the knowledgeable assistance of its modem archivist, Michael Halls. Among the London libraries, I wish to thank the staff at the India Office, the London School of Economics and the School of Oriental and African Studies.

Thanks are also due to Marjorie S. Turner for generously allowing me to quote from her interview with Sir Austin before she published her book.

While I was working on this book, Mauro Boianovsky and Gerardo Serra sent an encouraging email, saying: 'JVR continues to be a mine of material for historians of thought. JVR (and Austin) in India is certainly an interesting topic'. I am really grateful for their encouragement.

Special thanks are due to the series editors and external reviewers whose critiques helped me to add value to the final product.

At Palgrave Macmillan, Wyndham Hacket Pain, Ruth Jenner, Karthika Devi and Sugapriya Jaganathan deserve all praise for scrupulously supervising and facilitating the editing and publishing of the book.

Lastly, no one but me is responsible for the errors of omission and commission.

Islamabad, Pakistan   Pervez Tahir
12 June 2022

NOTES

1. Aslanbeigui Nahid and Guy Oakes (2009) *The Provocative Joan Robinson: The Making of a Cambridge Economist*. Durham, NC: Duke University Press.
2. Pervez Tahir (2019) *Making Sense of Joan Robinson on China*. London: Palgrave Macmillan.
3. Cairncross, Alec (1993) *Austin Robinson: The Life of an Economic Adviser.* London: Palgrave Macmillan, p. 30. Although reprinted in 2016, I must confess I was completely unaware of the publication of the book.
4. Pervez Tahir (1988) Some Aspects of Development and Underdevelopment: Critical Perspectives on the Early Contributions of Joan Robinson. Unpublished manuscript.
5. *The British Crown and the Indian States* (1929), London: P.S. King & Son.
6. Pervez Tahir (1990) Some Aspects of Development and Underdevelopment: Critical Perspectives on Joan Robinson, PhD dissertation, University of Cambridge.

CONTENTS

About the Author

Pervez Tahir is the President of the Council of Social Sciences (COSS), Pakistan, and holds a PhD in Economics from the University of Cambridge. He has served in various economic ministries of the Government of Pakistan. He was the longest serving Chief Economist of the Planning Commission. He also served as the Chairman of the Bank of Punjab. Tahir held the Joan Robinson Memorial Lectureship at Cambridge, Mahbub-ul-Haq Chair at GCU, Lahore, and headed the Economics Department at FCC University, Lahore. He is a senior visiting fellow of Pakistan Institute of Development Economics. He was also a member of the Statistical Advisory Panel of UNDP's Human Development Report. Author of three and editor of three books, the latest just brought out by Palgrave Macmillan of London, he has published numerous journal and newspaper articles at home and abroad. He writes a weekly column for the *Express Tribune*.

ABBREVIATIONS

COP	Chamber of Princes
DCs	Developed countries
DCSP	Directorate of the Chamber's Special Organisation
DSO	Directorate of the Special Organisation
EAGR	Edward Austin Gossage Robinson
GNP	Gross national product
ICS	Indian Civil Service
IEA	International Economic Association
ILO	International Labour Office
IOR	India Office Records
IRTC	Indian Round Table Conference
ISC	Indian States Committee
ISEC (F)	Indian States Enquiry Committee (Financial)
ISFEC	Indian States Finance Enquiry Committee
JVRC	Joan Violet Robinson Collection
LDCs	Less developed countries
RCICF	Royal Commission on Indian Currency and Finance
RIIC	Report of the Indian Industrial Commission
SCCOP	Standing Committee of the Chamber of Princes
UN	United Nations

LIST OF TABLES

CHAPTER 1

Introduction

Joan Robinson was a great economist and an influential public intellectual. This book focuses on her earliest work and less known activities, relating directly or indirectly to economic development in the underdeveloped economies. A publication, *The British Crown and the Indian States*, that remained unnoticed until after the death of Joan Robinson in 1983 is the main source. It dealt with the economic relations between the British India and Princely India. This is not to say that her later work is ignored. The early contributions and experience determine the set of issues discussed here. The later work is introduced whenever an early insight or argument seems to link up with it, not only as a reflection of the intellectual development of their author but, more importantly, as essential elements of the critical perspectives presented in the following pages.

When an economist achieves the eminence that Joan Robinson did, especially against great odds, every aspect of the life and work of the person assumes significance. This book explores one such aspect. In her undergraduate days at Cambridge, she felt frustrated with what was being taught. From the study of history in school and economics at the university, she yearned to understand poverty and backwardness. Being a woman was a grave disadvantage. At the university, she was graded a poor second. She could not have been awarded a degree even if she got a first because of being a woman. Regardless, she refused to become a woman throughout her career. She understood it was a man's world. She worked and

© The Author(s), under exclusive license to Springer Nature Switzerland AG 2022
P. Tahir, *Joan Robinson in Princely India*, Palgrave Studies in the History of Economic Thought,
https://doi.org/10.1007/978-3-031-10905-8_1

behaved like a man, never using the woman card. So much so that she was accused of being a bad mother, although she was as good a mother as any other working woman and certainly a very good grandmother. It seems the critics actually wanted to say that she was not a good wife. However, this is said of all women who do better than their husbands in professional life.

After finishing her Tripos at Girton College, Cambridge, Joan Maurice married Austin Robinson in 1926. Then E.A.G. Robinson, Austin was a Fellow at Corpus Christi College. She was instrumental in finding a job for him in the princely state of Gwalior in colonial India. Officials Gwalior were searching for a suitable tutor for their minor Maharajah. They approached Theodore Morrison, who had headed the Osmania University in the princely state of Hyderabad, the largest state of Princely India. Joan Robinson, friends with Morrison's daughter, proposed her husband's name and brought the offer to him. The couple left for Gwalior in the same year. In the literature, she has routinely been described as a wife accompanying the husband. This book shows they went their separate ways professionally very early in their lives and work, with Joan displaying signs of prominence from the very beginning.

While in Gwalior, the Robinsons studied the economic relationship between the backward Princely India and relatively developed British India. Their contributions were published in 1929 in the book *The British Crown and the Indian States*. Part I looks at the controversy surrounding this book.

Chapter 2 sets the stage. During the colonial period, and long after the end of colonialism in the postwar world, many presumed that India then was British India. In fact, there were two Indias—British India and Princely India. Some described the latter as Indian India. British India, divided into provinces and districts, was ruled directly by London, appointing viceroys who in turn managed through the British governors of the provinces and the Indian Civil Service in the districts. Princely India, on the other hand, consisted of a large number of states. These states were ruled by the hereditary princes under various treaties and agreements signed with the paramount power. Other than the matters of defence and external affairs, these states enjoyed quasi-autonomy in their internal affairs. A British resident officer was stationed in the states to protect the imperial interests. These officers came from the Foreign and Political Department of the government of British India, with its Political wing dealing with the princely states. Due to its interference with impunity into the affairs of the states, the Political wing itself was a bone of contention.

The princely state of Gwalior, where Joan Robinson resided for about two years, was the fourth largest state of Princely India. In the event of a ruler dying without leaving an adult prince behind, the British seized on the opportunity to enforce direct rule by setting up a minority council, run effectively by the British Resident posted in the state, until the minor royal qualified to ascend to the throne. The heir to the throne was trained by the British tutors. In the case of Gwalior, the minority council was headed by the elder Maharani but managed by the resident. E.A.G. Robinson was appointed tutor to the minor Maharaja, who was born to the junior Maharani. Joan Robinson taught in a local college. When the Robinsons were not tutoring or teaching, it was a life of leisure and fun, of witnessing intrigues in the palace, with the two Maharanis competing for control over the minor Maharaja and the Darbar. Joan Robinson was bored with this lifestyle.

Soon she got a chance to be productive when a committee arrived from London to investigate the fiscal and financial relations between the British India and Princely India. The case of the princes presented before this committee was published in *The British Crown and the Indian States.* In Chap. 3, it is pointed out that neither Joan Robinson's writings nor her archives cited *The British Crown and the Indian States.* Same is true of Austin Robinson's writings. There were, however, indications and suggestions of Joan Robinson's involvement in the work related to this committee, commonly known as the Butler Committee, in the JVR Collection of archives and a few publications appearing soon after her death in 1983. It was for this committee that Joan Robinson was asked to assist in the preparation of the case for Princely India. Austin Robinson helped in his spare moments. Thus, before she could grapple with the problems of a serious, rational economics, she was presented with an opportunity to study poverty and backwardness at its worst.

Chapter 4 narrates the story of how this author discovered the existence of *The British Crown and the Indian States.* An Indian author, K.M. Panikkar, claimed in his autobiography that he had contributed the political part of the book and Joan Robinson had contributed the economic part. With this unequivocal attribution, this author completed his doctoral dissertation at Cambridge and submitted it in 1988. At that time, Austin Robinson claimed that he had contributed the major part of the study. Neither he nor anyone else challenged the contention of Panikkar. Chapter 5 reviews the developments after 1988. Austin Robinson's unpublished papers became available. These papers confirm that Austin

Robinson was not aware of the publication of the study. There is, however, a draft in the papers with some corrections made by Joan Robinson. In 1993, Austin Robinson's official biographer, Alec Cairncross, gave full credit to him for the authorship of the study. In 2009, Aslanbeigui and Oakes searched Austin Robinson's unpublished papers and attributed to Joan Robinson a joint note on an unidentified topic, separate notes on railways and salt. In the same archives, there exists a section on customs revenue. Of course, all these are topics in applied economics, a specialization of Austin Robinson. Joan Robinson was also working on a preface, besides her generally agreed role in the overall drafting of the report.

Part II places Joan Robinson in the perspective of her involvement in the study published in *The British Crown and the Indian States*. She participated in discussions of resource transfer in the context of poverty and backwardness of Princely India. An attempt is made to connect this experience to her later writings on development and underdevelopment. Chapter 6 deals with Joan Robinson's understanding of the problem of underdevelopment or backwardness, as it then was called. It is a precolonial condition, dominated by villages. The descriptive features of the village economy are similar to those in Marx's works on India. It is stagnant due to a social rather than a productive division of labour. The relevance of the vent-for-surplus theory is examined along with Marshall's problems with increasing returns. In the rejection of the evolutionist view implied in the interpretation of underdevelopment in India are seen the origins of her eventual break with Marshall. Like Marx, the village economy is viewed as lacking in autocentric dynamic. An analytical story is constructed to illustrate the relationship between caste, hereditary division of labour and static socio-economic organization.

Chapter 7 describes how colonial development brings about Western industrialism by breaking up the village economy and elimination of the hereditary division of labour. Marx is followed again, unknowingly. External forces or the international division of labour is forced by colonialism with the British Indian state providing the infrastructure. Princely India was backward relative to British India due to weaker external penetration. Marx had talked of the slower dissolving effects on the internal solidity of the precapitalist mode of production, but the study focuses on the continued predominance of agriculture and a slower development of internal trade. Nationalism is also examined as a theory of development. The study disputes the Indian nationalists' claim that India was perfectly adapted to industrialization. With a low per capita consumption of manufactures, the study asserts that India had a long way to go on the path of Western economic history. As the study was essentially examining the unfair treatment of Princely India by British India, it shied away from the arguments presented by the economic nationalists in British India.

On return from Gwalior to England, Joan Robinson was fascinated by analytical optimism. Subsequently, she was pessimistic about capitalist industrialization in underdeveloped economies. Chapter 8 relates the shift to the influence of the experience of the Indian reality. It is argued that the earlier scepticism about the pace of industrial development in colonial India was the source of her later search for alternatives to capitalist industrialization. *The British Crown and the Indian States* located the central focus on industrialization. In days to come, she would advocate the socialist alternative not as an ideology, but as an accelerator of industrialization.

These were some general considerations of development furnishing the background of the question of economic and financial relations between British India and Princely India. Next, Part III spells out the *raison d'etre* of *The British Crown and the Indian States*—the extent of resource transfer from Princely India to British India. It brings out the applied nature of the work and Austin Robinson's clear stamp on it. Joan Robinson was never known for this kind of work. However, she had no known specialization at the time. It was too early, anyway, for a fresh graduate. She did assist and contribute to a smaller extent, even in applied work. This is where, it seems, she developed a long-lasting distaste for applied work and a passion for theory. She would be acknowledged by Keynes in *General Theory*, not Austin Robinson, though both were active members of the Cambridge Circus.

Chapter 9 shows the estimates of the net resource outflow from Princely India to British India. The Robinsons thought and, in terms of policy, recommended prescriptions like modem applied development economists. The case was made on the basis of estimates by using whatever passed in the name of statistics in the princely states, or by making intelligent guesses, an experience that most early development economists would go through in countries with inadequate or no data at all. Fiscal transfers extracted by British India from Princely India were without, in most instances, any quid pro quo. The study worked out the liabilities of the states on account of defence and other major heads of expenditure; the method by which were estimated their contributions through customs and other taxes and state monopolies; and the way the net direction of resource transfer was kept towards British India. There was also an evaluation of the estimation procedure adopted.

The liabilities of the states consisted mainly of defence, debt servicing, transport and communications and public works. It will be seen in Chap. 10 that the study did not make a detailed analysis of liabilities. The states were not liable to contribute tax revenue towards defence expenditure and related debt as they had bartered their external sovereignty for it. Again, a quid pro quo existed between defence and direct tributes in cash and kind. Railways, ports and irrigation were profitable, self-financing ventures, and roads were not a central responsibility. To the extent they were able to cover their current costs and capital charges, the states were not liable. In regard to the British Indian public expenditure, the conclusion of the study was that no significant liability arose for the princely states. Still, British India exacted revenues out of the states, through its taxes, monopoly price policies and profits on currency and mints. To the extent that the states were making these contributions without being liable, there was taking place a net transfer of resources from Princely India to British India. Chapter 11 outlines the estimation procedures of revenue contribution, giving a flavour of the applied economist that Austin Robinson would become in future. We also see Joan Robinson attempting applied work in regard to salt monopoly and railways. Considering that the study was carried out before they embarked on proper academic careers at Cambridge, the exercise shows an impressive skill to analyse insufficient data to reach a plausible set of conclusions. They also display an early understanding of how policy can be influenced by keeping the sights low.

Indian nationalists blamed the drain of resources from India to the colonial power as the main reason for backwardness. The controversy over the drain of resources, its relationship with backwardness and the role of the state are covered in Part IV. We attempt an interpretation of the role the estimated resource transfer seems to play in *The British Crown and the Indian States* and Joan Robinson's views on development. Chapter 12 dwells on the drain controversy. It is argued that the analysis does not purport to explain backwardness in terms of resource transfers, as the early Indian drain theorists had done and as the surplus transfer theorists were to do later. Princely India was backward compared to British India because their relative political autonomy preserved their static economic organization longer than in British India. This did not prevent the authors of *The British Crown and the Indian States* from making a case for the reversal of the transfer of resources to the Princely India in order to implement a development strategy which was later dubbed as the modernization paradigm. The transfer of resources was not in the nature of drain, and the old or the modern interpretations of drain linked to backwardness did not hold. It was not the principal factor responsible for the backwardness of the states. The question of transfer of resources was kept separate from the causes of backwardness. The transfer was an unjust imposition, but its connection with backwardness is not easily proved. The states were backward because of their poor resource endowment and weak integration with British India. Economic backwardness was a pre-existing, precolonial condition that had persisted in the shape of self-sufficient villages. It began to change in British India earlier than in Princely India due to the archaic ruling structures allowed to persist by their quasi-autonomy. The analysis of resource transfer in *The British Crown and the Indian* States was based on the benefit principle of taxation. The states were being taxed without benefiting from public spending by British India. The presumption was that if these resources were made available to the states, they will be utilized for capital accumulation.

Chapter 13 brings out the role of the state and deals with the question as to who would utilize the reverse flow of resources and how. It investigates the role of the state in Princely India, especially in the somewhat progressive states. The rationale is provided, not necessarily by market failure, but by the modernizing and imitative goals of some rulers and their ministers, who eschewed conservatism as an economic creed. Joan Robinson is known as a great advocate of an effective role of the state, socialist or other, in accelerating capital accumulation in the developing countries. The case argued for the Princely India by Joan Robinson was constructed around the need for capital and its utilization for enabling them to emerge out of industrial backwardness. The concern here is with the *dramatis personae* of capital accumulation. With the persistence of earlier, static economic organization, development had to be made to happen. A role was being assumed by the state. A link does seem to exist between Joan Robinson's later view of a strong state and the earlier experience of a group of modernizing princely states which managed, to some extent, to overcome the corruption and anachronisms of the ruling oligarchies of the general body of the states.

Finally, we put it all together in the concluding Chap. 14. On the cover of *The British Crown and the Indian States,* the byline was 'The Directorate of the Chamber's Special Organisation'. The Chamber, of course, was the Chamber of Princes. By self-admission that has not been contradicted so far, 'PART L. A Consideration of the Evolution of Political Relationship Between the Crown and the States' was written by K.M. Panikkar. Panikkar attributed 'PART II. An Examination of Some Aspects of the Fiscal Questions at Issue Between the States and the Government of India' solely to Joan Robinson—'Mrs Austin Robinson,' as he put it. Panikkar's attribution to Joan Robinson has never been challenged specifically. However, Austin Robinson Papers at the Marshall Library of Economics suggest that most of the sections and the basic applied work were contributed by Austin Robinson. He himself claimed as much. Joan Robinson oversaw the process and reviewed and edited Austin Robinson's contributions in the light of the presentational requirements of the Directorate of the Chamber's Special Organisation, besides making specific contributions on state monopolies, namely, salt and railways.

All said and done, the experience in Princely India laid the origins of Joan Robinson's interest in the problems of underdevelopment and development. The last chapter juxtaposes her early exposure to the problems of underdevelopment and development in the Princely India and her later contributions to the economics of development. An effort is made to place the analysis and ideas of Joan Robinson in the perspective of the development notions prevailing at the time of drafting parts of *The British Crown and the Indian States* as well as the perspective of pioneering development economics.

To put her idea of progress in the Princely India study of the twenties in schematic terms: development was coextensive with European industrialization, which required capital formation to counteract the effect of growth of population. As the states were too poor to mobilize adequate resources, a case was prepared to keep within the states the resources being transferred to British India. A point of enormous contemporary significance is that the backwardness was blamed not on the externally manipulated resource transfer but on the internally preserved structure of the static village economy. The transfer of resources became significant only after the end of the free trade. Underdevelopment was a pre-existing condition, perpetuated by the laissez-faire attitude of the conservative rulers of the princely states. Surplus transfer or unequal exchange never appealed to her as the major determinants of backwardness.

The two well-known presumptions in Joan Robinson's later work on development are noticeable in her earliest confrontation with the problem of poverty and backwardness. These relate to the emphasis on fixed capital, referring essentially to the creation of industrial assets and supportive infrastructure, and the role of the state. Compared to the modern usage of underdevelopment, the term backwardness was not vague in suggesting what was involved in outgrowing it. Development was like a ladder: British India had to catch up with Europe, and the Princely India had to catch up with British India. The farther down the ladder a country was, the greater the role for the state accumulation.

At the time, a federation keeping the British connection and an all-India *Zollverein* seemed the best that could be hoped for by way of economic and political advance. The focus was on finding practical ways to overcome the obstacles to development in this direction. There were serious economic problems to be sorted out before an arrangement acceptable to the princes could be worked out, so as to elicit their willing cooperation for the federal project and an economic Zollverein. Joan Robinson's contribution must be seen in the light of these efforts to preserve an Indian economic community. The Indian nationalists would not hesitate to make short work of the princes, not the then Joan Robinson, who worked from the side of Princely India on the *Zollverein* project. Her connection was with Princely India, through an interest excited by the challenge of development in an extremely complex sociopolitical environment.

In the Land of Princes

CHAPTER 2

An Unseemly *Memsaab*

In the second half of 1920s, Joan and Austin Robinson sailed to India and spent about two years in the princely state of Gwalior in colonial India. During this period, the Robinsons studied the lopsided economic relationship between the backward Princely India and relatively advanced British India. Their contributions were published in book form, but both the Robinsons and the economics discipline were not aware of it for a long time. Part I tells the story of its discovery and the resulting controversy.

During her long and eventful career as an economist, Joan Robinson undertook many visits to the less developed countries (LDCs). While her main work focused on the theoretical formulations of the mature economies of the developed countries (DCs), which according to Paul Samuelson 'had a major impact on three generations of economists',[1] she visited the LDCs for first-hand impressions, information gathering and gaining insights and knowledge to be able to guide development policy-making in the Third World.

Her visits to China, Sri Lanka, North Korea, Pakistan and India after independence in 1947 and Latin America are well-known, as are many of the related writings. However, Joan Robinson's longest ever visit abroad was to Gwalior, one of the larger states of Princely India, in the late 1920s. Not much was known about this sojourn of hers until her death in 1983, except the bare facts that after completing her Tripos from Cambridge, she married E.A.G. Robinson and accompanied him to India. Mr Robinson

© The Author(s), under exclusive license to Springer Nature   13
Switzerland AG 2022
P. Tahir, *Joan Robinson in Princely India*, Palgrave Studies in the
History of Economic Thought,
https://doi.org/10.1007/978-3-031-10905-8_2

had been appointed tutor of the minor Maharaja of Gwalior. This chapter seeks to throw some light on this less known India in general and the Gwalior state in particular. The idea is to provide a background to the political, economic, administrative and cultural environment in which the Robinsons worked and performed their respective roles. More specifically, we ask the question whether Joan Robinson was just there as a *Memsaab*, an expression used for the wife of an English official.

GUN SALUTE STATES

Before 1947, there were two Indias, defined by their respective relationship with the British Crown. One, and the better known, was British India under the direct rule of the British Crown. The other, less known, was Princely India, comprising of some 600 semi-autonomous states of varying sizes. Around 60 per cent of the territory consisted of provinces that were part of the British India. The rest of the territory comprised of a large number of princely states under various treaties between the British Crown and the native princes. These treaties, concluded towards the end of the nineteenth century, allowed quasi-independence or internal autonomy. Under the Indian Independence Act of 1947, the suzerainty of the British Crown over the princely states lapsed. With the exception of Kashmir, the states acceded to India or Pakistan under various agreements, some becoming provinces of the newly independent countries and others merging into the provinces.

Following the nationalist opinion in the British India, the states have in general been condemned as anachronisms of the worst type, misruled, mismanaged, backward and not worthy of serious consideration. Not an insignificant proportion of the blame must, however, be shared by lack of information and, where it existed, by its sometimes ludicrous nature. How does one even begin to study these states whose exact number was also a matter for debate? The most quoted numbers—560, 562, 584, 600, 629—were only some of the numbers used. A range of 550–600 is also mentioned (India, 1929; Report, 1929, p. 10; Jeffrey, 1978, p. 8; Copland, 1982, p. 1; Hurd, 1975, p. 169). The area and population are sometimes given, which of course are affected by the choice of the total number of the states. In attempts to emphasize the existence of extreme variation, infinitesimal estates, for instance, as microscopic in area as 0.29 square mile and as minuscule as inhabited by 32 persons (India, 1929, pp. 44–5, 70–1), are frequently cited. This has made its own contribution to deter any serious study of development in the states. The most popular method of preparing league tables has been to arrange them in order of the number of gun salutes offered to the ruler when visiting the viceroy in Delhi.

A gloss is thus put over a good number of real economies that were striving to run a development race with British India. They are barely mentioned in the stories of long-term stagnation in pre-Partition India. If anything, their collective backwardness, which was observed by Joan Robinson to be a reality, is presumed to have contributed to the general decline of India before Partition. Large numbers and aggregative approaches fail to throw any light on the dynamic, or the absence of it, within the economies of the principal states. The economies that mattered were not as numerous as has been thought and certainly not too small to be ignored.

As late as in the 1980s, there were 35 countries in the world with population less than a million (10 lakh). At least 22 of these had an area less than 10,000 square miles. They included a cross-section of the categorization of the economies by the World Bank, with GNP per capita ranging from 180 to 17,570 US dollars per annum (World Bank, 1987, p. 269). Using these very criteria but on the higher side—a population of a million or higher, an area of 10,000 square miles or higher and, in the absence of GNP per capita figures, a revenue of Rs. 10 million (100 lakh=one crore) or more—Table 2.1 brings together the salient features of the principal economies in Princely India.

In all there were 21 of them, 7 satisfying all three criteria, 5 fulfilling two criteria and the rest only one. Together, these economies contributed 71 per cent of the total area of Princely India, 66 per cent of the population and a little over 66 per cent of the revenue. They included even a non-salute state, namely Bastar, none of the sixty-five 11-gun and below salute states, two of the thirteen 13-gun salute states, one of the seventeen 15-gun salute states, seven of the thirteen 17-gun salute states, five of the six 19-gun salute states and all of the five 21-gun salute states.

Comparisons with the contemporaries of the princely states also highlight the importance of the latter. Though smaller in area, Hyderabad had a larger population than Argentina, Mysore as much as Peru and Colombia, Gwalior larger than Bolivia and Venezuela, while Guatemala and El Salvador trailed behind Baroda and Patiala (Papers, 1930, p. 105).

The Robinsons landed in India in the 1920s. In the earlier two decades, the British policy of isolating the princely states from one and the other, British India and the world at large was weakening. 'The shackles of

Table 2.1 Main features of the major economies of Princely India, 1927–1928
(criteria satisfied = actual figure, els = 0)

No.	State	Population (million)	Area (000 sq. miles)	Revenue (Rs. million)
1	Hyderabad	12.47	82.70	65.71
2	Mysore	5.86	29.53	36.10
3	Jammu and Kashmir	3.67	85.89	24.67
4	Gwalior	3.20	26.38	21.40
5	Jaipur	2.34	16.68	13.20
6	Jodhpur (Marwar)	1.85	35.07	13.64
7	Indore	1.15	10.00ᵃ	12.40
8	Travancore	4.01	0	24.82
9	Baroda	2.13	0	26.21
10	Patiala	1.50	0	12.61
11	Rewa	1.40	13.00	0
12	Udaipur (Mewar)	1.38	12.69	0
13	Cochin	1.00ᵃ	0	0
14	Kolhapur	0	0	14.01
15	Nawanagar	0	0	11.26
16	Bhavnagar	0	0	11.09
17	Kalat	0	73.28	0
18	Bikaner	0	23.32	0
19	Jaisalmer	0	16.06	0
20	Bahawalpur	0	15.00	0
21	Bastar	0	13.06	0

Note: Except for no. 14, which is an average estimate from Indian States Enquiry (1932, Appendix IV, 245), the computations use basic information in India (1929), relating in general to 1927–1928
ᵃNearly

paramountcy' had begun to loosen somewhat. One of its manifestation was the emergence of a corporate culture and the formation of a Chamber of Princes (COP). By the time the Robinsons arrived, the paramount power was becoming weary of the expression of collective voice by the states and their increasing interaction with the nationalist leadership in British India. The issues that were later raised before the Butler Committee to reconsider these relations had begun to crystallize. These were mainly the outcome of an unbalanced fiscal relationship with British India. Excise taxes, customs duties, public services such as the railways and post office were seen to deny the states their rightful share. In response, the case was made that the loss was more than compensated by the fact that the states did not have to contribute to the defence spending. In the view of the states, this ignored the fact that they had paid more than their due in the form of tributes and cession of revenue-generating territories (Copland, 1997).

INDIA CONNECTION

What were the nature and social circumstances of Joan Robinson's Princely India connection? It does not seem to have been a regrettable necessity of an 'upper middle-class English family' background (Harcourt, 1979, p. 663) nor, if you will, a Cambridge education. Joan Robinson's upper-class relatives were present even in India. For instance, the governor of Sind province, L. Graham, was married to an aunt.[2] Narasimhan gives further details about Joan Robinson's class background and connections in India. 'Both her father and her grandfather were generals', and 'there were already family connections on both sides with India. On her side, there were Civil Service connections'. But it would be simplistic to conclude about a person, who would soon be labelled by *The Economist* (1949, p. 95) as 'being at once an economist of standing' and 'a socialist', that her interest in the issues of poverty, backwardness and unfair taxation was a mere reflection of leisure-class affinities. Narasimhan has a telling way of bearing this out:

> Connections like these produce their own pressures. One can only draw attention to the sheer weight of the burden of consciousness on a more than usually intelligent, growing girl. One heard from her happy stories of riding and walking, but one also sensed a consciousness of the reaches of power and human fallibility. Most important of all, though, is something she used to say in a voice of outraged dismissal, 'You know, there was an "us" and a "them"'. (1983, pp. 215–7)

Her interest in the problems of Princely India seems nothing like the pastime of a social classmate. Purely in terms of economic analysis, the existence of a great number of internally autonomous states surrounded by a de facto unitary economic state of the size of British India must have presented a challenge to Joan Robinson's 'incisive mind' (Harcourt, 1984, p. 640). It held out the prospects of investigating economies of scale, externalities and other benefits of a large economy. These were among the issues she focused on after returning from India. It was, in fact, the earliest opportunity to analyse *Zollverein*-type possibilities in a backward economy. The complex fiscal dimension, with an utterly wanting statistical base of the princely states of the 1920s, was by no means a task for an analyst with no taste for challenge. The most important dimension of the challenge was the requirement to apply economic theory in a developmental context, a task lacking any precedence worthy of note.

During 1927–1932, the period in which Joan Robinson was intimately connected with the issues of an Indian *Zollverein*, none of the parties with stakes in the future of India could have imagined that within a decade and a half would take place the Partition of India and the end of the British raj.[3] A federation keeping the British connection and an all-India *Zollverein* seemed the best that could be hoped for in the way of economic and political advance. The focus was on finding practical ways to overcome the obstacles to development in this direction. There were serious economic problems to be sorted out before an arrangement acceptable to the princes could be worked out, so as to elicit their willing cooperation for the federal project and an economic *Zollverein*. Joan Robinson's contribution must be seen in the light of these efforts to preserve an Indian economic community. The nationalists would not hesitate to make short work of the princes. For Joan Robinson to work from the side of Princely India on the *Zollverein* project and to maintain a nationalist stance at the same time would be contradictory.

Yet this very position has been suggested. Marcuzzo (1985, p. 6) quotes from an obituary in an unspecified issue of *Economic and Political Weekly* to the effect that Joan Robinson 'attracted the grave displeasure of the authorities by her support and friendship with (sic) the leaders of the movement for Indian independence'. As was pointed out above, it was not yet clear whether or not there was an independence movement. Even the Nehru Report of 1928 stood for a dominion status, which 'will be as much the King's Government as the present Government of India'.[4] At any rate, no issue of that journal since Joan Robinson's death on 3 August 1983 contains the obituary from which Marcuzzo gleaned these observations. The journal did publish an obituary (A.M., 1983), but it does not touch on the subject. In her correspondence, one sees Gandhi and other names named and the *Harijans* and the Hindu-Muslim issues discussed, but no hint of a significant rapport with the nationalist leadership. After Joan Robinson's death, Narasimhan (1983, p. 217) mentioned Joan Robinson's association with Sarojini Naidu, a nationalist activist. In Garratt's correspondence with her, we find details of what is known as the Meerut case against the Indian communists.[5] However, this does not provide an adequate basis from which to deduce an active interest in the Indian nationalist or leftist movements. The connection rather was with Princely India, though an interest excited by the challenge of development in an extremely complex sociopolitical environment.

RESIDENT IN GWALIOR

Joan Robinson spent nearly two years in the princely state of Gwalior in the second half of the 1920s. Gwalior state was one of the two founding members of the COP. Among the big five states entitled to 21-gun salute, it was the fourth largest princely state in terms of population, area and revenue. Later, it acceded to India on the first day of independence to become part of the Madhya Pradesh province.

As noted earlier, Joan Robinson's husband, then E.A.G. Robinson, was appointed tutor to the minor Maharaja of the state. In the case of the ruler being a minor, the British appointed a Regent, which in this case was the elder Maharani Chinku Bai, and a British Resident who with a few other members formed a Regency Council to govern the state in the transition period. In effect, the British controlled the minority states directly and arranged to tutor the minor rulers in the tradition of English gentlemen. Gwalior enjoyed a somewhat benign treatment because the Scindias, the last dynasty of rulers of the state, had sided with the British in the first war of independence in 1857.

Gwalior had a Cambridge connection. Madhu Rao Scindia, who ruled during 1886–1925, had an honorary Doctor in Laws from the University of Cambridge. He was known as a progressive ruler who built Gwalior Light Railway, metalled roads and a postal system. A special fund was established for development projects in education, irrigation and famine relief (Kidwai, 2021). His son, Jiwajirao Scindia (1916–1961), was the minor Maharaja tutored by E.A.G. Robinson in 1927–1928. Joan Robinson did some teaching at the Victoria College in Gwalior.[6]

Choosing a minor as heir facilitated a longer than usual interregnum of direct rule over the princely states, with 'training programmes for young princes to be carefully supervised by British tutors' (Keen, 2003, p. 72). In 1915, the father of E.A.G. Robinson's trainee, Madhu Rao Scindia, had observed that the minority rule influenced the loyalty of the subjects towards the rulers. It had 'shaken the adherence of the people to their traditional customs and ways' (Ashton, 1982, p. 48).

Life for the Robinsons in Gwalior was a mix of privilege, leisure and work. They also witnessed the unending palace intrigues, with the two widows of the deceased Maharaja fighting to control the ten-year-old Maharajah and the affairs of the state. According to Harcourt and Kerr (2009, p. 3),

> Details of their life were recorded by both Joan and Austin in short memoirs of particular aspects of their daily routines. Austin records the day as beginning at around 6.30 a.m. with a tray of tea, followed immediately by him and Joan riding or perhaps driving through streets straggling with bullock carts, to the parade ground, where the Maharajah and his sister would be having their riding lesson and drill; Joan and Austin would ride as they pleased. At 7.30 a.m., everyone would assemble to ride back to the palace, with Joan and Austin and the four boys, who were educated with the Maharajah, trailing at the back. At home, after bathing in a tin bath, there would be breakfast and then Austin would go for three hours to the schoolroom. Joan occupied herself writing book reviews for the local papers.

'After lunch together and a siesta', continue Harcourt and Kerr (2009, pp. 3–4), 'there were Hindi lessons, and then Austin played cricket with the boys and Joan took the girls to play badminton and another palace game at which she was not very skilled. They exercised themselves and the children for several hours. In the early evening, perhaps at 6.30 or 7 p.m., they motored to the Club where they met other expatriates; Joan would have a gin and lemonade, read out-of-date newspapers, socialise with the other members, perhaps take a swim or play a game of tennis. Austin notes that some "conversation is conducted in a low tone as it savours of the intellectual and is therefore not really suitable for the Club" (EAGR 7/1/2/23[7])'.

It seems Joan did not savour the lifestyle of a *memsaab*. In the words of Harcourt and Kerr (2009, p. 4):

> The Robinsons would return home and bathe and dress for dinner. Joan recounts a dinner one night at the palace. Her awkwardness and inability to generate small talk and her discomfort in such socially precious situations are apparent even then. Joan describes her 'flagging spirits' at one dinner and her dismay 'when I take a bite, I find it is full of meat, which unluckily I dislike' (EAGR 7/1/2/41[8]) She continues to say '[M]y brain is quite congealed. I cannot think of a word to say to anyone' and she politely waits until it is 'seemly for us to go' (EAGR 7/1/2/46[9]).

In July 1928, Joan Robinson returned to London and eventually to Cambridge, followed by E.A.G. Robinson who became a university lecturer in 1929. Despite passing Tripos, she was not awarded the degree. Women were not yet eligible to receive degrees at Cambridge. She had to be content with occasional supervisions of students. It took some eight years before she was accepted as an assistant lecturer in 1937.

NOTES

1. Quoted in Graham and Harcourt (2020).
2. See his letter of 8 January 1931 in the JVR Collection, King's Modern Archives, which touches on the Round Table Conference.
3. See Copland (1982, p. 313).
4. Quoted in Menon (1956, p. 25).
5. G.T. Garratt's letter to Joan Robinson, 2 July 1931. There is some evidence also of the interest she showed in events on the eve of the Partition. See Harry M. Bull's pessimistic letter to Joan Robinson, 26 June 1947. JVR Collection, King's Modern Archives.
6. Referring to the Joan Robinson Memorial Lecture in the proceedings of the 79th Annual Conference of the Indian Economic Association held in Gwalior in 1996, *The Indian Economic Journal* (1997, p. 163) gives this information. The College has since been renamed as Maharani Laxmi Bai Government College of Excellence.
7. Austin Robinson Papers, Marshall Library, University of Cambridge.
8. Ibid.
9. Ibid.

REFERENCES

UNPUBLISHED MATERIAL

EAGR 7/1/2/23, Austin Robinson Papers, Marshall Library, University of Cambridge.
EAGR 7/1/2/41, Austin Robinson Papers, Marshall Library, University of Cambridge.
EAGR 7/1/2/46, Austin Robinson Papers, Marshall Library, University of Cambridge.
G.T. Garratt's letter to Joan Robinson. (1931, July 2). JVR Collection, King's Modern Archives.

Harry M. Bull's letter to Joan Robinson. (1947, June 26). JVR Collection, King's Modern Archives.

Keen, C. (2003). *The Power Behind the Throne: Relations Between the British and the Indian States 1870–1909*. Thesis submitted for the degree of Ph.D. at the School of Oriental and African Studies, University of London.

L Graham's Letter. (1931, January 8). JVR Collection, King's Modern Archives.

PUBLISHED WORKS

A.M. (1983). Obituary: The One Who Said Boo. *Economic and Political Weekly, 18*, 1461–1462.

Ashton, S. R. (1982). *British Policy Towards the Indian States, 1905–1939*. Curzon Press London.

Copland, I. (1982). *The British Raj and the Indian States*. Orient Longman.

Copland, I. (1997). *The Princes of India in the Endgame of Empire, 1917–1947*. Cambridge University Press.

Graham, H., & Harcourt, G. C. (2020). Keynesian Uncertainty: The Great Divide between Joan Robinson and Paul Samuelson in their Correspondence and Public Exchange. In R. Cord, R. Anderson, & W. Barnett (Eds.), *Paul Samuelson. Remaking Economics: Eminent Post-War Economists* (pp. 375–419). Palgrave Macmillan.

Harcourt, G. C. (1979). Robinson, Joan. In H. W. Spiegel & W. J. Samuels (Eds.), *International Encyclopaedia of the Social Sciences, Bibliographical Supplement* (Vol. 18). The Free Press.

Harcourt, G. C. (1984). Harcourt on Robinson. In *Contemporary Economists in Perspective* (Vol. 1, Part B). Jai Press.

Harcourt, G. C., & Kerr, P. (2009). *Joan Robinson*. Palgrave Macmillan.

Hurd, J., II. (1975). The Economic Consequences of the Indirect Rule in India. *Indian Economic and Social History Review, 12*, 169–181.

India, Government of. (1929). *The Indian States*. Central Publication Branch.

Indian States Enquiry Committee (Financial), The Report of. (1932). H.M.'s Stationery Office.

Jeffrey, R. (Ed.). (1978). *People, Princes and Paramount Power*. Oxford University Press.

Kidwai, R. (2021). *The House of Scindias: A Saga of Power, Politics and Intrigue*. Roli Books.

Marcuzzo, M. C. (1985). *Joan Violet Robinson*. Universita Degali Studi, Dipartimento di Economia Politica. Mimeo.

Menon, V. P. (1956). *The Story of the Integration of the Indian States*. Longmans, Green.

Narasimhan, S. (1983). Joan Robinson: In the Radical Vein a Laywoman's Homage. *Cambridge Journal of Economics, 7*, 213–219.

Papers on Indian States Development. (1930). East and West Ltd.
Report of Indian States Committee 1928–1929. (1929). H.M.'s Stationery Office.
The Economist. (1949). 156.
The Indian Economic Journal. (1997). 44, 161–164.
World Bank. (1987). *World Development Report*.

CHAPTER 3

A Tale of Two Robinsons

In the autumn of 1985, I completed the MPhil in the Economics and Politics of Development at Cambridge and started work on my doctoral dissertation on Joan Robinson's early contributions. The first question that I had asked myself was: What was Joan Robinson's first writing in economics and whether or not it was in any way connected with development, the area of my research. She herself remembered as her 'first publication' Robinson (1979, p. 110), the essay in which she made a case for economics as a serious subject (Robinson, 1932a). Actually, the first writing appearing in print under her name was the review of a book on industrial relations two years beforehand. In the course of this review, she criticizes the author for failing to 'examine the possibility that persons of the type whose inclinations and ability lead them to build up large fortunes would gradually leave a country in which his [egalitarian] policy was being carried out for others in which the doctrine of laissez-faire was still held in a pure form' (Robinson, 1930, p. 296).

Thus, her known career began by pinpointing the difficulties faced in tinkering with existing contracts and by seeking to turn economics into a rational subject. This research programme was a logical outcome of the frustration of her hope as an undergraduate at Cambridge during 1922–1925 that 'economics would offer more scope for a rational argument'. As a student she had had another hope, that economics would

P. Tahir, *Joan Robinson in Princely India*, Palgrave Studies in the History of Economic Thought, https://doi.org/10.1007/978-3-031-10905-8_3

enable her 'to understand poverty and how it could be cured'. She was to be 'disappointed' on this count as well:

> When I came up to Cambridge (in October 1921) to read economics, I did not have much idea of what it was about. I had some vague hope that it would help me to understand poverty and how it could be cured. And I hoped that it would offer more scope for rational argument than history (my school subject) as it was taught in those days.
>
> I was somewhat disappointed on both counts. Alfred Marshall was the all-dominating influence on the Cambridge faculty; the last item in this volume (24) indicates how I took to him. I felt smothered by the moralizing and mystified by the theory; in particular, no one seemed to know what was meant by the 'representative firm'.
>
> When I returned to Cambridge in 1929, they were still arguing about the representative firm (*Economic Journal*, March 1930) but meanwhile Piero Sraffa had turned up, rescued by Keynes from Mussolini. He was calmly committing the sacrilege of pointing out inconsistencies in Marshall, and, moreover, introducing us to other contemporary schools of thought (but they were no better). (Robinson, 1978, p. ix)

The Indian Sojourn

Before she could grapple with the problems of a serious, rational economics, she was presented with an opportunity to study poverty and backwardness at its most serious. In 1926,[1] the Robinsons left for India and stayed there until the summer of 1928.[2] As it is, Joan Robinson was in India for a long enough period to be excluded from the company of those pioneers in development who, according to Little, 'had little experience' of the underdeveloped economies (1982, p. 119).

But there is nothing in her writings in the immediate aftermath of the sojourn to India to indicate its impact directly. Except for mentioning *clichés* of 'colonial economics' like famine and overpopulation (Robinson, 1932a, p. 3) and a short review note on a book about Indian caste customs (Robinson, 1932b), writings about India or its backwardness are conspicuous by their absence and references very few. For instance, she refers to Wicksteed's claim regarding the prevalence of constant returns not only in the modem competitive industrial centres of the West but also in the customs-ruled villages in India (Robinson, 1934, p. 401). One searches in vain for any direct or indirect attempt to understand India's poverty and backwardness, let alone any possible cures. The fact is that she seldom referred specifically to her experience in Princely India in a career that was to spread well over half a century and one not without many reminiscences of one kind or the other. Was she then in Princely India for about two years just as a *memsaab* enjoying a life of leisure? It is difficult to accept this assumption about the author of such witty and insightful remarks about postcolonial India as, for example, the one quoted by Bhagwati (1985, p. 13)—'whatever you say about it, the opposite is equally true'.

Not only Joan Robinson, but, as far as I could search, Sir Austin also never mentioned the visit to Princely India and the work carried out there in his own writings. Nor did anyone else, until after the death of Joan Robinson in 1983 when Narasimhan remembered Joan Robinson having 'talked of this time' but not the work. Indeed, Narasimhan's moving personal account is the sole, albeit indirect, reminiscence of the first and the longest 'passage to India'. Narasimhan

> got the sense when she [Joan Robinson] talked of this time that the realities of poverty in a feudal state in Central India, as well as the land and the people, took hold of her imagination. (1983, p. 217)

So her interest in poverty and backwardness was established. But what did she contribute towards its understanding? Just about the time (December 1985) I was giving up hope of finding anything of relevance to my work, I came across the following information from a 'pioneer in development', Colin Clark.

> Austin and Joan Robinson had spent some time in India, where he had held the position of tutor to the crown prince of Gwalior in the 1920s. At that time about a quarter of India was ruled by hereditary princes, with only indirect supervision by the British authorities. Both of the Robinsons developed an active interest in India's economic problems. They were commissioned to prepare a report on the highly complex issue of the financial position of the princely states in a proposed reorganization of the Indian government. (Clark, 1984, p. 62)

This was the first indication to me that some work was done. Clark suggests joint authorship and vaguely hints at the nature of the work. He does not give any indication that the work was published.

In view of the hints thrown up by the Clark and Narasimhan stories, and the absence of any clues in the writings of the Robinsons, I was naturally thinking of interviewing Sir Austin. Fortunately, the opportunity itself came my way. In April 1986, Sir Austin chose me (or was I chosen for him?) to assist him in the editing of the second edition (Robinson, 1987) of the 1953 International Economic Association (IEA) conference on economic progress held in Santa Margherita Ligure, Italy, and published in 1955.[3] This work lasted for about two months. In my first meeting with him in this connection, I drew his attention to Clark (1984). I also informed him about my research topic and asked him a few questions about the India days. He said that he would talk to me about this when the work on his book would be over. During my subsequent visits, Sir Austin mentioned a name, Haksar, and Joan Robinson's close association with him. At some point, he specifically named Butler Committee. These were the only clues I got from him.

Long after I had finished my assignment, I received the following letter Sir Austin on the letterhead of Sidney Sussex College (Letter from Austin Robinson to the author, 18 June, 1986)

> Dear Tahir
> I enclose a cheque of £ 100 for the work you did on the I.E.A. volume about Economic Progress.
> May I say again how grateful I have been for your very thorough reading of it?
> I have not forgotten my promise to sit down with you and talk about my wife, Joan. I have been run off my legs and am off on Sunday for a short while to California for meeting of the Executive Committee of I.E.A. But I shall be back in about a fortnight and will ring you when I am back.
> Yours
> Austin Robinson

Sir Austin did not ring me up and the promised interview on Joan never took place. In the long list of acknowledgements for the IEA volume, my name could not find a place. I was left with no choice but to keep searching for material on my own. The name of Haksar and the Butler Committee mentioned by Sir Austin served as the starting points. I followed these up in an extensive search of records relating to the said Committee, the career and publications of Haksar and Joan Robinson's personal papers and records.[4]

JOAN'S FRIEND AND A COMMITTEE OF THE RAJ

During World War I, the princes cooperated with the British in the hope of regaining the autonomy they had been losing as a result of the Indian economic community that was emerging de facto. However, the end of the War only brought mounting public debt, increased taxation and the rupee muddle. It was against this background that the Butler Committee that Sir Austin referred to was set up.[5] At the centre of the controversy was the relationship between the British Crown and princely states, threatened by the financial and fiscal encroachment of these states by the government of British India. It commenced work in December 1927 and published its findings in March 1929.[6] The terms of reference were addressed to the main political and economic problems facing the princely states: (a) 'to report upon the relationship between the Paramount Power and the Indian States' and (b) 'to enquire into the financial and economic relations between British India and the States' (Report, 1929, p. 5). As is clear from (b), serious economic and fiscal issues were involved. In its annexures was contained the case presented on behalf of the princes by their counsel, Sir Leslie Scott. This could not have indicated the inputs of various individuals. I also checked the unpublished records of the proceedings of the Butler Committee at the India Office Library.[7] As the Robinsons did not (perhaps could not) appear before the Committee in person, nothing suggesting their exact contribution was found.

The search then turned to K.N. Haksar. He was political member (foreign secretary) in the Gwalior state government and assistant to Sir Leslie Scott, the counsel for the group of states for which Haksar was the chief coordinator. The coordination was carried out by the Special Organization of the Chamber of Princes. Haksar was the director of this organization. As pointed out by Sir Austin to me, Joan Robinson had come to develop a close contact with Haksar. In the context of Gwalior, Haksar wrote a number of articles on what was then understood by 'economic development', a concept related to the development of natural resources, and on the fiscal problems of the states (Haksar, 1928, 1929, 1930). It could not be ascertained whether Joan Robinson was consulted by him in the writing of these articles. Nor did his letters to Joan Robinson and his published works help clear up the role Joan Robinson played in connection with the states' case.

Joan Robinson's correspondence with contacts in India indicates her interest in many topical issues—economic, political and social—leading me to suspect that she must have written something herself on India. Garratt (1932a) was encouraged by her to write an article in the *Economic Journal* on the working class in India.[8] Furthermore, Garratt acknowledges Joan Robinson's assistance in enabling him to put together a consistent account of first trade contacts between Europe and India (Letter to Joan Robinson, 27 September 1932b; Thompson and Garrat, 1934).[9] Bull (1931) kept her informed on the state of the Indian economy and the problems such as the rupee ratio and the behaviour of *ryots*.[10]

Two letters indicate the extent of Joan Robinson's involvement. The first was from Garratt (1931, April 13). He informed Joan Robinson that Haksar believed her to have had done more for the princes than any other European.[11] There is no indication as to what she had done. What could an economist have done? The presumption is that it referred to the preparatory study done for the princes' case before the Butler Committee, unless one is prepared to believe that Joan 'Robinson's incisive mind' (Harcourt, 1984, p. 640) was indulging in a mere public relations exercise. The second letter is that of Bull (1931), co-author with K.N. Haksar of a book on the charismatic and development-oriented Maharaja Scindia of Gwalior (Bull & Haksar, 1926). Scindia was the father of the minor Maharaja under the tutorship of the then E.A.G. Robinson. The letter warned Joan Robinson about the hard work awaiting her with the start of the preliminary discussions between the princely states and British India.[12] These discussions were followed by the deliberations of technical bodies such as the Peel Subcommittee on federal finance set up by the second session of the Indian Round Table Conference (1931, 1932a, 1932b) and a financial enquiry committee (Indian States, 1932). It is doubtful that without having worked on the financial and economic matters before the Butler Committee, she could be of any useful assistance to the states in these deliberations. Haksar, by all accounts the closest associate of Joan Robinson, was a member of the Peel Subcommittee. He was also instrumental in the setting up of the financial enquiry. Held in England, these discussions at the start of the 1930s seem to have interested Joan Robinson even after returning from India.[13]

The correspondence is silent on the role of Sir Austin. The only indication of the part played by him was in Clark's account mentioned above.[14] Around this time, two further developments took place. First, Lord Kahn kindly granted me an interview (1986, December 1). According to him, Joan Robinson had returned from India with a deep imprint of its poverty and backwardness on her mind. He recalled that she was not the kind of person who would not write about what she felt. I am unable to say

whether he was referring to the India days or was connecting the argument with Joan Robinson's later interest in the socialistic alternative
because both arguments got mixed up due to my bad questioning.[15]
Secondly, Geoff Harcourt passed on to me for comments the manuscript
of a forthcoming book by Marjorie Turner. It contained an interview with
Sir Austin, held in 1984. It was after the death of Joan Robinson in 1983.
Here is what he had to say:

> It so happened that there was an argument going on between the Indian
> States, the parts of India which were still governed by Maharajahs and peo-
> ple like that and the Government of [British] India over the rights of the
> Government to tax their imports and that sort of thing. One of our special
> friends was the foreign secretary so to speak, [*sic*] the minority administra-
> tion of the Gwalior state and he at the same time was acting as secretary and
> organizer of a big group from a whole number of Indian States who were
> engaged in arguing this. An official committee came out from London to
> discuss this matter with the Indian States and thereafter the further discus-
> sions were carried on in London. Joan got all involved with the foreign
> secretary and others in the presentation of the Indian case for the Indian
> States. *I worked on the memoranda in my spare moments, but I was very busy*
> *with the tutoring of the Maharajah* [emphasis added]. Joan also went back to
> London to help the foreign secretary present the case. (Turner, 1986/
> manuscript)

In the interview with Turner, Sir Austin states that 'he worked in his
spare time' only as he was 'very busy' with the Maharaja, while 'Joan got
all involved'. From the suggestion of equal contribution in Clark (1984),
we move to the indication of major contribution by Joan Robinson, unless
we are willing to make the implausible assumption that Joan Robinson was
just doing the running around. Again, Sir Austin is talking about the work
on the memoranda, in other words, the fine-tuning of the documentation
prepared finally as per administrative and legal requirements, not the background analyses carried out for the case. Austin Robinson Papers, his
archival collection at the Marshall Library, were not available at that time,
that is, 1988.

In short, neither Joan Robinson's writings nor her archives cited any
serious work. Same was true of Sir Austin's writings. There were, however,
indications and suggestions of Joan Robinson's involvement in the work
related to the Butler Committee in the JVR Collection and a few publications appearing soon after her death in 1983.

NOTES

1. Coincidentally, this was also the year when Joan Robinson's mentor, Keynes, gave evidence before the Royal Commission on Indian Currency and Finance (Keynes, 1981, pp. 477–524). Keynes never visited India, but he wrote an authoritative book on its monetary and financial problems (Keynes, 1913).
2. Pasinetti (1987, p. 212) indicates the same period.
3. Robinson, Austin. (ed.) (1987) *Economic Progress. Second edition.* New York: St. Martin's Press.
4. Joan Robinson's personal papers and records are available in the Joan Violet Robinson Collection of the Modem Archives of King's College Library, Cambridge. Hereinafter, it will be referred to as JVR Collection, King's Modern Archives.
5. Throughout the book, it is referred to as Report (1929).
6. For a good summary, see *Near East* (1929, pp. 524-5). Butler (1930) is a precis by the Committee chairman himself.
7. See IOR V/26/272/2–3.
8. G.T. Garratt's letter to Joan Robinson, 3 August 1932a. JVR Collection, King's Modem Archives. The article for which he received Joan Robinson's encouragement is Garratt (1932), which argues for a de-casualization of the Indian industrial worker. Garratt (1888–1942) had been a member of the Indian Civil Service and political secretary of the Round Table Conference. He was associated with the League Against Imperialism and wrote frequently on Indian affairs. See, for instance, Garratt (1930).
9. G.T. Garratt's letter to Joan Robinson, 27 September 1932b. JVR Collection, King's Modem Archives. Most probably, the book under reference is *Rise and Fulfilment of British Rule in India* (1934), which Garratt co-authored with the historian E. Thompson.
10. Harry M. Bull's letters to Joan Robinson, 1931–51. JVR Collection, King's Modem Archives. Bull was associated with the college in Gwalior city and then with the state's customs and excise office. He carried out a number of socio-economic surveys of villages in the state.
11. Letter to Joan Robinson, 13 April 1931. JVR Collection, King's Modem Archives.
12. Letter to Joan Robinson, 7 June 1931. JVR Collection, King's Modem Archives.
13. See Appendix 1, focusing on the problems of an Indian Zollverein.
14. To get an idea of Sir Austin's assessment of Clark's work, see his highly critical review of Clark's *The Economics of 1960*. 'I am constantly carried back ten years in my memories, and see myself again with my head round Mr. Clark's door in the Marshall Library at Cambridge, trying to get him

to explain what exactly he has been doing, and being fobbed off with some quite unintelligible answer while he waits with hand poised to rattle out the next calculation on the machine' (Robinson, 1943, p. 239).
15. Lord Kahn's (1986) interview with the author. 1 December.

REFERENCES

UNPUBLISHED MATERIAL

Austin Robinson's letter to the author. (1986, June 18).
G.T. Garrat's letter to Joan Robinson. (1931, April 13). JVR Collection, King's Modern Archives.
G.T. Garratt's letter to Joan Robinson. (1932a, August 3). JVR Collection, King's Modern Archives.
G.T. Garratt's letter to Joan Robinson. (1932b, September 27). JVR Collection, King's Modern Archives.
Harry M. Bull's letter to Joan Robinson. (1931, June 7). JVR Collection, King's Modern Archives.
Lord Kahn's interview with the author. (1986, December 1).

PUBLISHED WORKS

Bhagwati, J. N. (1985). *Wealth and Poverty*. Basil Blackwell.
Bull, H. M., & Haksar, K. N. (1926). *Madhavrao Scindia of Gwalior*. Alijah Darbar Press.
Butler, H. (1930). The Indian States and the Crown. In *India*. The Times Publishing Company.
Clark, C. (1984). Development Economics: The Early Years. In Meier, G. M., & Seers, D. (Eds.) *Pioneers in Development*. Oxford University Press.
Garratt, G. T. (1930). Indian India. *Asia, 30,* 783–789–804–805.
Garratt, G. T. (1932). The Indian Industrial Worker. *Economic Journal, 42,* 399–406.
Haksar, K. N. (1928). Fiscal Inter-relation of Indian States and the Empire. *Asiatic Review, 24,* 539–543.
Haksar, K. N. (1929). The Salt Revenue and the Indian States. *Asiatic Review, 25,* 7–16.
Haksar, K. N. (1930). Economic Development in Gwalior State. *Asiatic Review, 26,* 150–157.
Harcourt, G. C. (1984). Harcourt on Robinson. In *Contemporary Economists in Perspective* (Vol. 1, Part B). Jai Press.
Indian Round Table Conference. (1931). *Proceedings of Sub-committees, November 1930–January 1931.* H.M.'s Stationery Office.

Indian Round Table Conference. (1932a). *Proceedings, September–December 1931.* H.M.'s Stationery Office.

Indian Round Table Conference. (1932b). *Proceedings of Federal Structure Committee, September-December 1931.* H.M.'s Stationery Office.

Indian States Enquiry Committee (Financial), The Report of. (1932). H.M.'s Stationery Office.

Keynes, J. M. (1913). *Indian Currency and Finance.* Macmillan.

Keynes, J. M. (1981). *The Collected Writings,* Vol. 19, Part II (D. Moggridge, Ed.). Macmillan.

Little, I. M. D. (1982). *Economic Development.* Basic Books.

Narasimhan, S. (1983). Joan Robinson: In the Radical Vein a Laywoman's Homage. *Cambridge Journal of Economics, 7,* 213–219.

Near East and India. (1929). 35, 524–525.

Pasinetti, L. L. (1987). Robinson, Joan Violet. In J. Eatwell, M. Milgate, & P. Newman (Eds.), *The New Palgrave: A Dictionary of Economics* (Vol. 4). Macmillan.

Report of Indian States Committee 1928–1929. (1929). H.M.'s Stationery Office.

Robinson, A. (Ed.). (1987). *Economic Progress* (2nd ed.). Macmillan.

Robinson, A. (1943). Review of C. Clark, *The Economics of 1960. Economic Journal, 53,* 238–242.

Robinson, J. (1930). Review of H. Clay. *The Problem of Industrial Relations, in Political Quarterly, 1,* 293–296.

Robinson, J. (1932a). *Economics is a Serious Subject.* W. Heifer and Sons.

Robinson, J. (1932b). Review of O'Malley (1932). *Cambridge Review, 54,* 138.

Robinson, J. (1934). Euler's Theorem and the Problem of Distribution. *Economic Journal, 44,* 398–414.

Robinson, J. (1978). Reminiscences. In J. Robinson (Ed.), *Contributions to Modern Economics.* Basil Blackwell.

Robinson, (1979). *Collected Economic Papers* (Vol. 5). Basil Blackwell.

Thompson, E., & Garratt, G. T. (1934). *Rise and Fulfilment of British Rule in India.* Macmillan.

Turner, M. S. (1986). *Joan Robinson and the Americans.* Manuscript.

CHAPTER 4

Discovering a Book

Towards the end of 1986, I had reasons to suspect that Joan Robinson had written something on the issues before the Butler Committee. On the assumption that some work was done, that Joan Robinson was totally committed and that the man on the spot, Sir Austin, must have been of valuable assistance when he, according to himself, could spare the time, I proceeded to the next step of following up the work and activities of the names mentioned in Joan Robinson's correspondence with colleagues in India.

AUTOBIOGRAPHY OF A CO-AUTHOR

In Joan Robinson's correspondence, the name K.M. Panikkar is mentioned a number of times,[1] but there are no letters from him in the records. Panikkar was a highly respected Indian author and diplomat. Copland (1997, pp. 79, 147) talks of the 'imagination, foresight and political acumen of Haksar and Panikkar' and described the latter as 'astute'. Panikkar's academic credentials were impeccable. He won a scholarship to Christ Church, Oxford, and achieved a first. Perusing the rather extensive writings of Panikkar proved productive.[2] His autobiography provided the definitive clue to Joan Robinson's contribution during the time she was in Princely India. Panikkar states:

© The Author(s), under exclusive license to Springer Nature   35
Switzerland AG 2022
P. Tahir, *Joan Robinson in Princely India*, Palgrave Studies in the
History of Economic Thought,
https://doi.org/10.1007/978-3-031-10905-8_4

Haksar had entrusted me with the task of writing a history of the develop-ment and present condition of the Indian States. The early historical section of the book *British Crown and the Indian States* came to be written in this way. The second part of the book dealt with finance and was written by a scholar named MRS AUSTIN ROBINSON [emphasis added]. Sir Leslie Scott's legal arguments before the Butler Committee were based on this work of ours. (Panikkar, 1979, p. 79)

The Part II of *The British Crown and the Indian States* (1929, pp. 133–215), which according to Panikkar was authored by Joan Robinson, bears a long title: An Examination of Some Aspects of the Fiscal Questions at Issue Between the States and the Government of India. There were two main writers—K.M. Panikkar and Joan Robinson—who worked on clearly demarcated parts. On the basis of this direct and unam-biguous evidence furnished by a co-author, I naturally concluded that the 82-page Part II of *The British Crown and the Indian States* was Joan Robinson's first published attempt at economic writing. The writing was in the field of poverty and backwardness and an unjust fiscal dispensation. As Panikkar describes Joan Robinson as a scholar, it clarified the misunder-standing that might have been created by the emphasis on Joan Robinson's contribution to the 'presentation' aspect in the Turner (1986) interview. This was specific evidence from a man on the spot. He was a participant in the negotiations and the debate taking place on the economic and fiscal relations between the British India and the Princely India. It is a co-author making it clear as to who was the other author and what were the respec-tive contribution.

What about the possibility of a misprint? The books from Indian pub-lishing houses are not known for error-free printing. However, the auto-biography of Panikkar was published by the Oxford University Press. The possibility that even Oxford University Press may have been less careful is discounted by the fact that the Panikkar quote is from the edition which it announces as 'Reprinted with correction 1979'. An English reader may suspect a misprint because Panikkar mentions 'Mrs. Austin Robinson' rather than Mrs Joan Robinson. However, Panikkar was merely adhering to the common Indian practice of referring, out of respect, to a wife by prefixing 'Mrs.' to the name of the husband. It did not seem to be a case of an 's' suffixed to 'Mr' by the printer's devil. Perhaps Keynes' authority should dispose of the matter. The address he wrote on the letters to Joan Robinson opened as 'Mrs. Austin Robinson'.[3]

Reading the relevant pages many times over indicated striking stylistic similarities to the later works by Joan Robinson. A certain assertiveness, an impatience with detail, repeated use of some words and the tenor and manner of the argument convinced me that a computer simulation of the literary style of Part II of *The British Crown and the Indian States* and her later writings would confirm the consistency. I could see what Shove (1933, p. 661) meant by suggesting that Joan Robinson was 'too prone to attribute fallacies to other writers' when I came across dismissive expressions like 'meaningless' or 'confusion'.

I had been minutely reading Joan Robinson's works only for three years. But I had had the good fortune of being supervised by Geoff Harcourt, the highly respected authority on Joan Robinson and the (unofficial) trustee of her papers. He read my work based on *The British Crown and the Indian States* for about a year so meticulously that I have simply been amazed by his eye for detail. I was encouraged by the fact that at no point did he sense a variation in style consistency. None, I thought, existed.

The terms of reference of the Butler Committee indicated that serious economic issues were involved. More relevant for my research, the discussion of these issues was carried out in the perspective of the problems of poverty and backwardness in British and Princely India. Further, the finding that Joan Robinson dealt with the problems of underdeveloped economies before she pioneered imperfect competition, contributed to Keynesian revolution and got involved in the debates on long-period development was extremely important. The earliest writing and activity in a field not yet boasting any high theory escaped the attention of researchers. The publication was missed practically by everyone, except the economic historian (Anstey, 1929) and other historians who mainly refer to the historical and political part written by Panikkar.[4]

Panikkar originally wrote and published his autobiography in 1954 in Malayalam, the language of Kerala, a state in postcolonial India with whose economy as well as economists Joan Robinson had had a special relationship. They had also missed it.[5] The possibility that the translator might have made a mistake was doubly checked. There was none.

With the confidence based on the evidence provided by a co-author of *The British Crown and the India States*, consistency of style, the hints in the correspondence and the absence of anything to the contrary in the India Office Records, I leave it to the reader to judge whether a conclusion contrary to mine could have been arrived at, unless there existed an insider's knowledge to which I had no access. Yet this is what seems to have happened.

Not Much of a Discovery, After All

After *The British Crown and the Indian States* became known following my dissertation in 1988, a reprint appeared in the same year in India. It showed the Chamber of Princes as the author. Strangely, no writer ever noticed Panikkar's specific attribution to Joan Robinson, although his autobiography was published much earlier in 1977. His claim has not even been considered in the economics discipline, what to speak of rejection.

At every stage I believed that Joan Robinson had the benefit of valuable advice from Sir Austin. It is difficult to imagine otherwise. Clark (1984) and Turner (1986/manuscript) point towards it. The applied nature of the work demanded it, as Sir Austin was a pioneering applied economist.

In view of the evidence I had gathered by January 1987, I had not thought of asking Sir Austin to confirm the authorship of *The British Crown and the Indian States*. It did not seem to me at all possible that he could claim sole authorship. I was seeking the interview to go beyond to discuss the background of the issues before the Butler Committee in a general sort of way. My specific question about the authorship would have related to an article published in the *Nation and Athenaeum* of 22 June 1929. It was signed 'E.A.J. Robinson'. My first reaction was that it was a misprint of 'E.A.G. Robinson'. However, the four subsequent issues of the magazine did not contain any correction. Then I checked the Who's Who from 1929 to 50 years on. There was no entry for E.A.J. Robinson. To guard against the likelihood of the name not being included, I made a random check for a few other names in the magazine. All were found in the Who's Who. I, therefore, tentatively concluded, that it was a pseudonym combining the initials 'E.A.' from E.A.G. Robinson and 'J.' from Joan Robinson. Suspecting it to be the only joint writing by the Robinsons, I had hoped to have it confirmed by Sir Austin. However, I was not able to talk with him. It was relevant, but not absolutely essential for my work.

This article, more political than economic, is not in Joan Robinson's style. Joan and Sir Austin were the only Robinsons connected with the princely states in the latter half of the 1920s. Only they could have, therefore, dealt with the subject of the article—the Indian states. Keynes had a special relationship with the *Nation*, according to Sir Austin himself (Austin Robinson, 1977, p. 26). It could reasonably be conjectured that Sir Austin wrote the article, at least the main part of it. It is very different in style from that of the writer of the second part of *The British Crown and the Indian States*.

Just a few weeks before the submission of my dissertation, I was informed of Sir Austin Robinson's contention that he, and not Joan Robinson, was the major contributor to the economic part of *The British Crown and the Indian States*. It reminded me of his words uttered in regard to Keynes:

He [Keynes] never believed in private property in arguments, and was never very certain which were his own and which were other people's arguments. (Austin Robinson, 1977, p. 32)

At that stage, all that lay in the realm of the possible was to recheck my sources and explain in detail what led me to infer that the major contribution was Joan Robinson's. However, when the dissertation was submitted, the Chairman of the Degree Committee, Professor William Brown, wrote to me on 4 May 1988:

I understand that a substantial part of your Ph.D. dissertation relied on a paper to which, you had reason to believe, Joan Robinson had made a major contribution. Professor Austin Robinson, on hearing of your work, has recalled that the major economics contribution was in fact his and not Joan Robinson's.

Clearly you will have to qualify your interpretations and conclusions in the light of this new information. Because the form and the emphasis of the thesis will not be what it would have been had you known this at the outset, you should explain in detail in the thesis what led you to believe that the major contribution was Joan Robinson's and hence to devote a good deal of your time to pursuing this line of research. I trust this will not seriously delay your completion of the work.

As noted above, after starting work on the dissertation, my first port of call was Sir Austin. He chose not to grant me the interview after making a verbal promise and, subsequently, a written commitment. I could understand the claims on his time were too much for his age. My supervisor, Geoff Harcourt, is considered an authority on the historical development of the contributions of the Robinsons. He had also known them personally. My work was meticulously read and checked by him. At no stage did he suspect that I was on the wrong track. I responded with a detailed explanatory note, which Geoff thought was an appropriate response. In his reply on 6 May 1988 to my note, Professor Brown observed as follows:

> In my judgement you present a very substantial case and I am happy to send the letter on to the external examiner. In the light of your letter it is unlikely that your thesis will need to be revised substantially and I hope that you will be able to meet the time table.

John Toye, the external examiner, thought otherwise, and I was asked to revise the dissertation. The elaborate and documented response given by me in a special chapter, 'The Story of a Discovery', [6] was not seen as a sufficient defence. I left Cambridge in August 1988 to think things out. When I returned in 1990, I chose to drop the material under dispute and instead contributed a new essay on Joan's China connection.[7] The title of the dissertation changed from 'Some Aspects of Development and Underdevelopment: Critical Perspectives on the Early Contributions of Joan Robinson' (Tahir, 1988) to 'Some Aspects of Development and Underdevelopment: Critical Perspectives on Joan Robinson' (Tahir, 1990).

STRANGE OSMOSIS

The authorship of *The British Crown and the Indian States* became a bone of contention because the book did not mention any names as authors. To reproduce its long byline: 'An outline sketch drawn up on behalf of the Standing Committee of the Chamber of Princes by the Directorate of the Chamber' Special Organization'. Haksar, a close associate of both Joan Robinson and Panikkar, was the director of this organization.

As noted above, the Robinsons never mentioned *The British Crown and the Indian States* in their respective works. Clark (1984) and Turner (1986/manuscripts) do not even hint at any work having been published. It is only when I discovered the book that the authorship was claimed. Until then, no economist knew that *The British Crown and the Indian States* ever existed. That Joan Robinson never looked back to this work is not hard to explain. She was known for repudiations and for 'almost nihilistic conclusion[s]' about her work (Harcourt, 1986, p. 98). Here was something that did not even bear her name. She did not have to repudiate it. If we assume that the memoranda mentioned by Sir Austin in his interview with Turner was the main case about the outflow of resources from the princely states and their estimation, then the only applied section of the dissertation would be affected as a result; the only argument affected would be that Joan Robinson started as an applied development economist: in other words, Harcourt's suggestion about the complementarity between Joan Robinson's theoretical work and her colleagues' applied work would hold in this case also. My work was not exactly about the estimates of fiscal transfers. It was focused rather on the story of underdevelopment and development knit around them and the impact on Joan Robinson's later work. This would be the case of a slight variation of what Keynes (1983, p. 866) thought of *The Economics of Imperfect Competition*: 'She is, in a sense, taking the cream off a new movement which has not yet found its own expositor in print'. The worst case would be that she did not even tell the story. Assuming that it is possible to dispose of the evidence presented above, and assuming further that the author of *The Structure of Competitive Industry* (Robinson, 1931) at that time thought that the railway-generated externalities were based on a confusion, a parallel of the following would still hold for Joan Robinson:

Neither of us [Humphrey Mynors and Austin Robinson] was right in the thick of the General Theory arguments, though we were not outside it. In my own case it was going on all around me and I could not escape it had I wished (which I certainly did not). I was, like others, arguing it incessantly and absorbing it by continuing osmosis. (Robinson, 1977, p. 27)

NOTES

1. See, for instance, G.T. Garratt's letter to Joan Robinson, 26 November 1932 and KN. Haksar's letter to Joan Robinson, 9 March 1933. JVR Collection, King's Modem Archives.

2. Panikkar (1894–1963) was the author of many books on princely states, including one jointly with Haksar (Haksar & Panikkar, 1930). Like Garratt, he had been associated with the League Against Imperialism. Haksar lured him into the states' bureaucracy to assist with the work related to the Butler Committee. In postcolonial India, Panikkar was ambassador to China. His later works include Panikkar (1953, 1962, 1977).

3. For instance, see Keynes' letter to Joan Robinson, 20 August 1942. Keynes' Papers, King's College Library, Cambridge.

4. See Copland (1982, pp. 96–7). An economic historian, Anstey (1929), also mentions it in a footnote.

5. I had intended to go to Kerala. When I visited the Indian High Commission in London for visa, I was told that the Communist-ruled state was out of bounds for foreigners. An official who spoke my native Punjabi told me: 'You can go to Delhi or some other place, but not Kerala. We don't go there ourselves!'

6. Tahir (1988).
7. It was elaborated further in a monograph completed while the author was Joan Robinson Memorial Lecturer at the Faculty of Economics and Politics, University of Cambridge, in 1990. A shorter version was published as Tahir et al. (2002). Later, the full version with a postscript was published as Tahir (2019).

References

Unpublished Material

G.T. Garratt's letter to Joan Robinson. (1932, November 26). JVR Collection, King's Modem Archives.

K.N. Haksar's letter to Joan Robinson. (1933, March 9). JVR Collection, King's Modem Archives.

Keynes' letter to Joan Robinson. (1942, August 20). *Keynes' Papers*. King's College Library.

Turner, M. S. (1986). *Joan Robinson and the Americans*. Manuscript.

William Brown's letter to the author. (1988, May 4).

Published Works

Anstey, V. (1929). *The Economic Development of India*. Longmans and Green.

Clark, C. (1984). Development Economics: The Early Years. In *Meier and Seers (1984)*.

Copland, I. (1982). *The British Raj and the Indian Princes*. Orient Longman.

Copland, I. (1997). *The Princes of India in the Endgame of Empire, 1917–1947*. Cambridge University Press.

Haksar, K. N., & Panikkar, K. M. (1930). *Federal India*. Martin Hopkinson.

Harcourt, G. C. (1986). On the Influence of Piero Sraffa on the Contributions of Joan Robinson to Economic Theory. *Economic Journal, 96*(Supplement), 96–108.

Keynes, J. M. (1983) *The Collected Writings* (Vol. 12.) (D. Moggridge, Ed.). Macmillan.

Panikkar, K. M. (1953). *Asia and the Western Dominance*. Allen and Unwin.

Panikkar, K. M. (1962). *In Defence of Liberalism*. Asia Publishing House.

Panikkar, K. M. (1979). *An Autobiography*. Oxford University Press. First printed in 1977.

Robinson, A. (1977). Keynes and His Cambridge Colleagues. In D. Patinkin & J. C. Leith (Eds.), *Keynes, Cambridge and the General Theory*. Macmillan.

Robinson, E. A. G. (1931). *The Structure of Competitive Industry*. Nisbet & Co. Ltd.

Robinson, J. (1933). *The Economics of Imperfect Competition*. Macmillan.

Shove, G. F. (1933). Review of Robinson (1933). *Economic Journal, 43*, 657–661.

Tahir, P. (1988). *Some Aspects of Development and Underdevelopment: Critical Perspectives on the Early Contributions of Joan Robinson*. Unpublished.

Tahir, P. (1990). *Some Aspects of Development and Underdevelopment: Critical Perspectives on Joan Robinson*. PhD dissertation. Faculty of Economics and Politics, University of Cambridge.

Tahir, P., Harcourt, G. C., & Kerr, P. (2002). On Joan Robinson and China. In P. Kerr (Ed.), With the collaboration of G.C. Harcourt. *Joan Robinson: Critical Assessments of Leading Economists* (Vol. 5, pp. 267–280). Routledge.

Tahir, P. (2019). *Making Sense of Joan Robinson on China*. Palgrave Macmillan.

The British Crown and the Indian States. (1929). P.S. King and Son. Reprinted in India as Chamber of Princes (1988, 2013) *British Crown and the Indian States*. Gyan Publishing House.

Turner, M. S. (1986). *Joan Robinson and the Americans*. Manuscript.

CHAPTER 5

Austin Carries the Day

Before 1988, no substantive information existed about the economic work that the Robinsons were doing in the Princely India. Their work was published in 1929, the year following the Robinsons returned to England, in book form with the title, *The British Crown and the Indian States*. The Robinsons as well as the economics profession were unaware of it. After 1929, the book went out of print. Joan Robinson died in 1983. None of her extensive writings ever mentioned it. Her archival collections at King's College are also silent in this regard. Of course, Sir Austin came to know of the book after the submission of my dissertation in 1988 and claimed authorship of parts of it. But his archival collections at the Marshall Library, Cambridge, also contain no reference to the printed book. There are, however, material and references available in these archives about the work of the Robinsons during their time in Princely India. In 1988, when I submitted my dissertation, this collection was not available.

Since 1988, a number of authors have reviewed Austin Robinson Papers at Marshall Library of Economics and Churchill College at Cambridge to assess the Robinsons' role in the context of Butler Committee and their contribution to *The British Crown and the Indian States*.

OFFICIAL BIOGRAPHER

The most important work was the official biography of Sir Austin by Alec Cairncross. In the context of the time spent in Princely India, he made the following emphatic statement:

© The Author(s), under exclusive license to Springer Nature   45
Switzerland AG 2022
P. Tahir, *Joan Robinson in Princely India*, Palgrave Studies in the
History of Economic Thought,
https://doi.org/10.1007/978-3-031-10905-8_5

The difficulty of establishing the authorship of particular passages is illustrated by the experience of the unfortunate student who submitted a PhD dissertation at Cambridge with the firm conviction that *The British Crown and the Indian States* was the work of Joan, not Austin, Robinson because 'the style was recognizably hers. (1993, p. 30)

Now my claim of authorship by Joan Robinson was not just based on stylistic similarities, as suggested by Cairncross. It rested on the evidence provided by Panikkar who, as noted in Chap. 4, was a respected Indian writer and later a diplomat. He was a key player in the debate raging in the 1920s on the relations between the British Crown and the princely states. He was a co-author of *The British Crown and the Indian States*. Cairncross does not even cite Panikkar (1979).

He observes that Joan was 'eager to see something of India', confirming my view that she had an early interest in the issues of poverty and backwardness. He goes on to say that Joan wrote reviews for the Indian press and Austin drafted memoranda for the princely states (p. 20). This is the same position that Sir Austin took in an interview with Marjorie Turner in 1984 for her book (Turner, 1986, 1989): 'Joan got all involved with the foreign secretary and others in the presentation of the Indian case for the Indian States. I worked on the memoranda in my spare moments, but I was very busy with the tutoring of the Maharajah. Joan also went back to London to help the foreign secretary present the case'.[1]

Cairncross maintains further:

In addition to helping in the preparation of the Princes' case, Austin also drafted an article on the subject for the The Nation which was not published. This pointed out that the terms of reference of the Butler Committee made no provision for a discussion of the future position of the States in a self-governing India and that this subject had also been excluded by the government from consideration by the Simon Commission. Yet if Indian elected members were given greater administrative powers after the Simon Commission reported, there were bound to be repercussions on the States, and without any prior consultation. (Cairncross, 1993, pp. 33–4)

As a matter of fact, this article was published on 22 June 1929 in *The Nation and Athenaeum*, a predecessor of what later became the *New Statesman* (Robinson, E.A.J, 1929). Keynes had an ownership interest in it. The magazine carried at least 16 articles by him between 1923 and 1930.[2] During this time, the editor was a Liberal economist, Hubert Douglas

Henderson. It is noteworthy that the author's name was given as 'E.A.J. Robinson'. There is nothing to contradict my conclusion that it was a pseudonym combining the initials 'E.A.' from E.A.G. Robinson and 'J' from Joan Robinson. The article deals with the issues that are more political than economic. It is not in Joan Robinson's style. Joan and Sir Austin were the only Robinsons connected with the princely states in the latter half of the 1920s. Only they could have, therefore, dealt with the subject of the article—the Indian states. According to Sir Austin himself, Keynes had a special relationship with the *Nation* (Robinson, 1977, p. 26). It can reasonably be conjectured that he wrote the article, at least the main part of it. It is very different in style from that of *The British Crown and the Indian States*.

There is no record of the press reviews by Joan that Cairncross mentions. We only know of her activities, as told by Sir Austin. She was seen reading the old editions of newspapers.

Regardless, Austin Robinson carried the day. My contribution, it seems, was merely to have brought into the public domain what had been forgotten and deemed to have been of not much significance. My attribution of the authorship to Joan Robinson, based on K.M. Panikkar's unambiguous naming of 'Mrs. Austin Robinson', was dismissed. The work itself became important, with Joan Robinson's role reduced to a minor helper in editing and proofreading of the report. There was, however, an acknowledgement of her active facilitation of the presentation of the report at the relevant forums.

Cairncross fully credits Austin with the authorship of Part II of *The British Crown and the Indian States*. He places it in the bibliography under the section entitled 'Contributions to Books and Reports'. But he gives 1928 as the year of publication, although every other source mentions 1929 (1993, p. 183).

NOT THE JOAN OF PROVOCATIVENESS

Aslanbeigui and Oakes, the authors of *The Provocative Joan Robinson*, gleaned through the Austin Robinson Papers related to the Indian sojourn and came out with some interesting observations about the contribution of Joan Robinson to *The British Crown and the Indian States*. Curiously, like Panikkar, they referred to her as 'Mrs. Robinson'. Based on her correspondence after returning from India in July 1928 while Austin was still there, they find her to be 'a reflective, well read, intellectually engaged' person (Aslanbeigui & Oakes, 2009, p. 32).

Acknowledging Austin's contribution, these authors mention a draft prepared by him but presented and discussed by Joan, in these words:

> In April 1928, Austin prepared a draft on the economics of the case for the princely states intended for inclusion in part 2 of the report. In late June, his draft was discussed in Delhi by the standing committee. Since his tutorial responsibilities in Gwalior limited his freedom to travel, Robinson went to Delhi in his stead to help finish the draft. At the invitation of the standing committee, she sailed with the committee members to London in order to assist in completing the report and presenting the economic brief. On July 20, two days before arriving in London, she noted that she had written a preface for the report (eagr/Box 8/2/1/13/13–16).[3] (Aslanbeigui & Oakes, 2009, p. 33)

Not only that Joan helped with the draft, she wrote its preface as well. She also shared the draft with William Beveridge, who was then the Director of the London School of Economics (eagr/Box 8/2/1/13/17–21). At the same time, Joan continued to work on the draft as and when the ongoing proceedings of the Butler Committee required. She wrote a joint note on a subject not identified and separate notes on railways and salt, two major issues between the British India and Princely India.

> The Butler Committee met on July 25 but accomplished virtually nothing and adjourned until October. In the intervening months, Robinson continued her work on part 2. By mid-October, an unidentified note on which she had been laboring had become "our note."[4] However, her work seems to have ended in disappointment. In the presentation to the Butler Committee, the note in question was reduced to a "mangled remnant," and although she had added notes on railways and salt, she was dissatisfied with her results.[5] (Aslanbeigui & Oakes, 2009, p. 32)

Thus, Aslanbeigui and Oakes (2009) identified specific contributions made by Joan Robinson to *The British Crown and the Indian States*. First, she drafted a preface which for some reason was not included in the printed version. Secondly, she wrote notes on the vexed issue of salt taxation and the inroads that the development of railways was making into the economies of Princely India. These notes formed part of the book. Thirdly, there was a note she started but ended up as a joint effort. The subject of the note is not known.

In view of these clear and not so clear contributions by Joan Robinson, Aslanbeigui and Oakes refrained from attributing sole authorship to Austin Robinson. They rather used the collective authorship printed in the book, *The Directorate of the Chamber's Special Organization*. They also give the correct year of publication, that is, 1929.

BLOGS ON BOTH OF THEM

In my interactions with Austin Robinson, there was not even a hint of the existence of a manuscript, what to talk of a typescript in his possession. Was he going to talk about it in the interview he promised, I do not know. As stated above, the interview never took place, despite a written acknowledgement of the promise. Be that as it may, his archives at the Marshall Library, Cambridge, include a manuscript. A blog devoted to Austin Robinson's India connection appeared on its website dated 1 November 2016. It was titled 'Austin Robinson's Indian sojourn', [6]

> Amongst the varied and extensive material contained within the Austin Robinson archives held by the Marshall Library, there is an unassuming brown marbled folder containing 112 typewritten foolscap pages. This is the draft report produced by Austin in 1928 at the behest of the Indian States and which was incorporated into "The British Crown and the Indian States" published in 1929. It is significant in that it not only represents Austin's first involvement in the practical problems of development economics but also provides an early example of his belief in the importance of quantifying economic arguments.

The blog continues to claim that Austin's role was to draft the full report, despite his admission to Marjorie Turner that he 'was very busy with the tutoring of the Maharajah' and, therefore, could only work 'on the memoranda in [his] spare moments'. [7] It also attempts to specify the part played by Joan Robinson in the entire episode, which differs from Aslanbeigui and Oakes (2009) that was also sourced in Austin Robinson Papers:

> After reviewing Austin's work the group acting for the States realized that the economic arguments were more complex than they had initially imagined and, in June 1928, asked Joan to accompany them to London to assist in the presentation of their case. Austin was not involved in any subsequent

amendments or the final presentation of the document which was later published by P.S. King as 'The British Crown and the Indian States' in 1929.

A link is given to access *The British Crown and the Indian States*.
Strangely enough, it is not Marshall Library but the Osmania University
that, as noted earlier, was once headed by Morrison, the gentleman
responsible for recommending Austin as tutor to the minor Maharaja
Jivajiro Scindia of Gwalior. Interestingly, Austin's preface to the memorandum showing some of Joan's amendments is also pictured in the blog.
The blog informs that the memorandum 'was eventually much revised and
re-written and was never actually attributed to him in the final published
version which appeared in 1929'. The blogger fails to recognize that it was
not attributed to the other major contributor, K.M. Panikkar, either—nor
of course to Joan Robinson. Austin Robinson could have clarified it in his
lifetime, but did not until I had completed my work. He could have convinced me with evidence to not move in this direction, but did not. He
woke up to it after I had presented alternative evidence. Like his biographer, Austin never challenged Panikkar's statement.

In a later blog on Joan Robinson, [8] the line of her playing the second
fiddle was reasserted: 'Joan assisted Austin in the drafting of a review of
the relations between the Indian states and the British Crown and was
invited to London for the presentation of the Princes' case'. From no role
in the drafting of the memorandum to corrections and then to assistance
and a larger role in presentation and advocacy is the refrain sourced in
Austin Robinson Papers. The other source, K.M. Pannikar, is not even
mentioned, much less contested. There is no reference to my research either.

SOME RECOGNITION: FINALLY

My research found a mention in Amdekar and Singh (2017). [9] They recognized the contribution to an area and period of little or no information.
The attribution controversy ignored the fact that, at the least, I discovered, analysed and contextualized this material. They noted:

> It remains difficult to find research material on India in the 1920s and
> 1930s. It is therefore fortunate that we have some research for this period
> through the efforts of Marshall, Joan Robinson and Austin Robinson as well
> as Pervez Tahir, who completed a Ph.D. at Cambridge in the late 1990s
> with the title 'Some Aspects of Development and Underdevelopment:

Critical Perspectives on Joan Robinson.' Joan and Austin had lived in the then Indian Princely state of Gwalior and participated in the controversy over the question of the division of resources between Gwalior and the government of India. While in Gwalior, Austin wrote drafts of a memorandum covering the major applied economics topics found in Part II of the Economics Tripos, which Joan contributed to through discussion and possible minor revisions. In this sense there can be no doubt that both Joan and Austin developed an active interest in India's economic problems during their stay in Gwalior.[10]

These authors caught the gist of my argument that Joan Robinson was distinct from the company of those economists who had little experience of underdeveloped economies. She looked at these economies to understand global capitalism.

In this sense, Joan Robinson embodied the trail of thinking as it emerged from Malthusian, Marshallian and Keynesian ideas on how humanity might optimally progress, taking these ideas into a new industrial and global dimension. Giving importance to industrialisation, taking active measures for capital accumulation, and the role of a hard state, the Robinsons (like the other Post-Keynesians) drove the idea of human development as a phenomenon of optimisation and aspiration rather than a steady-state process under natural law.[11]

When it came to attribution, they were somewhat more accommodating than the others. According to them, 'In her and Austin Robinson's contribution to *The British Crown and the Indian States*, she presented', and these are my words from the dissertation, 'a realistic, non-Keynesian view of unemployment in the underdeveloped countries, an emphasis on the population problem, optimism about export prospects under international co-operative arrangements … [S]he tended to overemphasize the role of the state'. One of the authors, Ajit Singh, knew Joan Robinson and her works very well. He could see that the issues mentioned here defined the future Joan Robinson. The world of Austin Robinson was completely different. He might have a role in doing the math, something Joan Robinson never claimed to know; so 'she had to think'. Think she did a lot, the origins of which can be seen in the following pages.

Curiously, an item in the Austin Robinson Papers mentions 'undated preface and sections on Customs Revenue and salt production by JVR for draft on Princely States; typed section on salt, single page on relationship between States and Crown'. It suggests that she was also doing applied work.[12] Three questions, however, remain unanswered. One, why did Austin Robinson not give the interview he promised to this writer? Two, why the statement made by K.M. Panikkar was never challenged by anyone, including Austin Robinson? Thirdly, why was there no knowledge about any economic engagement or writing by the Robinsons in India until 1988, when this writer first submitted his doctoral dissertation at Cambridge (Tahir, 1988). [13]

One thing is clear, though. Joan participated in discussions of resource transfer in the context of poverty and backwardness. She also reviewed the material produced in the process. Chapters 6 and 7 seek to connect her experience of Princely and British India on her later writings on development. The early exposure and experience determine the set of issues discussed here. The later work is introduced whenever an early insight or argument seems to link up with it, not only as a reflection of the intellectual development of their author but more importantly as essential elements of the critical perspectives presented in the following pages. When an economist achieves the eminence that Joan Robinson did, especially against great odds, every aspect of the life and work of the person assumes significance. The following chapters explore one such aspect. In her undergraduate days at Cambridge, she felt a concern for the poor and thought that study of economics would help in understanding the causes of poverty.

NOTES

1. The book was published in 1989 by M.E. Sharpe, London. I was given the manuscript for a reading in 1986. Marjorie did the opposite of what Sir Austin said. She acknowledged my effort but paid no money! In the book, what Austin did is not part of the text of the interview but a statement made by the author based on the interview.
2. Sir Austin also mentioned Keynes' special relationship with the magazine. Robinson (1977, p. 26).
3. 'Robinson's preface does not seem to have survived in the published report. The general foreword is written by another author. Although part 2 begins with a brief introduction (The Directorate, 1929, pp. 135–37), it includes constitutional and diplomatic matters that lie outside Robinson's competence' (Aslanbeigui & Oakes, 2009, 33, *n.22*).
4. 'Letter from Robinson to Austin, 10/3/28, eagr/Box 8/2/1/13/26–32' (Aslanbeigui & Oakes, 2009, p. 32, *n.23*).

5. 'Letter from Robinson to Austin, 11/13/28, eagr/Box 8/2/1/13/78–81'. See The Directorate (1929, pp. 197–201) ('The Salt Monopoly') and 201–05 ('Railways')' (Aslanbeigui & Oakes, 2009, p. 32, *n.24*).
6. Marshall Library (2016).
7. Turner (1986/manuscript).
8. Marshall Library (2018).
9. Amdekar and Singh (2017).
10. Ibid., 88.
11. Ibid.
12. Marshall Library, Austin Robinson Papers, Part 1 India, Box 75 7/1/11914–1992.
13. Tahir (1988).

REFERENCES

UNPUBLISHED MATERIAL

Austin Robinson Papers, Marshall Library. Faculty of Economics, University of Cambridge Part 1 India, Box 75 7/1/1 1914–1992.
(eagr/Box 8/2/1/13/13–16).
(eagr/Box 8/2/1/13/17–21).
(eagr/Box 8/2/1/13/26–32).
eagr/Box 8/2/1/13/78–81.
11/13/28.
Turner, M. S. (1986). *Joan Robinson and the Americans*. Manuscript.

PUBLISHED WORKS

Amdekar, S., & Singh, A. (2017). Cambridge and Development Economics. In R. A. Cord (Ed.), *The Palgrave Companion to Cambridge Economics* (pp. 73–92). Palgrave Macmillan.
Aslanbeigui, N., & Oakes, G. (2009). *The Provocative Joan Robinson: The Making of a Cambridge Economist*. Duke University Press.
Cairncross, A. (1993). *Austin Robinson: The Life of an Economic Adviser*. Palgrave.
Marshall Library. (2016). *Faculty of Economics*. University of Cambridge. http://marshlib.blogspot.com/2016/11/austin-robinsons-indian-sojourn.html
Marshall Library. (2018). *Faculty of Economics*. University of Cambridge. http://marshlib.blogspot.com/2018/
Panikkar, K. M. (1979). *An Autobiography*. Oxford University Press.

Robinson, A. (1977). Keynes and his Cambridge Colleagues. In D. Patinkin & J. C. Leith (Eds.), *Keynes, Cambridge and The General Theory*. Macmillan.

Robinson, E. A. J. (1929). The Indian States. *The Nation and Athenaeum, 45*, 392–393.

Tahir, P. (1988). *Some Aspects of Development and Underdevelopment: Critical Perspectives on the Early Contributions of Joan Robinson*. Unpublished.

The British Crown and the Indian States. (1929). P.S. King and Son. Reprinted in India as Chamber of Princes (1988, 2013) *British Crown and the Indian States.* Gyan Publishing House.

Turner, M. S. (1989). *Joan Robinson and the Americans*. M.E. Sharpe.

PART II

Thinking Development: Then and Later

CHAPTER 6

Precolonial Underdevelopment

The larger part of colonial India, as noted in the earlier chapters, was governed directly by the British, but a significant part was ruled by the Indian princes in numerous quasi-autonomous states. Joan Robinson was in the Princely India for about two years in the latter half of the 1920s. In 1927–1928, she was part of the process of preparing the basis for the economic part of the case for the princely states of India in connection with an official committee constituted to rethink their fiscal and political relations with British India. This study was included in a publication, *The British Crown and the Indian States*, in 1929. In providing some general considerations on the economy of India under the British in an historical perspective, the study touched on the key issues of underdevelopment and development that have interested the grand theorists for a long time and which continue to baffle their modern-day descendants and opponents alike.

The significance of the views emanates not so much from their being refined theories, which they were not, but as being the initial exposure of a theorist of Joan Robinson's stature and influence in the making of serious economic and development issues. The fact that she struggled with the problems of poverty and backwardness when Marshall's *Principles* was all that she knew of economics makes the analysis of these views an historically interesting study, for, as Lewis (1955, 9. 6) maintained, the study of development had ceased to be important since Mill's *Principles* was

© The Author(s), under exclusive license to Springer Nature   57
Switzerland AG 2022
P. Tahir, *Joan Robinson in Princely India*, Palgrave Studies in the
History of Economic Thought,
https://doi.org/10.1007/978-3-031-10905-8_6

published in 1848. Further, one will be looking at an 'unspoiled' Joan Robinson, who had not yet started to tread the road paved by imperfect competition, 'left Keynesianism' and 'Robinsonian Marxism'. Even the knowledge of Smith was not handed down by Marshall. An attempt is made to maintain a comparative perspective with the Marshall she knew, the Smith she should have known and the Marx she did not know, together with the possible linkages that emerge with her own later work.

The Concept

Underdevelopment is a state of affairs, a condition found by the study to sit still in the self-sufficiency of the village economy. Marx's social division of labour exists, but it does not display the Smithian dynamic, derived from division of labour and growth of productivity. There is specialization, symbolized in functional castes, but such exchange as would lead Marshallian supply and demand to form prices is nowhere to be seen.

Descriptive Features of the Village Economy

Here one begins to get the tidings of an original state of backwardness or, as in the latter-day usage, underdevelopment. It rests, according to the study, in 'earlier economic organizations' called villages.

> In a vast country possessing few natural waterways, where the temperature is unfavourable to great exertion, where wants are of the simplest, where war made elaborate interdependence risky, it was natural that the unit of economic self-sufficiency should be the smallest, the village. The village grew its crops, spun and wove its cotton, made and mended its simple ploughs and looms, and built by its own labour the mud-walled and thatched cottages which gave such shelter as was needed in a climate where the sky is the natural roof. The village artisans were the servants of the village, paid a recognised yearly tribute of grain per plough and doing in return whatever work was called for. (The British Crown, 1929, pp. 138–9)

The picture drawn here is very close to that painted by Marx in his early writings on India. To him as well, the village was isolated without and self-sufficient within. The isolation without was attributed by Marx to a geography that necessitated centralized, non-voluntary 'care of the great public works, the prime condition of [Indian] agriculture' (Marx, 1853b, p. 128). There was thus no need for village-to-village contact. According to him, the 'village isolation produced the absence of roads in India, and the absence of roads perpetuated the village isolation' and 'the community existed with a given scale of low conveniences' (Marx, 1853c, p. 220). In the study, the vast geographical expanse of India, the absence of natural waterways and a climate 'unfavourable to great exertion' contributed to village isolation, as also the risk that war posed if there were to be interdependence between the villages. With the simplest of wants, the study considered a small village to be the natural unit of self-dependence. Similarly, if to Marx the 'combination of hand-weaving, hand-spinning and hand-tilling agriculture gave [the village] self-supporting power' (Marx, 1853c, p. 131), the study's 'village grew its crops, spun and wove its cotton, made and mended its simple ploughs and looms' so as to be a self-supportive unit.

Joan Robinson had not yet read Marx.[1] The similar manner in which the study comes to look at the village economy as isolated and self-dependent may have more to do with similar access to the literature that had existed for a long time to form part of the Western folklore about the stasis of the East than to any specific influence of Marx. It is difficult to say with any degree of confidence as to what was Joan Robinson reading on the subject. The bases of Marx's indirect information are well-known.[2] She had the advantage of being in India, suggesting the possibility that observation played a greater role in the formulation of the image of the village economy. Being in Princely India, whose isolation had led to the survival of precolonial economic formations, she could observe what the village economy must have looked like before the British intervention. Some of Marx's assumptions have since been challenged.

Habib (1963, p. 119) presents some evidence against communal land ownership. Thorner (1966, p. 57) found Marx's description of the self-sufficient villages 'not, in fact, at all typical of the actual communities'. Naqvi (1972, pp. 393–412) maintains that Marx's conclusions did not follow even from the material used by him. None of these critiques follows up the logic of the argument to show why pre-capitalist forms persisted for so long in precolonial India and, as Joan Robinson directly observed, in Princely India.

ANALYTICS OF STAGNATION

The study's start with an undifferentiated, Durkheimian state of the village economy raises the prospect that it will take an evolutionary course of continuity and development through progressist differentiation. Joan

Robinson had not yet read Marx, so that the question of her following a dialectical or unilineal path did not arise. Still, the study bears comparison with that of Marx not only because of relevance to the questions of development and underdevelopment in general but also for the significance that Joan Robinson's views before reading Marx may have for understanding her position after having read him. For the period relevant to this study, one thing is certain, though. She could not have ignored Adam Smith and, of course, Marshall. To what extent is the study's view of development and underdevelopment an evolutionist view is only an alternative way of asking how much was she influenced by Marshall. 'Marshall', as she remembered her undergraduate days at Cambridge, 'was economics' (Robinson, 1951, p. vii). Until 1929, incidentally the year *The British Crown and the Indian States* was published, economics was nothing but 'the discussion and interpretation' of Marshall's *Principles* (Hutchison, 1953, p. 62). Marshall declared in the preface to the first edition that it was the influence of 'the notion of continuity with regard to development' which 'affected, more than any other, the substance of the views expressed' in the *Principles* (1890, pp. ix–x). By the time the last edition came out, he had adopted continuity and evolution as a motto. 'Economic evolution is gradual'. Hence 'the motto Natura non facit saltum is especially appropriate to a volume on Economic Foundations' (1920, p. xiii).

To know whether Joan Robinson followed this motto, one has to look at the forces and factors the study emphasized for the emergence of Indian society from the undifferentiated village economy. In other words, one must look at the elements that held the village economy together and its potential for change. According to the study, the village 'organization had very much to recommend it' for the following reasons.

> The workers were dealing and thinking in terms of real goods, they shared alike in the good and the bad fortunes of agriculture. The market was at their own door, or in their own bellies. To misjudge it was impossible. There might be gluts and famines, but starvation in the midst of plenty was at least unknown. But its full virtues can only be recognised if it be remembered that budgets of Indian worker's consumption have, in exceptional circumstances, shown a proportion even so high as 95 per cent. on food. (*The British Crown*, 1929, p. 139)

In the village economy of the study, the agents 'buy' goods with goods. No transactions are intermediated by a market with a cash nexus. Gluts or famines, the share-alike ethic prevails. There is no question of failed coordination. The stability of the village economy critically hinged on the empirically observed tendency of an Indian worker's budget to concentrate heavily on food. This was reflected in the fact that the great bulk of the population was nearly completely specialized.

This division of labour as a basis of development was found to be inadequate. Even after 'the growth and advance seen in the last three generations in British India', the nature of specialization had not altered significantly. The study continued:

> Even to-day 73 per cent. of the Indian population is agricultural, and only some 20 per cent. of its products are exported. *The argument for division of labour and specialization as a ground for a new organisation of Indian society is therefore meaningless* [emphasis added]. (*The British Crown*, 1929, pp. 138–9)

This is a strong assertion and must be understood in its proper perspective. The study is not denying the acknowledged role played by the division of labour in economic growth. What it is saying is that even after colonial intervention, the nature of specialization remains significantly the same. To suggest, therefore, that the precolonial village economy would, of its own accord, have developed productivity and the consequent division of labour to pull out of its stagnant equilibrium was not very plausible. The idea of division of labour as the basis of development goes back to Smith. According to him, 'In every improved society, the farmer is generally nothing but a farmer, the manufacturer, nothing but a manufacturer. The labour, too, which is necessary to produce any one complete manufacture, is almost always divided among a great number of hands'. In the village economy, a near-complete specialization existed; a farmer was nothing but a farmer and an artisan largely an artisan. There was thus a division of labour, but it did not seem to have been a consequence of higher productivity, as Smith would have it.

> The division of labour, however, so far as it can be introduced, occasions, in every art, a proportionable increase of the productive powers of labour. *The separation of different trades and employments from one another, seems to have taken place, in consequence of this advantage. This separation, too, is generally carried furthest in those countries which enjoy the highest degree of industry and improvement; what is the work of one man in a rude state of society, being that of several in an improved one* [emphasis added]. (Smith, 1776, p. 5)

The rude state of society had the following characteristics.

> In that rude state of society in which there is no division of labour, in which exchanges are seldom made, and in which every man provides everything for himself, it is not necessary that any stock should be accumulated or stored up beforehand, in order to carry on the business of the society. Every man endeavours to supply by his own industry his own occasional wants as they occur. (Smith, 1776, p. 207)

In village India, although the individual did not produce for himself alone, accumulation of stock beforehand was not deemed necessary as in the rude state. This is what the study had in view when it doubted division of labour as the basis for development. Smith's rude state refers to self-sufficient individuals, while the study is looking at a community which is geared towards self-sufficiency. Neither is the village economy in the rude state because it has division of labour, nor is it out of this state because there is no accumulation of stock. Since there is specialization, there is exchange, but it is largely the predictable intra-village transactions. The preponderance of food in the consumer budgets severely restricts the uncertain inter-trade or exchange.

Productivity theory has been described as one, though an important, aspect of Smith's theory. The study refers to the 20 per cent of the agricultural produce that was exported. This is not a small percentage. How did these exports emerge? Is this assertion based on a vent-for-surplus theory, which has been claimed to be more relevant to the colonial situations than the productivity theory? Simply stated, in this theory opening of trade provides a vent for the gap between the production possibility and actual production.[3]

The reason to suspect this as the explanation for the assertion in the study is occasioned by its sketch of the village economy.[4] However, the other rather Keynesian requirements are not met by this view. The vent-for-surplus theory assumed a latent surplus capacity which was utilized in response to the effective demand when the colonial state developed the physical infrastructure and ensured peace and security.

In the village economy of the study, the division of labour was limited by the extent of the market in Smith's sense, but this market did not extend beyond the agents' 'own door' or 'their own bellies'. The cultivators fed themselves, and the artisans who, as the servants of the village, shared the produce of the village and supplied whatever number of ploughs, among others, were required. The artisans owned their means of production. Access to means of production as well as subsistence was not through the market with a cash nexus. There was no money and nothing in the nature of a sales problem.

Future Keynesians involved in the study observed that 'starvation in the midst of plenty was at least unknown.' It is hardly possible to discern a demand constraint here.

As a Keynesian, Joan Robinson would observe:

> In an economy in which there is specialisation and exchange the principle of effective demand comes into play, and unemployment may occur. If, however, there are no debts, no form of money and no negotiable capital instruments, the output of the community will be in neutral equilibrium. (Robinson, 1936, p. 223)

Indeed, her view of the village economy never changed, despite the evidence noted earlier. A later exposition brings it out more sharply.

> For the peasant economy to be viable it is necessary that each local community should support the tradesmen it requires - one blacksmith, two barbers, five priests, or whatever it may be, and they must receive a living wage per man year ... The simplest plan is one that still persists in an unmodernized Indian village: the village specialists have a right to a certain percentage share in the harvest and must do as much or as little work as happens to be required. (Robinson, 1962, p. 31)

These features of the village economy precluded any important role for the division of labour and specialization as a basis for change in the socioeconomic organization. Left to itself, the village economy had no urge to break up.

In expressing misgivings about division of labour as the basis of an autocentric transition from the village economy, study's departure from Smith's grand design for development was in keeping with the general spirit of the time, dominated by Marshall. His problem with reconciling increasing returns and competitive equilibrium contributed to a lack of attention to the division of labour and problem of growth.[5]

Marshall himself made the division of labour the basis of his evolutionary perspective of development.[6]

Some sort of division of labour is indeed sure to grow up in any civilization that has held together for a long while, however primitive its form. Even in very backward countries we find highly specialised trades; but we do not find the work within each trade so divided up that the planning and arrangement of the business, its management and its risks, are borne by one set of people, while the manual work required for it is done by hired labour. This form of division of labour is at once characteristic of the modern world generally, and of English race in particular. It may be merely a passing phase in man's development; it may be swept away by the further growth of that free enterprise which has called it into existence. But for the present it stands out for good or for evil as the chief fact in the form of modern civilization, the kernel of the modem economic problem. (Marshall, 1890, p. 37)

The existence of a certain division of labour is recognized in backward economies. It takes the form of specialized trades. Thus far the study and Marshall agree with each other. Marshall then goes on to distinguish the backward economies from the advanced economies by the absence or the presence of division of labour within trades. By that Marshall does not mean the technical specialization by workers in Smith's pin factory but the capitalist division of labour between entrepreneurs and the hired labour, which he considers to be 'the chief fact in the form of modem civilization'. Apparently, this division of labour, called forth by the growth of free enterprise, is prior to the technical division of labour. Against the study's pessimism about the division of labour as the basis of autocentric development from the village economy, Marshall envisages a process evolving.

He believed that life in early civilizations 'is pervaded almost unconsciously by a few simple ideas which are interwoven in that pleasant harmony that gives their charm to Oriental carpets'. In 'such a civilization the ablest men look down on work; there are no bold free enterprising workmen, and no adventurous capitalists; despised industry is regulated by custom, and even looks to custom as its sole protector from arbitrary tyranny'. Furthermore,

> there is nothing in the first steps of progress that tends to break down the primitive habit of regarding the innovator as impious, and an enemy. *The influence of economic causes is pressed below the surface. There they work surely and slowly* [emphasis added]: but they take generations instead of years to produce their effect; and their action is so subtle as easily to escape observation altogether. They can indeed hardly be traced except by those who have

learnt where to look for them by watching the more conspicuous and rapid workings of similar causes in modem times. (Marshall, 1890, pp. 13–4)

Earlier, in his inaugural lecture at Cambridge, he had cited India as a place to look for the facts in modem times.

We are able to cross-examine the facts of modern India; and I believe that our science working on those facts will gradually produce a solvent, which will explain much that is now unintelligible in mediaeval history. (Marshall, 1885, p. 50)

The cross-examination of the facts of India in the study led to a different story.

India is already so organised that 73 per cent. of her population are specialists wholly, or almost wholly, occupied in agriculture, and a further 17 per cent. are resident in villages, and dependent for their living upon the village agriculture economy. *The urge to the break-up of the old village organisation was therefore in itself small* [emphasis added]. (*The British Crown*, 1929, p. 139)

Of course, the study did not directly mention Marshall, but the implicit rejection of his evolutionary view of development calls to mind an earlier attack on Marshall by Cunningham. Placing him with the nineteenth-century evolutionists such as Spencer, Cunningham lashed out at Marshall for perverting history. He doubted the existence of a 'royal road by which we may get to comprehend the evolution of social structure and of economic conceptions, which combined to bring about industrial progress'. Marshall, maintained Cunningham, was making the strong underlying assumption that 'the same motives have been at work in all ages, and have produced similar results, and that, therefore, it is possible to formulate economic laws which describe the action of economic causes at all times and in all places' (Cunningham, 1892, pp. 491–2).

This attack on his view of development was the only time Marshall had 'broken through my rule of not replying to criticisms'. He replied:

Those who know best the rural districts of England, or parts of the Continent or of India in which the mediaeval tone lingers most, recognise the most fully how under a very still surface there may be running many keen little pursuits of private gain; and they tell quaint stories of sly devices for getting the best of one's neighbour even in the quietest corners of the world. The very quiet affords time and opportunity for elaborate manoeuvring in small matters.

To hold this is quite consistent with the belief that in backward times and places there are many rights and dues which are, for a while at least, as rigidly fixed by custom as they could be by a modern law or a contract made out on stamped parchment. (Marshall, 1892, pp. 509–10, 18)

These two paragraphs from Marshall may aptly serve as the manifesto of the neoclassical resurgence in the field of development.[7] So far as Joan Robinson was concerned, her struggle to escape from Marshall's influence started during her undergraduate days at Cambridge and continued in Princely India as she grappled with the problems of development and underdevelopment. The only writing Joan Robinson had done before her engagement with *The British Crown* (1929) group, and which was published as well though not at the time but much later (Robinson & Morison, 1951), owed 'everything to Marshall' (Robinson, 1951, p. ix). In her words, this writing 'indicates how I took to him. I felt smothered by the moralizing and mystified by the theory' (Robinson, 1978, p. ix).

Smith was not free of 'moral preconceptions' either. Indeed, her attempt to penetrate these preconceptions (Robinson, 1962, pp. 30–3) brought an encounter between Willet (1968) and herself (Robinson, 1968), which is reminiscent of the Marshall-Cunningham polemic.[8] Criticizing Willett's defence of Smith, Joan Robinson had said:

Professor Willett's argument is an excellent example of the kind of doctrine I was attacking in my little book [Robinson (1962)]. He seeks to find one set of 'laws' that operate in all economies and apply equally to all societies - the hunters in Adam Smith's forest as well as capitalist firms in Marshall's England or Galbraith's America. (Robinson, 1968, p. 33)

Far from being a Marshallian evolution, 'the growth and advance seen in the last three generations in British India' was, in the words of *The British Crown*, a combined result of 'the upheaval of a rapid change in economic organisation' and 'the benefit of modern developments which in time br[ought] about readjustment'. These modern developments were identified as railways and other forms of physical infrastructure (1929, pp. 138, 143). In other words, exports did not constitute a vent for surplus. Their proportion was not significant anyway. More significant was the overall change in economic organization which was brought about by transport and other infrastructure. The maintenance of peace and security for a relatively long period also removed critical ground from underneath the arguments for village self-sufficiency.

It appears that the movement away from Marshall was unsuspectingly taking her towards Marx. It was seen above that she was not conversant with Marx while observing underdevelopment and development in India. In noting the similarities of their views on the way the village economy functioned, we speculated that the reason might be the common sources of information. But dismissal in *The British Crown* of division of labour as a ground for development from the village economy is not very different either from the analysis by Marx. There are crucially significant parallels in the role denied to the division of labour in the transition and the potential for development.

In the language of Marx, the division of labour that *The British Crown* considers incapable of brewing a new socio-economic organization is conceptualized as the social division of labour. 'This division of labour is a necessary condition for the production of commodities,' that is, production which is not for direct use, 'but it does not follow, conversely, that the production of commodities is a necessary condition for [the social] division of labour'. Marx then chooses India as an example: 'In the primitive Indian community there is social division of labour, without production of commodities'. He finds it to be 'an unalterable division of labour'. And this social division of labour in the Indian villages has the same role in Marx as in *The British Crown*; it causes stagnation, and the system keeps on reproducing itself without developing into a higher socio-economic form.

> The law that regulates the division of labour in the community acts with the irresistible authority of a law of Nature, at the same time that each individual artificer, the smith, the carpenter, and so on, conducts in his workshop all the operations of his handicraft in the traditional way, but independently, and without recognising any authority over him. The simplicity of the organisation for production in these self-sufficing communities that constantly reproduce themselves in the same form supplies the key to the secret of the unchangeableness of Asiatic societies. (Marx, 1867, pp. 42, 357–8)

The British Crown was thus closer to Marx than Smith or Marshall in its pessimism about the ability of the social division of labour to lead Indian society out of the precolonial village economy. As the social division of labour in the village economy struck many an observer as coinciding with the caste divisions, the next task is to analyse the extent to which these customs contributed to stabilizing the existing division of labour and to stunting the potential for development.

SOCIAL STATICS, CASTE AND HEREDITARY OCCUPATIONS

Following the procedure adopted so far in regard to caste as well, we look at the position taken in *The British Crown* in the perspective of the lines assumed by the grand theorists—Smith, Marx and Marshall. In addition, an attempt is made to infer from insights contained in Robinson (1933) an analytical rationale for the caste factor. Hopefully, it will throw further light on the grounds for pessimism in *The British Crown* about the ability of the division of labour to effect a change in the socio-economic status quo in precolonial India.

Joan Robinson's short review note on a book about caste customs evinced her interest in the 'most topical aspects of caste - untouchability, and the persistence of strong caste feeling in the face of the modern relaxation of caste rules among educated Hindus'. She was far from 'hazarding an opinion upon the fascinating and mysterious question of the origin of the caste system'. Significantly, she made none of what she described as the 'various popular errors, such as that caste is primarily based upon occupation' (Robinson, 1932, p. 138). Thus, it was not enough to know the caste to accurately tell the occupation. The author of the book she was reviewing also understood 'that many castes, in particular functional castes, have a hereditary calling, and that, in some cases, many of their members follow it'. He reckoned some of these to be 'either so high or so low that only certain castes engage in them'. Then this author went on to maintain that the pursuit of hereditary occupations by functional castes was more prevalent in villages, pointing out at the same time that 90 per cent of the Indian population resided in the villages. 'Certain handicraftsmen, such as potters, blacksmiths, barbers and washermen, have always been recognized members of the village community as well as inheritors of a caste calling, and are known generically as village servants' (O'Malley, 1932, pp. 122, 131–2).

Since it is the stagnation in the village economy that was holding up development in precolonial India, the focus has to be on the rigidity of functional castes and hereditary occupations in that economy. As a matter of fact, *The British Crown* had spoken of India as 'a country of hereditary employments and static organisation' (1929, p. 143). It was just noted that Joan Robinson did not see caste as based on occupation. But occupations were hereditary, which she seemed to suggest made the organization static. Since castes are hereditary, too, the question whether the incapacity of the division of labour to lift village economy up to a higher socioeconomic organization was related to the links between the caste customs and the hereditary nature of specialization wants further investigation.

In his writings on India, Marx forcefully described 'the hereditary division of labour, upon which rest the Indian castes' as 'decisive impediments to Indian progress' (Marx, 1853c, p. 221). He saw the hereditary division of labour as the economic basis and caste as a negative superstructural development (Marx, 1973, p. 500). Earlier, when in his view 'the crude form in which the division of labour' appears in India and 'calls forth the caste-system' of the Hindu religion, the historian who 'believes that the caste-system is the power which has produced this crude social form' was scoffed at as having 'had to *share the illusion of that epoch*' (Italics in original) (Marx & Engels, 1965, p. 51). It was a social division of labour for which commodity production was not necessary. His expectation was that the railway and its linkage with industrialization would dissolve the hereditary division of labour. Railways here symbolized mobility to which caste was a significant barrier, and industry was interpretable as leading to division of labour in the workshop. Joan Robinson's lumping together of hereditary employments and static organization may be seen in a similar light, the former being the basis of the latter, with the qualification that though Marx was not yet making a sharp distinction between class and division of labour as the basis of development, she was at the time not at all concerned with social class. She did not conflate caste and occupation invariably. But she did seem to believe in a connection between hereditary occupations and static socio-economic organization.

Smith noted the existence of castes in India: 'the whole body of the people was divided into different castes each of which was confined to a particular employment or class of employments' (Smith, 1776, p. 535). But his development framework remains unaffected by these features of caste. It was in the nature of the individuals to exchange, so that the society enjoyed a division of labour which was in harmony with individual interest. More and more of the same led to further development of the society. He drew no distinction between social division of labour and what Marx called division of labour in the workshop. Greater division of labour means further subdivision of tasks, but each task is performed by a separate individual as a distinct occupation. What must be the world's best-known factory, his pin factory, was used by him as an illustration to put in bold relief the higher productivity attending division of labour and not as the concept of division of labour.[9] In point of fact, Joan Robinson put it in bolder relief by using the caste factor at its most restrictive. It also suggests how, in her view, caste might fit in the trio of caste, hereditary division of labour and static socio-economic organization.

> The maximum rate of decreasing cost would occur if each unit of the factors was completely specialised and capable of performing only one task. If, in Adam Smith's pin factory, each of the workers had been bound by a rigid caste system to a single occupation, then to produce even one pin it would be necessary to employ the whole number of workers - one to draw out the wire, another to straight it, a third to cut it, and so forth. Then, if the wage per man were independent of his output,[10] the total cost of the capacity output of the team of workers would be equal to the cost of one pin, and the maximum possible rate of falling cost would be obtained. When the capacity output of one team was reached a fresh team would have to be employed and there would be no further possibilities of specialisation. (Robinson, 1933, p. 336)

This she thought was not normally the case. The units of a factor in practice were imperfectly specialized. At smaller outputs, 'a single indivisible unit of a factor, for instance, a man, may perform a number of different tasks. The Law of Increasing Returns is often associated with the fact that, as output increases, the number of tasks performed by the indivisible units of the factors is reduced'. Time saving in Smith's pin factory in moving from one to another operation and Marshall's example of waste involved in using a skilled worker at lower output when an unskilled worker would do were the instances given by Joan Robinson. With the increase of output, 'a method higher in the hierarchy of specialisation can be adopted' (Ibid.).

The principles underlying the above application by Joan Robinson of a caste rule in Smith's pin factory have an interesting analytical analogue in the 'village corporation',[11] given some important qualifications. Obviously, the village corporation does not produce a homogeneous output like the pin factory. But it will not be unreasonable to assume that the overriding concentration on food practically reduces it to a single-output unit. Similarly, it might look absurd to seek to apply the principle of increasing returns in an agricultural situation, reserved as it is usually for manufacturing concerns such as Smith's pin factory. It will not, it is hoped, seem as far-fetched if it is kept in view that the purpose is to understand why productivity is not rising in the village corporation, despite a clear-cut division of labour.

Caste rules in the village corporation are more strictly binding than the rules of a European guild. Entry or exit in the latter only requires the engagement or otherwise in the trade in question. In the case of village corporation, disengaging from the trade does not mean that a member of a functional caste ceases to be one; the membership is hereditary and the agent may be required to become functional at any time. Castes also reflect completely or nearly completely specialized agents, following hereditary occupations and performing, so far as the village is concerned, only one task. According to Joan Robinson's reasoning, the result of caste-based, specialized occupations would be that even to produce one unit of the output, all agents had to be employed. In the village corporation, all had to stand ready to contribute to the village output, as the need arose.

In a sense, all were 'employed'. 'Wage' in the village economy was independent of output, being share in whatever was produced. Just as in the pin factory with caste-enforced specialisms, it takes the entire team of workers in the village corporation to produce its output. The crucial difference is that the pin factory experiences falling costs if it produces more, but the village corporation only reproduces itself. Or, may it be said, producing more or less 'costs' the same per unit. While caste ties a worker to his specialization completely, there is actually no reduction of tasks performed. In fact, the members of the village corporation start where, according to Joan Robinson, the 'maximum rate of decreasing cost would occur'. It does not, because there is no fixed capacity when labour is the only productive source, and there are thus no economies of scale.

The presence of specialization suggests existence of exchange, though this too is limited by the predominance of food in consumption budgets. Money either does not exist or is not important as exchange in the village corporation has the semblance of intra-firm trade and there is no need to incur the cost of knowing what the prices are. That is how Marx's craft-agriculture unity is maintained. Hereditary employments imply complete specialization, but higher productivity and improved producing organization do not follow. This is one possible explanation of the pessimism in *The British Crown* about the division of labour as an agent of autocentric development. Nevertheless, Smith should not become totally irrelevant as the division of labour would be limited by the extent of the market. But if there were a market, its existence would be inseparable from the formation of prices. We have already noted that the market in the village was limited to, as *The British Crown* put it, the agent's belly or it was at his door. True, Smith's

> way lies ahead, through the increasing productivity that follows the division of labour ... [T]he main point is to argue the advantages of free trade and accumulation of stock. The important thing is increasing physical output, and prices do not really matter very much. (Robinson, 1962, pp. 32–3)

So far as Joan Robinson's reading of precolonial Indian conditions in *The British Crown* (1929) was concerned, the above did not obtain there. Neither accumulation nor prices mattered very much.

In regard to prices, Marshall would have sharply disagreed. Division of labour, market and prices were important ingredients of the evolutionary process of development. Custom ruled 'the general tenor of life in India', but it did not 'rule prices'. There were variations in prices of goods entering international trade, but the prices of internationally non-traded grains varied even more (Marshall, 1926, pp. 274–6). During its time, caste was excellently adapted for required specialization 'in spite of its great faults, the chief of which were its rigidity, and its sacrifice of the individual to the interest of society, or rather some special exigencies of society' (Marshall, 1890, pp. 304–7).

It is shown that the original state identified in the study is such as will fit the descriptions of underdevelopment in modem literature; the internal precolonial economic foundations are seen to possess little dynamic; and the long-term course of capitalist development, following external penetration, is found to be nationalistic and struggling to evolve after the known Western economic history. Development means Western industrialism and the question of going beyond capitalism or the possibility of alternatives to it did not arise.

KNITTING THE STORY

To recap: This chapter deals with Joan Robinson's understanding of the problem of underdevelopment or backwardness, as it then was called. It is a precolonial state, characterized by the predominance of the village economy. In the first place, the descriptive features of the village economy are spelled out and are shown to be similar to the picture painted by Marx. Secondly, the basis of the stagnation of the village economy of precolonial

India is identified as a social division of labour that is not an outcome of the Smithian productivity dynamic. Thirdly, the question of the relevance of the vent-for-surplus theory is examined. Fourthly, the discussion moves to the influence on Joan Robinson of the apparent paradox that though Marshall himself stressed the role of division of labour, his problems with increasing returns associated with the division of labour contributed to a lack of interest in the concept. Fifthly, it is pointed out that the Marshall-Cunningham encounter towards the end of the nineteenth century on history versus evolutionism reverberated in the rejection of the evolutionist view implied in the interpretation of underdevelopment in India. Her own later encounter with Willett is seen to reflect a break with Marshall. Sixthly, it is argued that the similarity with Marx is not confined to the descriptive features of the village economy; the absence of an autocentric dynamic is also asserted by both. Finally, an attempt is made to construct an analytical story to illustrate the relationship between caste, hereditary division of labour and static socio-economic organization. This division of labour entails a specialization that implies exchange, but this exchange does not lead to the formation of Marshallian supply and demand and an equilibrium price.

The upshot of the understanding in *The British Crown* of Indian underdevelopment is this. In the village economy, the existence of near-complete specialization suggests there must be exchange. The principal justification for a highly specialized occupation is that it supplies a large body of takers. Where the takers do not exist in large numbers, as in the village economy, specialized occupations have to be hereditary and denominated in castes, producing their products as and when required if they are artisans and sharing the food produced by the cultivating castes, which again supply themselves and the small number of village servants. Such a division of labour does not lead to the cumulative productivity improvements envisaged by Smith. The exchange that there is fails to throw up Marshallian prices either. Like Marx, the production organization in *The British Crown* is static, its arteries blocked by the hereditary division of labour.

NOTES

1. 'I began to read Marx after passing through the Keynesian Revolution' (Robinson, 1974, p. x).
2. See Hobsbawm (1964, pp. 21–2) and Mukhia (1985, p. 174) for the literature available to Marx on the village economy.

3. Myint (1958).
4. See S. Smith (1979, p. 55) for the link between the concept of the precolonial village economy and the vent-for-surplus theory, as well as a general critique of this 'mechanistic formulation of the export expansion process' (Sender & Smith, 1986, p. 15).
5. This would be the focus of her research on returning from India. See Robinson (1933). Interestingly, Joan Robinson was writing in the same year when Young (1928) revived interest in increasing returns and economic growth.
6. The material presented here from Book I of the first edition of the *Principles* underwent some editorial changes in the text in the later editions and was moved to Appendix 1 from the fifth edition. See Gillebaud (1961, p. 772).
7. See Toye (1984) for a summary and critique.
8. This is an issue that has seemed to confront all great development theorists. As we will see below, Ranade (1906)—the doyen of Indian economics and a pioneer of pioneers in development—had launched a similar attack on the classical school as early as in 1898. Seers' special case (1963) and Hirschman's monoeconomics (1981, p. 3) are the modern terms of reference of this old debate.
9. If there was a concept of division of labour which Smith valued most, it pertained to the division between town and country.
10. The device of paying a unit of a factor according to its output produces the same effect as though the unit were perfectly divisible. If Adam Smith's pin makers were paid at the same rate per pin when each worked separately as when they co-operated, the cost of pins would not alter as their output increased. [Footnote in original.]
11. See Marx (1858, p. 547) for this expression. Apparently, he picked it up from Raffles' *History of Java*, as is evident from Marx (1853c, p. 131). See Raffles (1817).

REFERENCES

Cunningham, W. (1892). The Perversion of Economic History. *Economic Journal, 2*, 491–506.
Guillebaud, C. W. (Ed.). (1961). *Marshall's Principles of Economics* (Vol. 2). Macmillan.
Habib, I. (1963). *The Agrarian System of Mughal India*. Asia Publishing House.
Hirschman, A. O. (1981). *Essays in Trespassing*. Cambridge University Press.
Hobsbawm, E. (Ed.). (1964). *Karl Marx: Pre-capitalist Economic Formations*. Lawrence and Wishart.

Hutchison, T. W. (1953). *A Review of Economic Doctrines 1870–1929.* Clarenden Press.

Lewis, W. A. (1955). *The Theory of Economic Growth.* George Allen and Unwin.

Marshall, A. (1885). *The Present Position of Economics.* Macmillan.

Marshall, A. (1890). *Principles of Economics* (Vol. 1, 1st ed.). Macmillan.

Marshall, A. (1892). A Reply. *Economic Journal, 2,* 507–519.

Marshall, A. (1920). *Principles of Economics* (8th ed.). Macmillan.

Marshall, A. (1926). *Official Papers.* Macmillan.

Marx, K. (1853b). The British Rule in India. In *Marx and Engels (1979).*

Marx, K. (1853c). The Future Results of British Rule in India. In *Marx and Engels (1979).*

Marx, K. (1858). Lord Canning's Proclamation and Land Tenure in India. In *Collected Works of Marx and Engels* (Vol. 15). Lawrence and Wishart, 1986.

Marx, K. (1867). *Capital* (Vol. 1). Lawrence and Wishart. Reprinted 1970.

Marx, K. (1973). *Grundrisse.* Penguin Books.

Marx, K., & Engels, F. (1965). *The German Ideology.* Lawrence and Wishart.

Mukhia, H. (1985). Marx on Pre-colonial India: An Evaluation. In D. Banerjee (Ed.), *Marxian Theory and the Third World.* Sage.

Myint, H. (1958). The "Classical Theory" of International Trade and Underdeveloped Countries. *Economic Journal, 68,* 317–337.

Naqvi, S. (1972). Marx on Pre-British Indian Society and Economy. *Indian Economic and Social History Review, 9,* 380–412.

O'Malley, L. S. S. (1932). *Indian Caste Customs.* Cambridge University Press.

Raffles, T. S. (1817). *The History of Java.* Gilbert and Rivington.

Ranade, M. G. (1906). *Essays in Indian Economics* (2nd ed.). G.A. Natesan.

Robinson, J. (1951). Introduction. In *Robinson (1951a).*

Robinson, J., & Morison, D. (1951). Beauty and the Beast. In *Robinson (1951a).*

Robinson, J. (1932). Review of O'Malley (1932). *Cambridge Review, 54,* 138.

Robinson, J. (1933). *The Economics of Imperfect Competition.* Macmillan.

Robinson, J. (1936). Disguised Unemployment. *Economic Journal, 46,* 223–237.

Robinson, J. (1962). *Economic Philosophy.* C.A. Watts.

Robinson, J. (1968). A Reply. *Journal of Economic Studies, 3,* 33.

Robinson, J. (1974). Introduction. In J. Robinson (Ed.), *Selected Economic Writings.* Oxford University Press.

Robinson, J. (1978). Reminiscences. In J. Robinson (Ed.), *Contributions to Modern Economics.* Basil Blackwell.

Seers, D. (1963). The Limitations of the Special Case. *Bulletin of the Oxford Institute of Economics and Statistics, 25,* 77–98.

Sender, J., & Smith, S. (1986). *The Development of Capitalism in Africa.* Methuen.

Smith, A. (1776). *An Inquiry Into the Nature and Causes of the Wealth of Nations.* George Routledge and Sons. Reprinted 1890.

Smith, S. (1979). Colonialism in Economic Theory: The Experience of Nigeria. In S. Smith & J. Toye (Eds.), *Trade and Poor Economies*. Frank Cass.

The British Crown and the Indian States. (1929). P.S. King and Son.

Thomer, D. (1966). Marx on India and the Asiatic Mode of Production. *Contributions to Indian Sociology, 9*, 33–66.

Toye, J. (1984). *A Defence of Development Economics*. University College.

Willet, T. D. (1968). A Defence of Adam Smith's Deer and Beaver Model. *Journal of Economic Studies, 3*, 29–32.

Young, A. A. (1928). Increasing Returns and Economic Progress. *Economic Journal, 38*, 527–542.

CHAPTER 7

Colonial Development

In this chapter, we outline Joan Robinson's early insights on development derived from the work on *The British Crown and the Indian States*. Development is considered to be the same thing as Western industrialism. How did the village economy break up is the question addressed here. As it lacked internal economic forces to outgrow itself, external penetration became inevitable. Colonialism played this role. Here again she seems to be following Marx unknowingly, which justifies the detailed comparisons made between the two. The external forces, it is pointed out, took the form of international division of labour forced by colonialism and the supportive role of the colonial state in providing the needed infrastructure. Money, exchange and the associated uncertainty disturb the life of an 'optimizing peasant', while the relatively cheap money-based machine-made goods undersell the village industries. The discussion then turns to the consequences of external economic impact. Whereas Marx had talked of the slower dissolving effects on the internal solidity of the pre-capitalist mode of production, the study focuses on the continued predominance of agriculture and a slower development of internal trade. The preconditions for an industrial revolution were being laid, but the industrial revolution itself was not round the corner.

At this point, nationalism is examined as a theory of development. It is argued that the main case in the study rests on an industrial revolution–type argument and not on transition to capitalism. It does not pose the

© The Author(s), under exclusive license to Springer Nature Switzerland AG 2022
P. Tahir, *Joan Robinson in Princely India*, Palgrave Studies in the History of Economic Thought,
https://doi.org/10.1007/978-3-031-10905-8_7

counterfactual question of what would have happened had a national industrial policy been adopted in the nineteenth century, nor does it follow Keynes's conclusion that India should specialize in agricultural exports (Keynes, 1911). Significantly, the study disputes the claim by the nationalists that India was perfectly adapted to industrialization. Basing the case on the low per capita consumption of manufactures, the study asserts that India had a long way to go on the path of Western economic history. The doubts are about the pace, not the path.

THE IDEA OF DEVELOPMENT

Thus far the implicit assumption has been that development to Joan Robinson meant capitalist development, in the way of which stood the weak urge to break up the village economy, embodied in an idyllic division of labour. At least during her sojourn to India in the latter half of the 1920s, it could not be expected to have been a concept of noncapitalist development. The fact that the analysis was to form the basis of a report for the Indian princes to be presented before an imperial committee, which obviously could not have been a socialist manifesto, was not the reason. As noted previously, she had not yet read Marx and there was no hint of any interest on her part in alternatives to Western-style capitalist development. Marx's interest was unequivocally the capitalist development of India. However, as will be seen later, the argument in *The British Crown* is basically an industrial revolution type; the emphasis is on industrial capitalism. Doubtless, both found nothing organic in the economic chemistry of the village system that would of itself lead to development. The breakthrough had to be injected externally.

> The urge to the break-up of the old village organisation was ... in itself small ... The urge was, in fact, at first as much sentimental and political in origin as economic. (*The British Crown*, 1929, p. 139)

According to Marx,

> Where the members of the community have already acquired separate existence as private proprietors from their collective existence ..., conditions already arise which allow the individual to *lose* his property, i.e. the double relationship which makes him both a citizen with equal status, a member of the community, and a *proprietor*. In the oriental form this loss is hardly possible, except as a result of entirely external influences, for the individual

member of the community never establishes so independent a relation to it as to enable him to lose his (objective, economic) tie with it. He is firmly rooted. This is also an aspect of the union of manufacture and agriculture [emphases in original]. (Hobsbawm, 1964, pp. 93–4)

Thus, Marx and *The British Crown* both see the significance of factors external to the village economy in leading the latter to the path of development. But this contradicts the earlier stated position about the impotence of autocentric economic forces by suggesting that they were as important as the other factors. A closer look at the context of these remarks indicates that the reference here is not, as in Marx, to an economic base. The 'economic' factors are part of the overall external influences on the village economy—which are economic, political and sentimental. Economic factors related largely to the British commercial supremacy and international division of labour, political factors encompassed colonialism in its role as a developer of infrastructure and resources and its modernizing sociocultural influences, and the sentimental factors seem to refer to economic nationalism of the non-populist type. The first two, being interlinked, are discussed together and the latter, in view of its pivotal importance in the would-be development economics, separately.

COLONIALISM AND THE TRANSITION TO THE WORLD ECONOMY

The British commercial supremacy forced on British India 'the transition from a village to a world economy' in the manner of economic shocks. The 'laborious products of the village artisans' failed to compete with the barrage of money-based 'machine-made goods'. Colonialism served the interests of this world division of labour by ensuring that the infrastructure lines did not run counter to it. Being 'Europeans, convinced without argument or experiment that whatever was best for Europe was best for India', the colonial rulers were concerned that direct links with the world market were quickly established. The resulting risks and uncertainties visited upon the self-sufficient village agriculture economy were left to find a resolution on their own. As the colonial state pursued a policy of providing modem physical infrastructure, such as railways, roads, post and telegraph, the village economy was exposed to external economic influences. The infrastructure development basically served the needs of security, but it was on 'the provision of security' that the 'whole development of India in the nineteenth and twentieth century has depended' (*The British Crown*, 1929, pp. 140–2,5). Whatever the original aim, the infrastructure development had its economic effects, too.

Similarly, in the early writings of Marx on India, British commercialism and colonialism were repeatedly emphasized as the external forces instrumental in destroying the unchanging village economy. After noting the hitherto preference in India of the British aristocracy for conquest, of moneyocracy for plunder and of millocracy for underselling, Marx ascribes to millocracy the discovery that 'the transformation of India into a reproductive country has become of vital importance to them'. Towards this end, 'They intend now drawing a net of railroads over India'. He continued:

> I know that the English millocracy intend to endow India with railways with the exclusive view of extracting at diminished expenses the cotton and the other raw materials for their manufactures. But when you have once introduced machinery into the locomotion of a country, which possesses iron and coals, you are unable to withhold it from its fabrication. You cannot maintain a net of railways over an immense country without introducing all those industrial processes necessary to meet the immediate and current wants of railway locomotion, and out of which there must grow the application of machinery to those branches of industry not immediately connected with railways. The railway system will therefore become, in India, truly the forerunner of modern industry. (Marx, 1853, pp. 218–20)

The British Crown leaves no doubt that the greater use of money is a sign of development. The emphasis is not only on machine-based goods. The goods that destroy the handicrafts are money-based, in addition to being machine-based. The argument is connected with the view that the insurmountable walls of the village were raised, among other things, to insure against the situation where 'war made elaborate interdependence risky' (*The British Crown*, 1929, p. 138). Marx's explanation consisted in viewing conquests as leaving the essential unity of crafts and agriculture in the village unimpaired 'since the individual in [the pre-capitalist Asian] form never becomes an owner but only a possessor' (Hobsbawm, 1964, pp. 91–2).

Earlier, it was noted that the social division of labour reflected in functional castes required some exchange, but not necessarily through an elaborate use of money. The overwhelming concentration on food in the budget of the average consumer made its need felt even less. Exchange with little or minimal intermediation of money was essentially part of the risk-averse fortification of the village. With the rise of the British, the direct link with the world market as well as their land policies exposed the village to the uncertainties of international trade and caused payments of rents and land taxes in money. The displacement of village craftsmen also meant payments for imported substitutes in terms of money. To do that, the cultivator had to sell his surplus for money, earned in many cases by shifting from food to cash crops. It even led to dependence for food and the need to purchase it with cash. Money itself was thus part of the externally thrust dynamic of the 'upheaval of a rapid change in economic organisation' (*The British Crown*, 1929, p. 143). Uncertainty, associated with the sudden increase of monetary transactions, eroded the collective risk-aversion of the village economy, as the following argument suggests.

> To one accustomed to think in terms of European conditions and standards, hesitancy to embark on such a trade would appear foolish. But it must be remembered that the Indian villager is in even worse position to carry risks and dangers than a European farmer. In an average year he secures barely enough to fill the mouths of his household. In a bad year they go short. So long as he is growing crops to feed himself and to pay his rent, he feels as safe as he can be in his circumstances. To grow crops for an unknown and uncertain market brings an additional risk which he was at first without more knowledge unwilling to accept. He is not slow to adopt a proved success, but he cannot afford to experiment. (*The British Crown*, 1929, p. 140)

The above algorithm is not a far cry from the security-conscious, optimizing peasant conceptualized by Lipton (1968).[1] A sudden turn of this economy to money-based and machine-made goods changes the environment in which the peasant is attempting to do his best to survive. This emphasis on money and uncertainty does not put the authors of *The British Crown* in the company derided by Marx as those out to 'discover a capitalist mode of production in every monetary economy' (1894, p. 787) but reflects Marx's own view that money 'dissolves a production whose object is primarily immediate use-value'. As noted earlier, the social division of labour is considered necessary by Marx for commodity production, but the reverse is not true. Commodity production necessarily implies exchange. The social division of labour facilitates the production of a surplus. Together, the social division of labour and a surplus make exchange happen. In the pre-capitalist formations, production and exchange are for reproducing the community and its members, that is, use-value. The role of money becomes important when products give way to commodities (Hobsbawm, 1964, pp. 13,112). However, in the Indian village economy, mass-produced commodities along with money were imposed externally, making the British conquest qualitatively different from the earlier conquests. 'Machinery and money' acted as 'destructive forces': these words are those of Marx and Engels (1965, p. 85) used in a different context; interestingly, here they serve to convey the gist of the argument in *The British Crown*. It summed up the transition from the old village economy to a higher economic plane as the rise of a more elaborate money economy.

> Gradually the experiment in British India has worked itself out. The old village economy has, to a great extent, come to be superseded by a more elaborate money economy. Rent and land revenue are now almost everywhere paid in money. The competition of machine-made goods has made itself felt in the furthest village, prices of country cloth are affected, and the old village industries depressed. (*The British Crown*, 1929, p. 141)

Marshall also saw the rising role of money as crucial in changing the character of the Indian economy, but the emphasis in *The British Crown* on the risk and uncertainty associated with an expanding monetary economy takes some crucial steps away from him.

> I believe that India is changing her economic character very rapidly. There is a great increase of what mediaeval economists call *adaoertions*, that is, the substitution of payments by cash for barter, for exchange of services, for labour dues, and for produce rents. This has caused a greatly extended need for currency. (Marshall, 1926, p. 181)

The core of Marx's argument is found in Volume 3 of *Capital*.

> The development of commerce and merchant's capital gives rise everywhere to the tendency towards production of exchange-values, increases its volume, multiplies it, makes it cosmopolitan, and develops money into world-money. Commerce, therefore, has a more or less dissolving influence everywhere on the producing organisation, which it finds at hand and whose different forms are mainly carried on with a view to use-value. To what extent it brings about the dissolution of the old mode of production depends on its solidity and internal structure. And whither this process of dissolution will lead, in other words, what new mode of production will replace the old, does not depend on commerce, but on the character of the old mode of production itself. (Marx, 1894, pp. 331–2)

The British Crown did not regard the division of labour per se as 'meaningless' but as the basis of a new organizational dynamic in the concrete historical situation of India. Adam Smith's model generates the optimistic prediction that the sophistication of the division of labour naturally leads to capitalist development. It is this naturalism and optimism that was found without substance when applied to India. The argument could not be termed 'neo-Smithian Marxism', which Brenner reserved for those using Smith's argument based on the world division of labour rather than Marx's class analysis, and derives pessimistic conclusions about capitalist development in the underdeveloped countries (Brenner, 1977). At least Joan Robinson never claimed to be a Marxist even after she familiarized herself with his works. The concern here is with the period before that. Still, she seems to have held a view which is closer to Marx than to the academic economists, in particular, Marshall and, as will be seen below, Keynes. Both Joan Robinson and Marx look askance at the simple Smithian theory that the division of labour will lead pre-capitalist economies out of backwardness. They saw the division of labour frozen in the constraints of the village economy—the social division of labour of Marx and the hereditary employments of Joan Robinson. It required shaking up by the external economic influences, particularly the international division of labour. This does not happen smoothly.

Whither this externally produced shake-up is the question that must be asked next. In the absence of an autocentric dynamic, were the Eurocentric intrusions leading British India on to a path of desired development? The facts examined in *The British Crown* did not lead to much optimism. At the culmination of three decades of rising commodity prices in 1913, India had not performed well in seizing on the export opportunities.[2]

> Even to-day 73 per cent. of Indian population is agricultural, and only some 20 per cent. of its products are exported ... India is already so organised that 73 per cent. of her population are specialists wholly, or almost wholly, occupied in agriculture, and a further 17 per cent. are resident in villages, and dependent for their living upon the village agriculture economy. (*The British Crown*, 1929, p. 139)

Capitalism thus was not expected to grow out of agriculture. Development entailed the planting of an industrial revolution in India. In terms of the facts presented, the prospects for it were not patently clear.

Marx also became cautious in his optimism as he moved from his journalistic writings on India to *Grundrisse* and *Capital*. Among the pre-capitalist formations, the 'Asiatic form necessarily survives longest and most stubbornly' because of the self-sustaining craft-agricultural unity' (Hobsbawm, 1964, p. 83). A more careful study of the inorganic intrusions leads to the conclusion that the introduction of monetary exchange via the international division of labour does not itself change the village economic organization.

> The chief part of the products is destined for direct use by the community itself, and does not take the form of a commodity. Hence, production here is independent of that division of labour brought about, in Indian society as a whole, by means of the exchange of commodities. It is the surplus alone that becomes a commodity, and a portion of even that, not until it has reached the hands of the State in the shape of rent in kind. (Marx, 1867, p. 357)

Commerce exercises a 'dissolving influence' on the mode of production, but India 'strikingly illustrated' the obstructions raised by the old mode of production to the 'corrosive influence' of British commerce, so that 'this work of dissolution proceeds very gradually' (Marx, 1894, pp. 331–4).

Division of labour based on international trade introduces significant dynamic elements. However, in Marx's terms, the further development of the commercially intruded economy critically hinges on the dynamics of internal response. The production for export must also be accompanied by market demand for new consumer goods, emergence of a labour market and the development of productive forces.[3] The outward form of this process is the development of internal trade, fostering linkages that work against the possibility of self-supporting villages being supplanted by mere enclaves for external trade. There was recognition of these dangers, as *The British Crown* underlined the risks of a sudden transition from the village to the world economy, aggravated by railways bringing the cotton areas closer to Manchester rather than to the other parts of India. However, it could not have stayed like that for long, as the intra-linkages were also beginning to take place.

> They [the railways] were built partly, no doubt, with an eye to military necessities, but even more with an eye to the development of an export and import trade. They were admirably devised to bring Manchester cottons to the areas which produced exportable goods. They were less well designed to develop an internal trade between one part of India and another. This has in

some measure been remedied in recent years, but a generation back the break-up of the village implied not the risks of specialisation inside an Indian economic unity, but the additional dangers of an international trade. (*The British Crown*, 1929, p. 140)

Notice the disregard here of the complementary significance of roads for internal trade. Railways were built by a central government, required to build them to protect British strategic and commercial interests and which was able to raise funds in the world capital market. Roads were the responsibility of the provincial governments that neither had the resource base nor had a significant interest in promoting internal trade to encourage a town and country division of labour bringing village cotton to Indian Manchesters.

ECONOMIC NATIONALISM

The discussion so far suggests that the understanding in *The British Crown* of the problems of developing the underdeveloped Indian economy was that the necessary economic elements for autonomous growth were rather weak, if at all they existed. The externally imposed colonial development, combining commercial intrusion and the building of productive forces in the form of physical infrastructure as well as a modicum of social services, did stir the economic elements but not strongly enough. To these economic and political factors were added 'sentimental' factors in the break-up of the village economy, meant to pave the transition towards capitalist industrialization. These were factors relating to 'a rising tide of nationalism which found an expression in the policy of protection advocated by the Fiscal Commission in 1922' (*The British Crown*, 1929, p. 184).

While Joan Robinson was in Princely India, nationalism had two broadly identified variants, one rooted in a populism summed up loosely under a variety of 'Eastern industrialisms' and the other in the desire to pursue the path of 'Western industrialism' but under the auspices of national autonomy.[4] A radical populist school owed its allegiance to Gandhi, advocating that 'instead of a more rapid forward rush into big capitalist business, a retreat to more primitive industry and social organisation' (Salter, 1925, p. xv). It would delink externally, encourage small scale in agriculture as well as manufacture in its pursuit of national autarky. Another strand, without dismissing large scale altogether, focused on the continued hold of the conservative elements such as family, caste and religion to formulate a programme based on 'the principle of integration' rather than Western industrialism based on the principle of division of labour (Mukerjee, 1916). Neither the tenor of this argument nor anything in Joan Robinson's correspondence related to her Princely India days leaves any impression of an interest she might have taken in populism of some kind. She seemed more concerned with the development of productive forces.

Did she then see eye to eye with what may, for want of a better term, be called the Western industrialism school? Not exactly, as *The British Crown* did not unreservedly see India's comparative advantage lying in industrialization. This is not to say that it did not use the expression Western industrialism; it was employed as the criterion by which the extent of backwardness or underdevelopment was to be judged (*The British Crown*, 1929, p. 138). The use of the expression seems deliberate to oppose it to the strong currents of populistic Eastern industrialism, but it confused the position with the Western industrialism school. The work of Wadia and Joshi (1925), cited for the value of British Indian agricultural produce,[5] duly represented the tradition of the Western industrialism school, which originated with Ranade. In a pioneering work on development, the latter rejected the claim of received economics for its principles to be the 'guides of conduct for all time and place whatever might be the stage of National advance' (Ranade, 1906, p. 2), a position to which Joan Robinson would strongly adhere in her later work.[6] In particular, he criticized the prediction of international trade theory that India should specialize in agriculture. The same conclusion was drawn in *The British Crown*. Ranade was puzzled by the British Indian government's contradictory policy of discouraging capitalist agriculture on the one hand and a laissez-faire attitude towards capitalist industry on the other. The benefit of the contact with Britain, in as much as it laid down the preconditions of industrialization, was recognized. But he lamented that India was not free like Germany or Japan to turn the contact to its advantage by formulating a national industrial policy. That was why the task of planting a Great Britain in India was proving difficult even after a century of British rule (ibid., pp. 70–71).

The authors of *The British Crown* were not so sure about the industrial future of India. They contended that despite British commercialism and colonialism, as well as 'sentimental' props of tariff protection after World War I, 90 per cent of the population continued to be engaged directly or indirectly in agriculture. In other words, the village economy was putting up resistance, with populist nationalism coming into conflict with the non-populist nationalism of the Western industrialism school. It was necessary to know the basis of the national policy of the latter so as to be able to distinguish the approach of the authors from the approach of this school. The talk of a sentimental urge to industrialize was, in fact, an allusion to this school. The facts presented in support of this point of view were the following.

> Manufactured products in any form covered less than 4 per cent. in a typical budget of a poor family, and only some 10–15 per cent. of a middle-class family … In 1913 imports of Manchester cottons represented less than Rs.2 per head of population, and in 1926 the total imports into India represented only Rs.7-6-0 [=Rs.7.4] per head of population. (*The British Crown*, 1929, p. 139)

As a late industrializer, the focus of India's nationalist policy would be on import substitution and the exploitation of demand generated by the earnings from agricultural exports. But the majority of the families spent precious little on manufactures, indigenous or foreign. The per capita import figures cited above correspond to this consumption pattern. With facts like these, the urge to break-up the village economy and to institute a national industrial policy cannot but have been a sentimental urge. It is well to note that the Indian nationalist opinion was not being singled out here; some elements in the government of British India at some point showed interest in a tariff policy, restrained by the predominant free traders and stopped by the Government in London. With the low per capita consumption of manufactures of any kind, a growth in large-scale industry of, say, 10 per cent per annum would have quickly exhausted the limited demand.[7]

Obviously, Joan Robinson had not yet read Kalecki's review of the Romanian protectionist, Manoilesco (Kalecki, 1938). Whether or not there was any influence of List on Joan Robinson, it is hard to say.[8] Germany was 'scarcely known' when she was a student at Cambridge (Robinson, 1951, p. vii). Once in India, she was inclined towards the idea that the process of transition could, if necessary, be eased by tariff policy. This is of course the infant industry argument, an exception recognized within the free trade framework, and by no means an argument for generalized import substitution or autarky. One ought to be clear here about an important distinction. Protecting nascent large-scale industries is one thing and easing the transition from the village to the world economy quite another. The latter predated the former. In both cases, large-scale industries drive out the small-scale village industries. In one case, the large-scale industries are entirely foreign and, in the other, both national and foreign. For the past a counterfactual point was raised but not discussed.

> Whether or not the transition from a village to a world economy could have been eased by a sympathetic use of the customs duties it is not the purpose to discuss. It is enough that during the vital period India happened to be ruled by a school of thought to which such an idea was inconceivable. (*The British Crown*, 1929, p. 141)

Despite considering the period as 'vital', the authors are content with merely pointing out that protection was an anathema to the ruling body of thought at the time, which held an inviolable belief in free trade—the so-called Manchester school. More than the counterfactual, the interest was in the factual as follows.

> Experience has now shown that industrially produced goods can undersell the laborious products of the village artisan …. [What] is really clear is that the village industry cannot, in its original form, compete on a money basis with machine-made goods. *The situation is in many ways analogous to that of England at the beginning of the Industrial Revolution, and India has many stages of European economic history yet to pass through* [Italics not in original]. (*The British Crown*, 1929, p. 141)

There is no readiness to gamble as to what would have happened had the reigning view been different in the past. Yet there is unequivocal assertion based on evidence, the sources of which unfortunately were not fully revealed, that the village crafts could not compete with the machine-made and money-based goods. Machinery permits labour productivity vastly superior to village crafts. The resulting lowering of costs makes possible money-denominated price reductions which could undersell the products of the labours of the artisans. A basic premise of the received theory of international trade—no country could undersell others all round—became inoperative.[9] The case for easing the pain of transition was thus well-founded. That done, the course of further development was charted by history—economic evolution *a' la* the first developed country.

These are not unfamiliar words. Marx, though earlier devastating in his criticism of List,[10] wrote in the preface of his major work.

> Intrinsically, it is not a question of the higher or lower degree of development of the social antagonisms that result from the natural laws of capitalist production. It is a question of these laws themselves, of these tendencies working with iron necessity towards inevitable results. The country that is more developed industrially only shows, to the less developed, the image of its own future.[11]

And further,

> One nation can and should learn from others. And even when a society has got upon the right track for the discovery of the natural laws of its movement ... it can neither clear by bold leaps, nor remove by legal enactments, the obstacles offered by the successive phases of its normal development. But *it can shorten and lessen the birth-pangs* [emphasis added]. (Marx, 1867, pp. 8–10)

India, as Joan Robinson concluded, had yet to go past the initial conditions of the stage of industrial revolution in the European economic history. The view of the similarity of preindustrial conditions and the resulting outcome, so far as India was concerned, was not uncommon. Morison who, of course, was known at Cambridge, being a recommended author for the Tripos (Morison, 1906),[12] had formulated this view in some detail (Morison, 1911). In a review of his book, Keynes had sharply censured Morison, so that on the issue of development of India, Joan Robinson held an essentially different view to that of Keynes.[13] While agreeing with the similarity of preconditions, Keynes doubted that they laid down the industrial 'royal road to prosperity'. He was emphatic in stating his view.

> But surely Sir Theodore Morison misreads the times when he regards Bombay rather than the never-ending fields as the presage of India's future. He rightly attributes the contemporary decay of village industries in India, as they have decayed formerly elsewhere, to the growth of specialization consequent on the improvement of communications. But this improvement has also led to some degree of specialization among nations, and, if regard be had to climatic conditions and to the aptitude and habits of her people, it seems hard to believe that India will not obtain more wealth by obtaining from the West, in exchange for her raw products, most of these commodities

she now obtains in this manner, than by diverting her capital and her peasants from the fields of the country to Bombay, in order to make them herself. (Keynes, 1911, p. 427)

Keynes accepted for India the dictates of international division of labour, which accompanied or followed the destruction of village industrial base under the impact of British commercialism and colonialism. With such complete specialization—agricultural India and industrial England—there was nothing to protect anyway and arguing a case for free trade would be a needless exercise.[14]Joan Robinson did not agree that India should completely specialize in agriculture, nor did she give blanket approval to the line of the Western industrialism school in India. While conceding that experience had demonstrated the ability of mass-produced imported goods to undersell village industrial products and accepting their fate as a fact of history, she took a position which was at variance with that of Keynes. By the same token, she had rejected populism as a basis for national economic development.

It [experience] has not shown, as has sometimes been claimed, that ... India should concentrate all her efforts upon agriculture, and import all industrial products from abroad. (*The British Crown*, 1929, p. 141)

But she was not sentimental either, like the Western industrialism school. She went on to infer:

On the other hand, it [experience] has not shown yet, what many politicians have claimed, that India is perfectly adapted for an industrial future. (*The British Crown*, 1929, p. 141)

What are we to make of all this? The destruction of village industries is accepted by her as a verdict of history, though the process could be protracted. Populist roots of national development thus had no place in the view of development outlined in *The British Crown*. It must be noted that she had put an important qualification before the argument about the underselling of village industries—they could not compete with money-based and machine-made goods in their 'original form'. In fact, these industries also underwent a change with the rise of modern industry. The use of fly-shuttle, the reliance on yarn produced by the large-scale industry and market rather than custom sales gave a very different look to the indigenous cotton industry. The scenario was not one of being swamped by the mass-produced goods.[15]

The international division of labour and colonial development of infrastructure make a dent in the statically organized social division of labour in the village economy. It does not, however, follow that she accepts complete specialization for India in agriculture. What British commercial penetration and colonial policies did was to lay down the conditions similar to those in England at the start of industrial revolution. The way forward is shown by known Western economic history, of which German economic nationalism is a part. But an industrial revolution is not yet in sight. As her whole approach is based on pragmatic conclusions from experience, she dismisses the Western industrialism school as sentimental. There are more stages of Western economic history that India would have to go through. In that history, there was no stage called socialism. It was only later in her career that she would argue for socialism as a substitute for capitalism in her theory of development. The most important stage was industrial revolution, for which India was not yet fully ready. In other words, the study by Joan Robinson was closer to the Dobb (1946) story of a long period of transition rather than the Morison (1911) story of the takeover of village industries by mass-produced goods being only a matter of time. She ignored the implications of British India being a colony and the princely states semi-autonomous.

WESTERN INDUSTRIALISM

In *The British Crown and the Indian States*, development implies Western industrialism. Colonial penetration began to disturb the village economy. As in Marx, colonialism ushered in the international division of labour. The colonial state provided the requisite infrastructure. While Marx envisaged its slow dissolving effects on the village economy, *The British Crown* focuses on cheaper foreign goods driving the village crafts out of the market. Agriculture was still dominant and internal trade was slow to develop. The preconditions of industrial revolution had begun to be laid, but the progress was slow. It was a case of how an industrial revolution begins rather than the Marxian transition to capitalism. The study does not go into the question of whether a national industrial policy would have moved the economy closer to industrial revolution. Concerned as it was with Princely India, the study stayed away from the arguments presented by the economic nationalists in British India.

According to *The British Crown*, the caste-enforced, hereditary division of labour within the village economy lacked the potential for increased productivity. The externally forced international division of labour introduced money, specialization and exchange, but had not yet provided any degree of confidence to say, even if aided by protectionist sentiment, that India was fully adapted to an industrial future. On the contrary, Marshall was unambiguous about the economic future of India.[16] It was similar to Keynes's prescription for India as a specialist in agriculture. This prescription was contrary to experience.

Western industrialization is taken as development, underdevelopment or backwardness indicating the economic distance from it. There is, however, not a clear prognosis on offer. *The British Crown* noted the 'beginning in British India' of the 'Industrial Revolution', its broad similarity to 'England at the beginning of the Industrial Revolution', with 'much of the initial dislocation ... gradually beginning to adjust itself' (1929, pp. 141–142). This is true as far as it goes. After all, it was analysing an economy which by 1914 had become the world's second largest producer of jute manufactures and the fourth largest producer of cotton textiles.[17] The contention about the similarity of the initial conditions of the industrial revolution in England and India but the absence at the same time of visible evidence of the existence of major industrial potential seems contradictory. It was not (yet at least) an expression of pessimism that Indian development will not proceed after the Western development, but that India's industrial future is not yet clear. The essence of the argument is that despite industrial beginnings, there are forces at work which keep the process slow or arrested. These forces are not analysed in any detail, but a statistical explanation in the form of a very low per capita consumption of manufactures is provided, such that the urge to industrialize is regarded as sentimental. Important though this explanation is, it does not exhaust the problematic of the transition towards capitalism. The suggestion that the village industries could change form implies their attempts to survive. The transition would have to be long as was the experience elsewhere.[18] In any case, as Joan Robinson observed later, capitalism does not concentrate its invasion on the most vulnerable village industries but attacks on a broad front (Robinson, 1966, p. xi). The village industries thus have a greater chance to survive.

NOTES

1. This point was suggested by Peter Nolan, the Founding Director of the Centre of Development Studies at University of Cambridge and the Director of Jesus College's China Centre. In 1985–1988, Professor Nolan was the Faculty Adviser of the author.

2. A later study of the period noted that India was 'completely defeated by population density. She did some irrigation, but little in relation to total cultivated area; most of her small farmers continued to farm wholly for subsistence; and her agricultural exports were the slowest growing in the tropical world' (Lewis, 1970, p. 23).

3. Sender and Smith (1986, p. 5).

4. See Kitching (1982, pp. 142–52) for a critical discussion of nationalism and populism as theories of development.

5. *The British Crown* (1929, p. 139, n.1).

6. See above for similar views expressed by Cunningham and by Joan Robinson in her later writings. The reference to Ranade pertains to the second edition. The first edition was published as early as in 1898, just six years after the Cunningham-Marshall encounter.

7. Lidman and Domrese (1970, p. 328).

8. List's own verdict on 'nationalities' like India was that they were not 'worthy or capable of maintenance and regeneration'. Their 'entire dissolution' was 'inevitable, and a regeneration...only possible by means of an infusion of European vital power' (1841, p. 419).

9. For a later elaboration of this point, see Robinson (1946/1947, pp. 104–5).

10. See Marx (1975).

11. It may be noted that the economic history of the Third World told a different story.

12. See Cambridge (1922, p. 391).

13. Nobody was yet a Keynesian, not even Keynes! Keynes was not Keynes in 1911; he was still a neoclassical under Marshall's influence.

14. 'If the two countries produced different commodities, neither would have a motive for protecting its own from competition; there would be no need to argue the case for free trade' (Robinson & Eatwell, 1973, p. 243).

15. See Bagchi (1972, pp. 219–27) and Morris (1984, pp. 673–75).

16. See Pigou (1925, p. 458).

17. Lidman and Domrese (1970, p. 321).

18. Sender and Smith (1986, pp. 13, 37).

References

Bagchi, A. K. (1972). *Private Investment in India 1900–39*. Cambridge University Press.

Brenner, R. (1977). The Origins of Capitalist Development: A Critique of neo-Smithian Marxism. *New Left Review, 104,* 25–92.

Cambridge, University of. (1922). *The Student's Handbook*. Cambridge University Press.

Dobb, M. (1946). *Studies in the Development of Capitalism*. Routledge and Kegan Paul.

Hobsbawm, E. (Ed.). (1964). *Karl Marx: Pre-capitalist Economic Formations*. Lawrence and Wishart.

Kalecki, M. (1938). Review of *Die Nationalen Produktivkraefte and der Aussenhandel* by M. Manoilesco. in *Economic Journal, 48,* 708–711.

Keynes, J. M. (1911). Review of T. Morison. *The Economic Transition in India. Economic Journal, 21,* 426–431.

Kitching, G. (1982). *Development and Underdevelopment*. Methuen.

Lewis, W. A. (1970). *Tropical Development 1880–1913*. George Allen and Unwin.

Lidman, R., & Domrese, R. I. (1970). India. In *Lewis (1970)*.

Lipton, M. (1968). The Theory of the Optimizing Peasant. *Journal of Development Studies, 4,* 327–351.

List, F. (1841). *The National System of Political Economy*. Longman and Green. Reprinted 1885.

Marshall, A. (1926). *Official Papers*. Macmillan.

Marx, K. (1853). The Future Results of British Rule in India. In *Marx and Engels (1979)*.

Marx, K. (1867). *Capital* (Vol. 1). Lawrence and Wishart. Reprinted 1970.

Marx, K. (1894). *Capital* (Vol. 3). Lawrence and Wishart. Reprinted 1972.

Marx, K. (1975). Draft of an article on Friedrich List's book. In K. Marx & F. Engels (Eds.), *Collected Works* (Vol. 4). Lawrence and Wishart.

Marx, K., & Engels, F. (1965). *The German Ideology*. Lawrence and Wishart.

Morison, T. (1906). *The Industrial Organization of an Indian Province*. John Murray.

Morison, T. (1911). *Economic Transition in India*. John Murray.

Morris, M. D. (1984). The Growth of Large-scale Industry to 1947. In *Kumar (1984)*.

Mukerjee, R. (1916). *The Foundations of Indian Economics*. Longmans and Green.

Pigou, A. C. (Ed.). (1925). *Memorials of Alfred Marshall*. Macmillan.

Ranade, M. G. (1906). *Essays in Indian Economics* (2nd ed.). G.A. Nateson.

Robinson, J. (1946–1947). The Pure Theory of International Trade. *Review of Economic Studies, 14,* 98–112.

Robinson, J. (1951). *Collected Economic Papers* (Vol. 1). Basil Blackwell.

Robinson, J. (1966). *Economics: An Awkward Corner*. George Allen and Unwin.

Robinson, J., & Eatwell, J. (1973). *An Introduction to Modern Economics*. McGraw-Hill.

Salter, G. (1925). Introductory Note. In P. P. Pillai (Ed.), *Economic Conditions in India*. George Routledge.

Sender, J., & Smith, S. (1986). *The Development of Capitalism in Africa*. Methuen.

The British Crown and the Indian States. (1929). P.S. King and Son.

Wadia, P. A., & Joshi, G. N. (1925). *The Wealth of India*. Macmillan.

CHAPTER 8

Is There a Common Thread?

This chapter attempts to relate the experience of the Indian reality to Joan Robinson's short-lived fascination for analytical optimism on return to England and subsequent pessimism about capitalist development in underdeveloped countries. It is argued that the earlier scepticism about the pace of industrial development in colonial India was the source of her later search for alternatives to capitalist industrialization.

After returning to Cambridge, Joan Robinson turned immediately to issues other than underdevelopment and development. Not that her interest in poverty and backwardness waned. The sojourn to India had further developed this early interest. Within about two years of completing the Economics Tripos at Cambridge, which in scope and method was Marshallian to the hilt, she was confronted with a challenge to apply her mind and the theory she learned to conditions which were not in the view its authors. The experience of India seems to have sown the initial seeds of doubt in her mind about the validity of the assumptions of orthodox economics. This is borne out by her inability to get unambiguous inferences about future Indian development while experiencing its reality, as opposed to Marshall's confidence about the economic course of events in India without first-hand knowledge.

In the process, she seems to be struggling to cast off Marshall's influence—struggling because she did not succeed in completely dissociating

P. Tahir, *Joan Robinson in Princely India*, Palgrave Studies in the History of Economic Thought, https://doi.org/10.1007/978-3-031-10905-8_8

herself from Marshall's dismissiveness of the impact of history on present and future, nor did she move fully, albeit subconsciously as she was ignorant of him at the time, to Marx's view of 'present as history'.[1] She certainly shared the evolutionism of both: there are stages that all nations go through, linearly in a Smith-Marshall framework and dialectically for Marx.[2] There is a model to learn from and to follow, the model of Western Europe. India was put on this path during the colonial period; its evolution started only after that. She moved closer to Marx in that the original state of underdevelopment, the self-sufficient village economy, had to be subjected to the cataclysm of external forces. Marshallian supply and demand, in this vision of society, fail to evolve out of the stiff joints of the village economy. Once the village economy lays prostrate before colonial and commercial penetration, she reverted to the Marshallian vision of an elaborate money economy as a distinct sign of progress. Instead of looking at the determining dynamic of the internal mode of production interacting with the international division of labour, as Marx would do, she attempted to apply division of labour and productivity *a'la* Smith as the basis for development in the concrete situation of India. This is where her problems began; she found specific constraints on the realization of the Smithian dynamic.

It must be understood that we are dealing here with a report, not systematic theory.[2] At best, *The British Crown* was a semi-official study, incorporating a set of assertions and observations informed, no doubt, by the economic theory learned at Cambridge and its application to the real-life situation of India. Our concern has been to interpret and analyse the use of available economic ideas in the context of Indian development. The originality lies, therefore, not in ideas but in intuitively testing them in conditions whose systematized study had not yet been pioneered, that is, the so-called development economics. The study ought to be seen as among the earliest attempts by a modern economist from the West to understand the nature of underdevelopment and development in the world's second-largest underdeveloped economy. It helps to take a fresh look at two aspects of the evolution of Joan Robinson economic ideas: analytical optimism and pessimism about capitalist development. The following pages discuss these in turn.

ANALYTICAL OPTIMISM

The experience of India was bound to create tension between the theory Joan Robinson had learned and its realism. The paucity of facts in India of the 1920s and the quality of whatever statistics were available may not entirely explain the tension. There appears to be a link between Joan Robinson's work on methodology and imperfect competition in the early 1930s and the study on Princely India in the late 1920s. It also shows how hard it was to get away from Marshall's influence. She set out to improve on the Marshallian framework as a critical disciple. According to Harcourt, the salient features of Marshall's method were to prove long-lasting.

> [M]uch of her theoretical work is based on Marshallian-type generaliza-tions—that is to say, broad qualitative statements that constitute either the basis for the development of a logical argument or the puzzles that are to be explained by theoretical reasoning. (Harcourt, 1984, p. 652)

In her essay on methodology (Robinson, 1932), she argued for analyti-cal optimism, a step-by-step comprehension of reality by gradually improv-ing on the realism of assumptions as and when the technique applied was capable of handling them. The historians of social thought, indeed, classify this essay by Joan Robinson as one written by a critical disciple of Marshall and reflecting a general conviction of the time 'that existing theory failed from a want of reality because it was based on a series of assumptions very imperfectly connected with the observed facts of life' (Soffer, 1970, pp. 1940–58). At the time of writing this essay and judging by her writ-ings, Joan Robinson had been a keener observer of the facts of the econ-omy of colonial India than that of England. If anything, she was aiming to improve the capability of the theoretical technique to capture undivided reality, not just the Indian or English reality, by introducing more lifelike assumptions. The analytical optimist in her went on to write *The Economics of Imperfect Competition*. Perfect competition was considered unrealistic and the assumption was dropped. But the crucial assumption of an eco-nomic individual was retained, justified by the argument that more com-plicated motives would abolish economists in favour of psychologists. Similarly, erratic actions would need not economists but statisticians to discover economic laws (Robinson, 1933, p. 6).

In India she had witnessed custom rather than economic motives ruling economic life. She had also found factual experience giving her the opposite of what the theory predicted, namely, the comparative advantage of India not necessarily lying in agricultural commodities. In reaching the conclusion that the break-up of the village economy was the outcome of political and sentimental factors, she could not at the same time have believed in Marshall's verdict that the influence of economic causes in India was pressed below the surface. Not surprisingly, the wary optimist in Gwalior had put a rider of 'not yet' on the prospects of industrial revolution in India. There was thus a latent conflict between the analytical optimist in her and the pessimism-prone keen observer of the theoretically intractable reality. Shove, the methodological pessimist, had got an inkling of it. He had doubted whether she seriously meant economists to wait until the technique was perfected for solving real problems.[3] Interestingly, Gifford, himself a more militant analytical optimist and extremely appreciative of Joan Robinson's essay on methodology, also suspected a streak of Shove-like pessimism.[4] Later she repudiated *The Economics of Imperfect Competition* and never reissued the essay on methodology. For Joan Robinson, here was the foundation of two kinds of economics, one for the developed economies and the other for the underdeveloped economies. Over time, she was to question the relevance of orthodox economics anywhere, not just in underdeveloped economies.[5]

Pessimism About Capitalist Development

Commissioned as it was by the quasi-autonomous princely states of India, the study in India may well be the first view on development from the 'periphery', albeit by economists from the 'centre'. The study locates the origin of her perennial doubts about capitalist development in the underdeveloped countries, which of course was the predominant view from the 'periphery' when the 'centre-periphery' debates started in their Baran-Frank version.[6] Frank and his followers turned the division-of-labour-based optimistic conclusion of Smith into a pessimistic view of capitalist development in underdeveloped countries without changing the basis. Brenner (1977) called it neo-Smithian Marxism. The disregard of class in Joan Robinson's first foray into development was similar. About industrial capitalism there was a certain wariness but not yet the unequivocal pessimism of her subsequent approach. In regard to the precolonial village economy, the Indian study expressed doubts about the existence of the dynamic of productivity and the division of labour. Colonialism was, therefore, seen as doing the progressive work of breaking up the village economy. To use her later terminology,[7] it was not 'colonial-distorted development' but an improvement from 'pre-capitalist underdevelopment' to 'incipient modern development'. The study does not see India specializing in raw materials, nor does it jump to the opposite conclusion of a completely industrial India. The failure of the division of labour to lift village India out of stagnation, and the relative success of colonial India in this direction, did provide some basis to suggest the existence of the conditions for a successful industrial policy. That makes it possible to describe the approach as wary optimism.

A reviewer of her essay on methodology stated:

> At a time when the most violent changes in the conditions under which contracts may be made are being carried out in England, when contracts have almost been declared illegal in Russia, how useful is the advice likely to be of the economist whose technique assumes that the conditions of contract are unalterable? (Watson, 1932, p. 108)

In a sense the reviewer raises a question about her analytical optimism which had implications for wary optimism about development in colonial India: could contracts be assumed as given, sanctioned by law or tradition? What is possible to deduce from her writings at the time about the conditions of contract is the following. The tradition-bound implicit contracts had to be compelled to be made explicit. The rise of an elaborate money economy and exchange under colonialism was a development in this direction. With contracts becoming explicit and widespread, as in England, tinkering with them would lead to the flight of the capitalists, the accumulators, unless tinkering was global. This was an important message of the first-ever review she wrote.[8] It was followed by the essay on methodology, which assumed contracts as given for generating analytically optimistic conclusions. It is not stated in so many words, but it can safely be assumed that these contracts take the capitalistic form. Also important is the fact that capitalism coincides with an industrial economy. There are no transitions here, merely 'the manageable set' of assumptions for 'the optimistic, analytical, English, economist' (Robinson, 1932, p. 6).

The fact is that transitions never seem to have interested her, from whatever-it-is to capitalism as well as to socialism from capitalism. The study on India in the late 1920s provided its genesis, messy as it was in its set of assumptions. In that study, the word 'capitalism' does not occur; development is the same thing as 'industrial revolution'. In her later writings, it changed to 'industrial capitalism'. The argument turns on industrial revolution rather than the transition to capitalism. In her *magnum opus*, the basic assumption is that 'the capitalist rules of the game are well established and have long been played' (Robinson, 1956, p. 69). In *Exercises*, the analysis of family and socialist economies 'lays the foundation for a discussion of the problems of under-developed countries'. Though she grants the possibility of 'many interesting exercises to be done in working out the development of industrial capitalism from the embryo', she decides instead to 'jump ahead and consider capitalism when it is full blown' (Robinson, 1960c, pp. vi, 70). She cited with approval Ayres' theory[9] to conclude that the essential difference between Western Europe and 'the older civilizations' lay, respectively, in the weakness and strength of the 'ceremonial patterns' of behaviour as obstacles to productivity and innovation (Robinson, 1962c, p. 106). What is this but a confirmation of her earlier reference to the economies of 'highly complex ancient civilizations' as those 'which somehow failed to develop the capitalist rules of the game' (Robinson, 1956, p. 368).

The study of India was Joan Robinson's first exposure to the problems of development and underdevelopment. More important, this is the only writing on development associated with her where she was not looking for an alternative to capitalism. The term Western industrialism could be interpreted as capitalism, since she had not yet revealed her preference for any other type of industrialism. The context, however, makes it clear that the case is for an industrial revolution, not a transition towards capitalism. The unknown Joan Robinson is different from the known Joan Robinson in an important respect: she is not yet arguing that a socialistic framework, and not the 'Indian mixture', is required 'to jump a thousand years of economic history'. In 1929, *The British Crown* had identified the division of labour and specialization as the basis of development, but found it meaningless in the Indian context. It confronted the Indian nationalist sentiment for industrialization with experience to suggest it was hasty in its prognosis. In about three decades, Joan Robinson was confirming her pessimistic prognosis (Robinson, 1957b, p. 844).

The focus on Western industrialization suggests not a transition from one set of productive forces and relations of production to another but a technological jump from traditional crafts tied to a primitive agriculture to modem industry, as would be the case in development economics in about two decades. The movement from the undifferentiated village economy to industrialization had to be brought about by the force of colonialism and the props of nationalism. Even so, 90 per cent of the population continued to be directly or indirectly dependent on agriculture. In time, the predominance of agriculture would also be recognized in development economics as a characteristic feature of underdeveloped economies. It must be kept in mind that once the process of differentiation started, it was considered irreversible: she did not expect it to lead to a socialist, undifferentiated state. In the 1929 study, the historical sequence for Joan Robinson is the village economy, the transition to the world economy under colonialism, pre-industrial revolution conditions but uncertainty about future industrialization.

This was before she had read Marx. After having read him, she stated his view of imperialism and development as follows.

> He [Marx] sees the capitalist system fulfilling a historic mission to draw out the productive power of combined and specialised labour. From its birthplace in Europe it stretches out tentacles over the world to find its nourishment. It forces the accumulation of capital, and develops productive technique, and by that means raises the wealth of mankind to heights undreamed of in the peasant, feudal or slave economies. (Robinson, 1942, p. 3)

The above is not a full statement of Marx's optimistic view of the spread of capitalism over the world.[9] She emphasizes the 'nourishment' that capitalism at its birthplace gets by its penetration of the world outside Europe, but the impact on these territories in terms of capitalist development is not clearly brought out. In her analysis of Luxemberg's theory, even this nourishment effect is somewhat reduced by the emphatic conclusion that capitalism does not live by imperialism alone (Robinson, 1951a, b). What is more significant is Luxemberg's theory of 'capitalist emancipation of the *hinterland*' (emphasis in original) (Luxemberg, 1913, p. 419) is ignored by Joan Robinson. In her own *Accumulation*, she conceptualizes 'primitive stagnation' as a common characteristic of pre-capitalist economies. Production is less than the potential, indicated by the existence of disguised unemployment and the 'purchasing power equal to many years income' with wealth owners. The concept of disguised unemployment in this context has the same meaning as in standard development economics.[10] But it is not inconsistent with her more general concept presented in Robinson (1936) that it occurs in any stagnant economy, capitalist in its downturn and pre-capitalist in its normal state. Primitive stagnation signifies that surplus labour as well as finance to employ it is there. However, the economy fails to emerge out of stagnation because of its inability to get going 'the idea of accumulation and a class of entrepreneurs to play according to the capitalist rules' (Robinson, 1956, pp. 256–7).

Joan Robinson's primitive stagnation is different from Marx's primitive accumulation. In Marx's view, the emergence of primitive accumulation meant the rise of capitalist relations of production, that is, the emergence of dispossessed workers hired by the capitalists. Both Marx and Joan Robinson first saw in colonialism a force capable of making a dent into pre-capitalist stagnation but later became cautious in their optimism. The only time she raised some prospect of capitalism developing was quickly followed by remarks reminiscent of the pejorative use of sentimentalism for nationalism in the study of Princely India in 1929.

> Local entrepreneurs may come into being under the influence of the foreigners, and local rentiers may begin to place their savings in business instead of gold, so that the economy is brought under the sway of the capitalist rules of the game, and after a time the local capitalists become nationalists and set up a movement to expropriate the foreigners. (Robinson, 1956, p. 371)

It appears that her reference was to colonial India, a society which had failed to develop the capitalist rules of the game in the precolonial period, and the colonial period and the national emergence had, according to her, not contributed much in this direction.

> It is easy enough to make suggestions and counter-suggestions as to the causes why capitalism has flourished in some societies and not in others, but whatever the causes, the fact is plain—India has been part of the world market as long as any country, and the problem of development is still on her hands. (Robinson, 1957b, p. 844)

Many a time in history, the potential for investment appears in societies, but for investment to go into 'technical progress and increasing mechanisation … to raise productivity' rather than 'creating temples and palaces', it 'is necessary, to start the game, that there should be thrifty rentiers as well as active entrepreneurs' (Robinson, 1956, pp. 256–7). Her emphasis on the emergence of capitalists is more like Schumpeter (1943, p. 16) than Marx, the latter's focus being on proletarianization.[11]

However, even when she agreed with the main thesis of Baran, whose pessimistic prognosis provided the fuel for the fire of later neo-Marxist and dependency theories, she insisted on the factual rather than the counterfactual, just as she had done when the question of easing the transition by tariff in the free trade phase of the Anglo-Indian economic history came up.

I do not myself see much point in the history of 'if only …' It seems to me that if, for example, the world had been such that a European power had not dominated India things would have been so radically different from all that we know that there is only idle amusement to be got from speculating about how matters would have turned out in any particular respect.

Even for the purpose of amusing speculators, to compare India and Japan is not much good. Where there are comparable cases—say, Siam, Burma and Indo-China—Baran's case that political independence makes up for economic development, would not be easy to support. (Robinson, 1957a, opposite 1)

Yet again,

In history, every event has its consequences, and the question, what would have happened if that event had not occurred? is only an idle speculation. (Robinson, 1962, p. 75)

So much for nationalism. There is also a parallel between her early view of colonialism and the later view of socialism in underdeveloped countries. Like Marx, she had seen colonialism as a powerful external force to destroy the hold of tradition. Thirty years on, she observed that the liberalism of the West 'only warmed the surface of the deep waters of Indian tradition'.[12] As she was comparing India with China, it is straightforward to infer that what colonialism with all its ruthlessness failed to do could hardly be achieved by liberal democracy. She saw in socialism a far more penetrating force to get to the bottom 'of the deep waters of Indian tradition'.

I believe that the clue to economic history is to be found in the interaction of the 'forces of production' and the 'relations of production'. The communist 'relations' seem to be highly suitable for doing the job of developing the countries which missed development under capitalism. (Robinson, 1957a, opposite 1)

LEAPFROGGING

In the above we find the clearest statement of the general conclusion that there are no transitions in Joan Robinson's view of development, only leapfrogging.

The motto for Joan Robinson was not *Natura non facit saltum* but *Natura facit saltum*.[13] The correspondence of the forces of production and the relations of production at any stage constitutes an equilibrium. The disequilibrium dynamics scarcely interested her. And the origins of her pessimistic prognosis about capitalist development go back to the unsure prediction about colonial India's industrial future in her maiden exposure to the development literature, *The British Crown* (1929). The same study locates the central focus on industrialization, for the faster achievement of which she would emphasize a socialist strategy in days to come.[1415]

NOTES

1. This phrase is due to Sweezy (1953).
2. Furtado (1973) challenged this view.
3. This is not to suggest that reports carry no weight. Some reports profoundly influenced economic thinking. See, for example, Hamilton (1791).
4. G.F. Shove's letter to Joan Robinson, 19 October 1932. JVR Collection, King's Modem Archives.
5. C. Gifford, Letter to Joan Robinson, 26 November 1932. JVR Collection, King's Modem Archives
6. See Seers (1979, p. 713).
7. Baran (1957), Frank (1967).
8. Robinson and Eatwell (1973, p. 323).
9. Robinson (1930, p. 296).
10. Ayres (1944). She had a series of exchanges with Ayres on this subject. See JVR Collection, King's Modem Archives viii/Ayres for the relevant correspondence.
11. See Warren (1980) for a fuller treatment.
12. Some evidence from India shows that proletarianization is not necessarily related with higher capital accumulation (P. Bardhan, 1986, p. 67).
13. Robinson (1962, p. 106). The lectures on which this book was based were delivered in 1959, that is, exactly 30 years on from *The British Crown* (1929).
14. See Rosenstein-Rodan (1984).
15. It was not necessarily an ideological stance. The objective was not socialism per se but as a means to rapid capital accumulation. For instance, her advice

to the socialist government of (then) Ceylon was that there was 'nothing to be gained from interfering with' the foreign-owned tea plantations as they were 'well run' and 'exceptionally efficient' (Robinson, 1959, p. 69). Her views on the Chinese development fall in a different category. Considerable research is required to make sense of them. See Tahir (2019).

REFERENCES

UNPUBLISHED MATERIAL

C. Gifford's letter to Joan Robinson. (1932, November 26). JVR Collection, King's Modem Archives.

G.F. Shove's letter to Joan Robinson. (1932, October 19). JVR Collection, King's Modem Archives.

PUBLISHED WORKS

Ayres, C. E. (1944). *The Theory of Economic Progress*. University of North Carolina Press.

Baran, P. (1957). *The Political Economy of Growth*. Monthly Review Press.

Bardhan, P. (1986). Marxist Ideas in Development Economics: An Evaluation. In J. Roemer (Ed.), *Analytical Marxism*. Cambridge University Press.

Brenner, R. (1977). The Origins of Capitalist Development: A Critique of neo-Smithian Marxism. *New Left Review, 104*, 25–92.

Frank A.G. (1967). *Capitalism and Underdevelopment in Latin America*. Monthly Review Press.

Furtado, C. (1973). The Concept of External Dependence in the Study of Underdevelopment. In C. K. Wilber (Ed.), *The Political Economy of Development and Underdevelopment* (pp. 118–123). Random House.

Hamilton, A. (1791). *Report on Manufactures*. U.S. Government Printing Office, 1913.

Harcourt, G.C. (1984). Harcourt on Robinson. In *Contemporary Economists in Perspective* (Vol.1, Part B). Jai Press.

Luxemberg, R. (1913). *The Accumulation of Capital*. Routledge and Kegan Paul. Reprinted 1951.

Robinson, J. (1957a). Clues to History. Letter to the Editor. *Nation* 185 (U.S.), Opposite 1.

Robinson, J. (1930). Review of H. Clay. *The Problem of Industrial Relations, in Political Quarterly, 1*, 293–296.

Robinson, J. (1932). *Economics is a Serious Subject*. W. Heifer and Sons.

Robinson, J. (1933). *The Economics of Imperfect Competition*. Macmillan.

Robinson, J. (1936). Disguised Unemployment. *Economic Journal, 46*, 223–237.

Robinson, J. (1942). *An Essay on Marxian Economics*. Macmillan.

Robinson, J. (1951a). *Collected Economic Papers* (Vol. 1). Basil Blackwell.

Robinson, J. (1951b). Introduction. In *Robinson (1951a)*.

Robinson, J. (1956). *The Accumulation of Capital* (1st. ed.). Macmillan.

Robinson, J. (1957b). The Indian Mixture. Review of M. Zinkin. *Development for free Asia*. In *New Statesman and Nation, 54*, 844–845.

Robinson, J. (1959). Economic Possibilities of Ceylon. In *Papers by Visiting Economists*. National Planning Council.

Robinson, J. (1960c). *Exercises in Economic Analysis*. Macmillan.

Robinson, J. (1962). *Economic Philosophy*. C.A. Watts.

Robinson, J., & Eatwell, J. (1973). *An Introduction to Modern Economics*. McGraw-Hill.

Rosenstein-Rodan, P. N. (1984). Natura Facit Saltum: Analysis of the Disequilibrium Growth Process. In *Meier and Seers (1984)*.

Schumpeter, J. A. (1943). *Capitalism, Socialism and Democracy*. Allen and Unwin.

Seers, D. (1979). The Birth, Life and death of Development Economics. *Development and Change, 10*, 707–719.

Soffer, R. N. (1970). The Revolution in English Social Thought, 1880–1914. *American Historical Review, 75*, 1938–1964.

Sweezy, P. M. (1953). *The Present as History*. Monthly Review Press.

Tahir, P. (2019). *Making Sense of Joan Robinson on China*. Palgrave Macmillan.

The British Crown and the Indian States. (1929). P.S. King and Son.

Warren, B. (1980). *Imperialism: Pioneer of Capitalism*. Verso.

Watson, A. G. D. (1932). Review of Robinson (1932a). *Cambridge Review, 54*, 107–108.

Transfer of Resources from Princely India to British India

CHAPTER 9

Net Resource Outflow

The contribution of Joan Robinson during her stay in Princely India in the second half of the 1920s has two important aspects. Her treatment of the general considerations of the question of economic and financial relations between British India and Princely India serves as an indication of her early insights into the issues of underdevelopment and development in colonial India. Part II dealt with this aspect. Part III finds, on the basis of the case formulated in the study on India—*The British Crown and the Indian States*—for a return flow of resources from British India to the princely states, that both Robinsons thought and, in terms of policy, recommended prescriptions like modern applied development economists about a decade and a half before the birth of development economics[1] and two decades before the first World Bank adviser set foot in an underdeveloped country. [2]The case was made on the basis of estimates by using whatever passed in the name of statistics in the princely states or by making intelligent guesses, an experience that most early development economists would go through in countries with inadequate or no data at all.

Austin Robinson's Applied Work

It is important to emphasize the applied nature of the work, something that Joan Robinson was never known for.[3] In contrast, Austin Robinson's training began as an applied economist. As he told his biographer: 'By the

© The Author(s), under exclusive license to Springer Nature
Switzerland AG 2022
P. Tahir, *Joan Robinson in Princely India*, Palgrave Studies in the
History of Economic Thought,
https://doi.org/10.1007/978-3-031-10905-8_9

time I came back to Cambridge in October 1920 and attended for the first time lectures in economics... I was well on the way to becoming an applied political economist'. [4] Not only the thinking was of a development economist, the methodology was that of an applied development economist. [5] Obviously, the future founder of the Department of Applied Economics at Cambridge, Austin Robinson, had a large footprint in the estimation of the inflows and outflows of resources. Joan Robinson added a few notes, besides helping with editing, presentations and advocacy.

According to the study, Princely India occupied 38.8 per cent of the all-India area and contained 22.5 per cent of the population (*The British Crown*, 1929, p. 138). [6] It comprised a large number of internally autonomous and not necessarily contiguous states.[7] This chapter sets out the main case in terms of fiscal transfers extracted by British India from Princely India without, in most instances, any quid pro quo. It shows how the study worked out the liabilities of the states on account of defence and other major heads of expenditure; the method by which were estimated their contributions through customs and other taxes and state monopolies; and the way the net direction of resource transfer was kept towards British India. Then there is an evaluation of the estimation procedure adopted, underlining that it was the first-ever professional work of the Robinsons in the field of applied development economics.

THE ASSUMPTIONS

The study selected 1926–1927 as the year of analysis. After making a thorough examination of the liability of the states on account of the major categories of common interest—defence and debt, transport and communications and public works—it worked out a rough quantum of tributes and their contribution to the principal revenue sources of British India, which included customs, excise duties, income tax and the profits of monopolies such as salt, railways, currency and mints. This made possible a global estimate of the net burden imposed on the states by the British Indian fiscal system. Its tentative nature was admitted, but a firmer estimate based on better data was unlikely to alter the 'fact that the subjects of Indian States do contribute to British Indian revenues' and that 'the task of enunciating the necessary principles of adjustment' required to be undertaken (*The British Crown*, 1929, p. 213). The study did not 'claim that our figures are exact', but it did 'believe that within reasonable limits' the estimates were fairly reliable.

Our object has been rather to show the nature of the problem from such data as have been available than to establish definite figures. Where figures have been used we have aimed at moderation. In not a few cases we believe that we have under-estimated the contributions of the States, and where for some reason we accept an estimated figure which we suspect to be over-favourable to them the effect of the error is not great. In any instance where it is thought that we have over-estimated we would ask the reader to substitute his own figure and to see how far, if at all, the change affects our general argument. (*The British Crown*, 1929, p. 135)

OVERALL TRANSFER: AN EVALUATION

After estimating the contributions of the states separately under various heads, the study put together the overall picture as in Table 9.1.

The total revenue contribution of the states to the British Indian exchequer stood at Rs. 1044 lakhs.[8] According to the study, the states had no liability to pay. This meant that the whole of revenue contribution constituted a net transfer of resources. It emphasized that 'these figures are only tentative', though a serviceable approximation to the 'fact that the subjects of Indian States do contribute to British Indian revenues' (*The British Crown*, 1929, p. 213).

The exercise carried out by the Robinsons related to a single year, 1926–1927, under assumptions not always brought out clearly and a method that was as crude and arbitrary as were the data deficient in coverage and lacking in quality. Estimation of a trend was out of question. Information on other years was provided, wherever possible, suggesting roughly that the chosen year was not the only time of the outflow of

Table 9.1 Overall contribution of states, 1926–1927

Items	Lakhs of rupees[a]
Sea customs	706
Excise duties	39
Income tax	–
Salt	93
Railways	120
Currency and mints	86
Total	1044

Source: The British Crown (1929, p. 213)

[a]10 lakhs = 1 million

resources. The impact of the Great Depression was felt much later. So, the year chosen was not exceptional. As the stated purpose was to illustrate the problem rather than establish precise orders of magnitude, it was not an unreasonable choice, more so because the data became weaker the farther back one went into the past. More relevant, the problem of resource transfer became serious only after the abandonment of the Manchester school policies of free trade and minimal taxation and state economic activity after World War I. The conscious decision to err towards underestimation rather than overestimation made the estimate conservative enough to be acceptable as a broad indication of a tendency of net resource transfer from Princely India to British India.

Most of the problems with the estimation procedure stemmed from the impossibility of solving them. Surprisingly, the study did not work out any relative measure of the resource transfer, something that was not completely beyond the realm of the possible. It was content with providing an absolute measure, which makes it difficult to evaluate the significance of the resource transfer. It is possible to say that the states' share thus estimated was 78 per cent of the share indicated by their population proportion.[9] This is not much help as nothing is revealed about the actual resource capacity of the states and the extent of the loss suffered. The share in proportion to population is in any case notional, or at best an indication of the potential, and what was calculated was an informed guess. Again, it would be too much to expect a figure as a ratio of the states' GDPs.[10] An idea of the resource transfer as a proportion of the total resources of the states would have been the next best thing. That was not attempted either.

This would be an extremely difficult task to accomplish. There were 560 states, with annual revenues ranging from a few thousands to hundreds of thousands of rupees. According to a leading authority on the Indian fiscal affairs before the Partition, a large number of the states did 'not indulge in any such "outlandish" customs' as the collection and publication of data. The same authority produced a no less outlandish guess by placing the annual revenues of all the states at Rs. 7500 lakhs. It was admitted to be sketchy, but not without a confident suggestion about the likelihood of it being an understatement of the true resource picture (Shah, 1927, pp. 524–9; Shah & Khambata, 1924, pp. 211, 256–7). The guess surpassed the total yield from principal revenue sources in British India by some 300 lakhs of rupees![11]

That it was not only wide off the mark but also in the wrong direction is borne out by a comparison with the estimate provided later by Visvesvaraya (1934, p. 310). There are good reasons to rely on his judgement. He had been the prime minister of Mysore, a state that was without any doubt among the 'notable exceptions' which, according to the Indian Economic Enquiry Committee, 'maintain statistics almost as complete as those prepared in British India'. [12] His own reputation as a progressive administrator, his intimate knowledge of the states in general and his impeccable credentials as the author of an all-India nationalist economic plan provide reasonable justification for choosing his estimate as nearer to the real state of affairs. Writing in 1934, he put the total revenue of the states at Rs. 4748 lakh. No specific period was mentioned. At the time the Robinsons were investigating the subject, the estimate by Shah had been published. It is probable that they disregarded it for its unrealism on the basis of whatever information they had been able to marshal. Visvesvaraya's estimate was made five years after her study. The officialdom in British India had started to publish overall statistics of the states only after the Butler Report.

India (1929) contained a detailed account of the revenues of the states, related in general to 1927–1928, a period closer to the year studied in *The British Crown*, that is, 1926–1927. Based on this source, the total revenue of all the states works out at Rs. 4886 lakhs. It is higher than Visvesvaraya's estimate, the most likely reason being the impact of the Great Depression on the latter. Even closer to the period of the Robinsons' study must be the Butler Report's estimate of Rs. 4579 lakhs (*Report*, 1929, p. 10).

One may choose an estimate to one's own taste, as any of these serves to illustrate the relative significance of the transfer of resources from the states to British India, the outflow being in the vicinity of 20 per cent of the revenues of the states.

THE HARCOURT PUZZLE

As mentioned by Harcourt (1984, p. 652), economists have often been puzzled by Joan Robinson's apparent lack of interest in applied or empirical work in her known career. The study analysed here goes some distance to resolve the Harcourt puzzle. It may not be the empirical work of 'the conventional kind', which it could not have been at any rate as one had not yet heard of econometric testing. But there need be no doubt about the applied nature of the work. The study tried out a number of useful hypotheses on whatever data were available in Princely India of the 1920s.

The estimation of the extent of the resource transfer was an applied exercise in every sense of the term. It would not be wrong to say that Joan Robinson participated in and contributed to an applied development exercise supervised by a budding applied economist, her husband E.A.G. Robinson. In time, Sir Austin Robinson became a pioneer in the field of applied economics (Turner, 1986).[13]

Although Joan Robinson never developed a taste for applied, empirical or mathematical work, she did taste the applied work in her early years. She prepared a joint note on an unidentified subject. More significantly, the working on and the analysis of the critically important areas of salt monopoly [14] and railways [15] in this and the following two chapters was done by her (Aslanbeigui & Oakes, 2009, p. 32, *n.*24). Later in her career, Joan Robinson carried out an applied development study of Sri Lanka (Robinson, 1959). [16] Parts of her work on China may also fall in the applied category.[17] Similarly, her name appears in the acknowledgements of an empirical study of Liberia (Clower et al., 1966, p. vii). However, in a letter to this writer (10 March 1987), Professor Clower informed that her contribution was not more than casual comments. While she was cut out for a theoretician *par excellence*, her early exposure to applied work does show up occasionally.

NOTES

1. See Arndt (1972, 1981) for the origins of development economics.
2. Currie (1981, pp. 54–58).
3. See Harcourt (1984, p. 652).
4. Cairncross (1993, p. 14).
5. The Robinsons were conscious of the fact that the analysis was 'the first in the whole history of India'. It dealt with 'the uncertainty that has hitherto cloaked the precise relations of the States to the Indian Empire' and 'put the economic relations between the States and British India in a conspectus of fact and law' (*The British Crown*, 1929, pp. 176, 136). Brebner (1931, p. 316) found it 'as a record practically unique in English'. Among other studies on the subject, Timmalachar (1929) was mainly concerned with Mysore state and involved a simple calculation on the basis of population, while Ramaiya (1930) did not attempt any estimates.
6. *The British Crown* (1929) includes Burma (now Myanmar), which was a part of the Indian empire. Its exclusion would increase the area of the states to 47 per cent and population by not more than half a per cent (India, 1932, p. 15). As it is population share that is crucial for her estimation procedure, the inclusion of Burma does not significantly affect results.

7. Due to the existence of many states of small sizes, the total number of the states was a matter of some dispute. As a result, the population and area figures also differed in different studies. Two-fifths of the area and one-fifth of the population, as implied in figures, were widely used.

8. J.S. Mills (1929, p. 416) uses the same estimate of overall resource transfer given in Table 9.1.

9. Estimated share/share proportionate to population = Rs. 1044 lakh/Rs. 1332 lakh = 78% where the denominator is obtained by the total sharable revenue (Rs. 5919) multiplied by the states' population ratio (0.225).

10. See Heston (1984, pp. 401–37) for the serious difficulties in estimating the output and income of British India. Shah (1927, p. 529) guessed the total 'wealth' of the states to be one-sixth of the aggregate for India.

11. The principal sources of revenue in British India yielded in 1926–1927 (accounts) Rs. 7204 lakh (Indian Finance, 1932, p. 9). Kumar (1984, p. 927) believes that the tax incidence per head in some states was more than in British India, but gives no evidence. In any case, even a higher tax burden per capita in all states would still not leave British India behind in absolute terms, as was assumed by Shah.

12. India (1925, p. 53).

13. Turner (1986/manuscript).

14. *The British Crown* (1929, pp. 197–201).

15. *The British Crown* (1929, pp. 201–5).

16. See also *The Times* (1958) for the main points of this study.

17. See, for instance, Robinson (1973) and Robinson and Adler (1958).

References

Unpublished Material

Robert Clower's letters to the author. (1987, March 10, April 8).

Turner, M. S. (1986/manuscript). Joan Robinson and the Americans.

Published Works

Arndt, H. W. (1972). Development Economics Before 1945. In *J. Bhagwati and R.S.*

Aslanbeigui, N., & Oakes, G. (2009). *The Provocative Joan Robinson: The Making of a Cambridge Economist*. Duke University Press.

Brebner, J. B. (1931). Book note on *The British Crown and the Indian States*. *Political Science Quarterly, 46,* 315–316.

Cairncross, A. (1993). *Austin Robinson: The Life of an Economic Adviser.* Palgrave Macmillan.

Clower, R. W. et al. (1966). *Growth Without Development: An Economic Survey of Liberia.* Northwestern University Press.

Currie, L. (1981). *The Role of Economic Advisers in Developing Countries.* Greenwood Press.

Harcourt, G. C. (1984). Harcourt on Robinson. In *Contemporary Economists in Perspective* (Vol. 1, Part B). Jai Press.

Heston, A. (1984). National Income. In D. Kumar (Ed.), *The Cambridge Economic History of India* (Vol. 2). Bombay.

India, Government of. (1925). *Report of the Indian Economic Enquiry Committee.* Central Publications Branch.

India, Government of. (1929). *The Indian States.* Central Publication Branch.

India, Government of. (1932). *The Origin, Rise and Consolidation of the Indian States: A British Assessment 1929.* B.R. Publishing. Reprint 1975.

Indian Finance Year Book. (1932). *Annual Supplement of Indian Finance.* Central Publications Branch.

Kumar, D. (1984). The Fiscal System. In D. Kumar (Ed.), *The Cambridge Economic History of India* (Vol. 2). Bombay.

Mills, J. S. (1929). The Butler Report and the Indian Princes. *Asiatic Review, 25,* 413–420.

Ramaiya, A. (1930). The Indian States and British India: Their Financial Relations. *Empire Review, 51,* 208–211.

Robinson, J., & Adler, S. (1958). *China: An Economic Perspective.* Fabian International Bureau, Fabian Tract No. 314.

Robinson, J. (1959). Economic Possibilities of Ceylon. In *Papers by Visiting Economists.* National Planning Council.

Robinson, J. (1973). *Economic Management in China.* ACEI.

Shah, K. T. (1927). *Sixty Years of Indian Finance.* P.S. King and Son.

Shah, K. T., & Khambata, K. J. (1924). *Wealth and Taxable Capacity of India.* P.S. King and Son.

The British Crown and the Indian States. (1929). P.S. King and Son.

The Times. (1958, September 3). Economic Advice to Ceylon: Nationalization not Advised. 9.

Timmalachar, B. (1929). Fiscal Relations between the Indian States and the Government of India. *Indian Journal of Economics, 9,* 413–440.

Visvesvaraya, M. (1934). *Planned Economy for India.* Banglore Press.

CHAPTER 10

Liabilities of the States

The liabilities of the states consisted mainly of defence, debt servicing, transport and communications, and public works. However, the study did not take up the important examination of the extent to which the states could be made liable to shoulder the burden of public expenditure by British India.

DEFENCE AND INTERNAL SECURITY

Defence was 'the most important and the most expensive' service provided by British India, claiming 52 per cent of the total expenditures listed in the central budget (excluding railways) in 1926–1927. It was sometimes contended that the contribution of the states to British Indian revenues was broadly a means to discharge their liability for defence and security. 'The States contribute', the study went on to claim, 'a considerable sum to central revenues by various indirect means, and it is loosely assumed by some apologists for the Government of British India that the States' total contribution merely covers their obligation for defence' (*The British Crown*, 1929, p. 154). For instance, Shah (1927, p. 529) contended that British India would be justified in asking the states to contribute their quota for defence. He also believed that this quota would exceed any refunds on account of British Indian taxes. The study found the

© The Author(s), under exclusive license to Springer Nature   119
Switzerland AG 2022
P. Tahir, *Joan Robinson in Princely India*, Palgrave Studies in the
History of Economic Thought,
https://doi.org/10.1007/978-3-031-10905-8_10

assumption to be without any substance. By surrendering their sovereignty over external affairs, the states had excluded themselves from being the cause of external aggression and thus from the liability to pay for its prevention. They had traded their foreign policy for British protection. There was, therefore, no general obligation on the part of the states to contribute to defence expenditure.

> Indeed the fact that with many States the Crown has made special treaties and agreements containing express terms dealing with the amount of subsidy or tribute to be paid or the number of troops to be provided, makes it impossible to maintain that any such general obligation can be implied. (*The British Crown*, 1929, p. 148)

Maintaining internal peace was mutually beneficial, but 'no reason for one party to subsidize the other'. If the states were 'the gainers from the peace of India', 'the existence of the States in fact relieved the British Government of part of the cost of maintaining order' (*The British Crown*, 1929, pp. 150–1). A general obligation to contribute indirectly to external defence and internal security through taxation was untenable. With no significant military strength left with the states, protecting one state against another had become an obsolete function, and internal policing was a matter for the states themselves. Yet the states made direct payments and not merely through voluntary gifts.

> Some pay annual tributes in money, some ceded territories whose revenues were estimated to be adequate to support a given number of troops, some pay a subsidy for the same object. It is not known accurately what is the present yield of the territories ceded, but it is known that the revenue has very greatly increased, has increased indeed faster than the cost of maintaining troops. It was found, for instance, that in 1902, Berar, which had been assigned to Government in 1853, in order to discharge a payment of Rs.32 lakhs, was yielding a revenue of Rs.119 lakhs (an increase of 270 per cent.), while the total cost of the army in India had increased during that period by less than140 per cent. It is not possible to find comparable figures for other districts or other years, and we cannot exactly estimate the present share contributed by the States towards the cost of defence by their cessions of territory, their tributes and subsidies. But in any case the cessions, subsidies and tributes were designed to bring in a sufficient income, allowing in every case a handsome margin, to maintain certain stated forces. If the fixed trib-

utes and subsidies have proved a bad bargain for Government, the territories have turned out an exceedingly profitable one. (*The British Crown*, 1929, pp. 157, 163)

By minutely examining various treaties and arrangements that the British power entered into with the states at different times, the study attempted alternative estimates of their direct contribution to defence. One of these involved an elaborate exercise to estimate the number of troops that the territorial and pecuniary cessions of the past and the subsidies and tributes existing at the time of the writing would have supported under a reasonable set of assumptions. It placed the contribution at one-third of the total strength of the British Indian army, well above the one-fourth that the proportion of the states' population would dictate, but less than what could be squeezed out in situations like the uprising of 1857 when the states supported more than 40 per cent of the East India Company's army.

In another exercise, the study estimated the contribution that the states would have to make in the event of them joining a federation with British India. The argument of no liability would not hold in this case. But the interest of Princely India would only be in the defence against external threat. The study, therefore, deducted from the respective strength of both armies an estimated number required for internal security. The resulting aggregated strength was then assigned on the basis of population. Using the figures for the central budget for 1926–1927, the study imputed to the states a liability on account of defence of Rs. 400 lakhs out of a total of Rs. 4200 lakhs, 'if despite other considerations it were chargeable to the States'. These other considerations were of course the direct contributions in the form of territories and moneys ceded as well as tributes and subsidies (*The British Crown*, 1929, pp. 163–9).

As was seen in the previous chapter, the amount of Rs. 400 lakhs was only about 38 per cent of the estimated revenue transfer of Rs. 1044 lakh to British India, in contrast with Shah's conclusion to the contrary. Shah (1927, p. 213) also shows in the central budget an entry called tribute, a paltry sum of Rs. 84 lakh. These are the direct money payments which the study described as a bad bargain for British India. The good bargain, the territorial cessions, far outweighed the money payments. As was pointed out above, the territory of Berar alone contributed more than the entire tribute paid in money terms.

DEBT SERVICING

Absolved of the liability to contribute to defence expenditure, the states could not have been asked to share the burden of servicing debt incurred on account of defence. Interest payments, which amounted to only Rs. 67 lakh in 1914–1915, skyrocketed to around a thousand lakh within a matter of three years due to war debt and continued to be high after the war due to currency troubles. In 1926–1927, the year of the study, the interest liability stood at Rs. 1184 lakh. The study noted the following position in the case of war debts.

> As regards the war debts, the States' position has never been clearly established. But the liability of the Princes for the financial contributions to the costs of any war, however vast, cannot be different from their general liability for foreign defence… If defence is guaranteed to them by the Crown, they cannot be asked to pay the cost of that defence simply because British India accumulated debt instead of meeting its obligations immediately. (*The British Crown*, 1929, pp. 170–1)

Besides the burden caused by war, the mounting debt also reflected the failure of the British Indian authorities to ensure an elastic tax structure— 'inability to raise revenue to levels corresponding to the new and higher level of prices' (*The British Crown*, 1929, p. 170). Not the least important were the difficulties caused by an unstable rupee, but the study pleaded no liability for the states on this score as well.

> The debts incurred in the subsequent years (1919–1928) fall into a different category. In so far as the deficits of those years were due to currency causes, the States cannot be held responsible, since they enjoy no influence in deciding the currency policy of the financial authorities of British India. Moreover, they had felt the burden already, since each State has a budget of its own which also must be made to balance. Each State had to contend with just the same difficulties as the Central Government, although they had no hand in the currency policy, which caused them. (*The British Crown*, 1929, pp. 171–2)

The above assertion is hard to reconcile with the arguments, taken up in the following chapter, for the states share in the profits of currency and mints. If the states had, according to the study, a right to share in these profits, she did not explain why they should escape their share in the losses. However, the principle that the states could only be held responsible in proportion to the benefit of debt accrued to them remains valid.[1]

RAILWAYS

The railways, with a separate budget of their own, were the most important sector under head of transport and communications. The note in this regard was prepared by Joan Robinson. [2] 'The States', noted Joan Robinson, 'have by no means received the railways as a gift from Government' of British India. At the stage of construction, the states made available the requisite capital funds for the lines within their territories 'on not very favourable terms, and provided the necessary land free of cost, even forfeiting their sovereignty over it'. For instance, the state where the Robinsons resided, Gwalior, provided a loan of Rs. 75 lakh for the Gwalior-Agra section of the main line, 'less than half of which lies in Gwalior territory, and supplied not only the necessary land, but also materials for the construction of the line, free of charge'. In addition, the states forsook the right to levy transit duties on goods carried by trains (*The British Crown*, 1929, p. 174).

For many years the railways were not making profits and received contributions from the revenue budget. However, at the time Joan Robinson was writing, they had started to generate surpluses. If the states did not share the burden of deficits, the Government of India was not sharing its surpluses either. That was not the argument Joan Robinson made. She believed that an exercise like the one she was conducting would have, during the deficit phase, shown a matching of liabilities, 'including a fair share of the deficit', and contributions. Nevertheless, the important question was not the past but the existing liability: 'It is not, however, necessary to discuss in detail the liability of the States in the past any more than it is possible to claim considerations for past contributions'. As far as the existing liability was concerned, she pointed out that the railways were self-supporting, charging for the services provided and paying their own capital charges (*The British Crown*, 1929, p. 175).

PORTS AND HIGHWAYS

Ports were profitable concerns, not subsidized in any way. The states had no liability on this account.

Roads were an internal concern of the states and the provinces of British India. The mutuality of benefits ruled out any question of liability on either side. However,

Considerable distances of highways, such as the Agra-Bombay road, lie through States, and they are kept in better condition than local traffic demands, largely for the benefit of British-Indian motorists. Certain States, moreover, have been saddled with roads or bridges, originally built for strategic purposes, which bring the States no benefit comparable with their cost of upkeep and which have been superseded by railways since they were first made. The States provide their full share of roads and bridges and they are under no liability on this account. (*The British Crown*, 1929, pp. 176–7)

POST, TELEPHONES AND TELEGRAPH

The post office ran persistent deficits, which were met from the revenue budget. Despite this subsidy, the study concluded that the liability of the states was nil even in this case. Eleven of the states possessed their own independent postal services and another five operated them jointly with British India. As a result, a large portion of the population of the princely states did not use the Imperial Post Office and the states concerned had no liability in this regard. In the case of the states which 'are not permitted to manage their own postal system, there can obviously be no ground for saddling them with any portion of this deficit'. They had been denied the opportunity of running their own cheaper service, which the Travancore state had shown to be feasible by keeping the wage bill low. The states 'that desire to be served by the Imperial system' would be the only ones liable to share the deficit burden, but merely to the extent of 'the operation of the system within their borders'. An analysis of the structure of the deficit made further inroads into the extent of the states' liability. The study found that the post office itself was not in deficit, but its sister services, telephones and telegraphs, were. In addition, deficits arose due to capital expenditure on new post offices, which failed to be self-supporting. The telephone services were expected to become profitable soon. It followed that the 'extent to which the States desiring to be served by the Imperial system are liable for the expenses of the Post Office, therefore, is the extent to which they benefit from the Telegraph Service, and from capital expansion'. Because of their backwardness in commerce, the use of telegraph services in the states was very limited (*The British Crown*, 1929, pp. 177–9). With regard to capital expansion, she observed that the states could not justifiably be made to bear 'the losses upon new branches opened at the initiative of the Imperial Post Office, since when they themselves ask for a branch to be opened in a particular district they are required to provide a guarantee' (*The British Crown*, 1929, p. 180). On the basis of population served, the liability of the states was worked out at less than one lakh rupees for 1926–1927. In the subsequent year, when the pay hikes bloated the deficit, the states' liability was about Rs. 4 lakh.

> But before the States are debited with this amount it is necessary to remember that the deficit on the Post Office is incurred because new branches are opened which cannot immediately pay, so that none of the States served by guaranteed branches share in this liability, while presumably only profitable branches of the Imperial Post Office are opened in the States which run postal services for themselves. For this reason we do not include these four lakhs in our estimate of the States' liabilities. (*The British Crown*, 1929, p. 181)

Public Works

Under the head of public works, the most important service was irrigation. Various schemes were designed to be self-financing, showing profits when 'the additional land revenue due to their existence' was allowed for. Capital and current costs were stipulated to be shared, according to the treaties signed, 'in proportion to the benefit received' (*The British Crown*, 1929, pp. 181–2). Thus, the states were not liable to contribute to the central exchequer on this account. However, while the government of British India was 'accustomed to charge seigniorage' for the water rising in its territory and distributed to the states, the same was not considered necessary for the states.

> For instance, the surface water of a large area of the territory of Kishengarh State has been drained away to supply the Sambhar salt lake, and the district deprived of water has been reduced to a wilderness. During a minority administration the Darbar was prevented from constructing bundhs, or wells, on the ground that by such means their own water would have been kept within their own territory and prevented from flowing to swell the Sambhar lake. The Darbar has received no compensation for the water which it has lost. (*The British Crown*, 1929, p. 182)

This was not to deny that the states with no natural water of their own also benefited from irrigation schemes, but the user charges and incremental land revenue charged as well as the overall profitability of the schemes created no liability for the central budget.

On the whole, the states were not liable to contribute tax revenue towards defence expenditure and related debt as they had bartered their external sovereignty for it. Again, a quid pro quo existed between defence and direct tributes in cash and kind. Commercial services presented a different set of problems. Railways, ports and irrigation were profitable, self-financing ventures, and roads were not a central responsibility. To the extent they were able to cover their current costs and capital charges, the states were not liable. The services provided by the Imperial Post Office showed deficits met from general taxation, indicating the existence of grounds at least in this case for the liability of the states to contribute to the central revenue. The study came to the opposite conclusion, as the cause of deficit could not be located in the states.

Notes

1. See Khan (1937, pp. 156–7).
2. Aslanbeigui and Oakes (2009), p. 32, *n*.24).

References

Published Works

Aslanbeigui, N., & Oakes, G. (2009). *The Provocative Joan Robinson: The Making of a Cambridge Economist*. Duke University Press.
Khan, M. M. (1937). *Federal Finance*. Robert Hale.
Shah, K. T. (1927). *Sixty Years of Indian Finance*. P.S. King and Son.
The British Crown and the Indian States. (1929) P.S. King and Son.

CHAPTER 11

Revenue Contributions

In regard to the British Indian public expenditure, the conclusion of the study was that no significant liability arose for the princely states. But the government of British India still exacted revenues out of the states, 'the indirect and uncovenanted contributions' (*The British Crown*, 1929, p. 183), through its taxes, monopoly price policies and profits on currency and mints. To the extent that the states were making these contributions without being liable, there was taking place a net transfer of resources from Princely India to British India. The 'peoples of Indian States are at present subjected to a considerable burden of taxation for which they receive no return and for which there can be no justification' (*The British Crown*, 1929, p. 215).

The Assumptions

In view of the skimpy state in which data were held in princely states, the measurement of this transfer required an extraordinary set of assumptions and an ingenious technique. In broad terms, the study assumed the use of goods and density of services per capita in the states to be a lower proportion of the British Indian per capita levels in an attempt to capture the reality of their relative backwardness. Thus, British Indian per capita levels provided the ceiling, which were given the weight 100. The proportions for the states were worked out by sifting out from whatever information

© The Author(s), under exclusive license to Springer Nature Switzerland AG 2022
P. Tahir, *Joan Robinson in Princely India*, Palgrave Studies in the History of Economic Thought,
https://doi.org/10.1007/978-3-031-10905-8_11

was available an intuitively plausible set of weights normally below 100 and equal to 100 in some obvious cases.

Customs and excises were the major sources of indirect contribution by the states to the British Indian budget. Income tax was included in the analysis, but without any effort at estimating its contribution due to the non-availability of information from the British Indian authorities.

CUSTOMS

The largest item was customs revenue. However, to know the contribution of the states to the British Indian exchequer was not a simple matter of adding up the duty paid on the imports into the states. Most of the states added on their own import duties to incoming goods. This should have served as a relatively easy point to collect interesting statistics. The condition in which the study found the statistical systems of the states scarcely conformed to this expectation. The comments the study made on the quality and the coverage of information foreshadowed the common themes of frustration written down by the first crop of development planners in many first five-year plans.

In order to make a quantitative estimate of the contributions of the States, it is necessary to attempt to estimate the proportion of the total customs revenue which is derived immediately or ultimately from their population. The means to obtain accurate figures or even an intelligent estimate are [sic] lacking. The Government do not tabulate their sea customs according to destination, and if they did, the vast quantity of things which break bulk at the ports, and are re-consigned in smaller packages to the States, or are brought by individuals in the States from traders in British India, would escape tabulation. Nor do the States in general record their imports by countries of origin. The State import duties do not distinguish between English, Japanese and Bombay cotton goods or between sugar originating abroad and in British India or in another State. Few States indeed keep accurate statistics at all. Such as are available are extremely difficult to reconcile either with probability or with known facts. Further, the heads under which they record imports are wholly different from those used by the Imperial customs authorities, and differ also between State and State. Some have records of quantities only and not values. Some record values only, not quantities. The measures used are in many cases not easily changeable into the measures used by the Imperial customs. Imports of cotton may be reckoned in maunds, or yards, or values, and sometimes the only returns available show the yield of a specific duty on a miscellaneous group of goods. (*The British Crown*, 1929, pp. 187–8)

Though there were a few cases where information could be believed to have been collected with some care, it was still not a reliable record of all dutiable imports entering the ports of British India for destinations in the states. 'For all classes there are ways and means of avoiding tax'. The ordinary people could brave the long and difficult state borders where the attempt 'to prevent evasion entirely would, even if it were possible, be financially ruinous'. The employees of the Imperial Post Office used their parcel service for the purpose. With the rich residents of the states, the practice consisted in buying imported goods in British India and bringing them into the state territories as used items. Finally, the imports on the accounts of the state governments did not pay any duty anyway (*The British Crown*, 1929, pp. 188–9). In addition, there was the problem of making allowance for states like Kashmir which had been granted the special position of refunds of duty on goods consigned to them in return for not imposing their transit duties on goods entering British India through their territory.

Due to the above factors, any estimate based on whatever information the states made available would understate their import supply. A simple technique would be to apportion total imports between British India and the states on an equal per capita basis, implying that the states share customs revenue in proportion to their population. In 1926–1927, the share of the states in import duty yield would have amounted to nearly Rs. 900 lakh out of a total of about Rs. 4000 lakh (The British Crown, 1929, p. 186). While an exercise based exclusively on the defective statistics of the states, as noted earlier, would have been an underestimate, the per capita basis erred on the side of overestimation. Underlying such an estimate would be the assumption of similar levels as well as patterns of consumption and production.[1] This would assume what was intended to be proved that the states were backward relative to British India and needed to keep their resources with themselves in order to be able to mount an effort to catch up. To advance the analysis, the study had to find a way around this difficulty. The dilemma was stated in a nutshell: 'It is hard to estimate how much allowance should be made for the relative poverty of the States, and impossible to collect exact figures of the amount of overseas goods which cross the frontiers' (*The British Crown*, 1929, p. 186).

As a percentage of the total for India as a whole, the population of the states was 22.5 per cent. The aim was to discover some criteria by which to adjust this notional share of dutiable imports suggested by population proportion that would be consistent with the stage of development in the states. The data from the states, leaving much to be desired in homogeneity and coverage, provided an extremely poor basis for an overall estimate. Nevertheless, study 'employed the knowledge thus gained as the basis of an estimate for the whole area'. It could be described as intuition based on facts available with a certain, albeit low, degree of reliability. The method used was described in these terms.

> The method we have adopted in making this estimate is to take the various heads of customs revenue and group them into four classes according to our ideas of the probable consumption of each article in the States, compared with its consumption in British India. The result is mainly guesswork, but there is unfortunately no alternative, and our utmost hope is that the errors of our guesses may in some measure cancel out and that the total guess may be nearer the truth than if we guessed simply from one total to the other. (*The British Crown*, 1929, p. 189)

Having set the per capita consumption in British India as the upper limit, and using whatever information was available from the states to formulate 'ideas of the probable consumption', the study divided the import items into four categories in order of their importance. The weights reflected per capita consumption in states as a declining proportion of per capita consumption in British India. Table 11.1 portrays the method adopted, its assumptions and the predictions.

Row (3) in Table 11.1 gives the weights chosen, that is, the consumption in states as a proportion of consumption per capita in British India, and the corresponding footnotes work out row (2), which indicates the per cent of total imports taken by the states. Thus, for category I, the study assumed the equality of per capita consumption between the two Indias. In other words, both get a share in proportion to their populations, that is, 22.5 per cent for Princely India and 77.5 per cent for British India. Both are assigned the equal weight of 100 per cent such that the states' share is 22.5 per cent. Consistent with the relative backwardness of the states, their consumption of dutiable imports was in no case assumed to be more than the per capita consumption in British India. In regard to the other three categories, consumption per capita in the states was

Table 11.1 Yield of customs, 1926–1927

I		II		III		IV	
Articles 22.5% yield	Customs	Articles 18.0% yield	Customs	Articles 15.0% yield	Customs	Articles 10.0% yield	Customs
Sugar	701	Articles wholly or mainly manufactured (other than cotton or silk)	814	Liquor	261	Machinery	38
Mineral oil	129	Cars and cycles	105	Tobacco	191	Railway materials	24
Cotton yarn	36	Rubber tyres and tubes	39	Iron steel (10% duty)	43	Railway tracks	8
Cotton piece goods	621	Paper and stationery	24	Iron and steel (protective special duty)	268	Miscellaneous (10% duty)	1
Matches	89	Portland cement	9	Articles of food and drink	175		
Others (non-protective special duties)	15	Coal tubs	1	Raw materials	65		
				Miscellaneous (15% duty)	61		
				Miscellaneous (30% duty)	104		
				Silk	78		
(1) Total revenue	1591		992		1246		71
(2) Assumed % taken by states	22.5		18		15		10

(continued)

Table 11.1 (continued)

	I		II		III		IV	
	Customs	Articles 22.5% yield	Customs	Articles 18.0% yield	Customs	Articles 15.0% yield	Customs	Articles 10.0% yield	Customs
(3) Consumption in states as % of consumption in British India		100.0[a]		78.0[b]		62.0[c]			38.0[d]
(4) Tax paid by the population of states (Lakh Rs)	358		179		187				
(5) Total sea customs paid by the states (Lakh Rs)	731								

Source: The British Crown (1929, p. 190)

[a] $22.5 \times 100 / (22.5 \times 100) + (77.5 \times 100) = 22.5\%$

[b] $22.5 \times 78 / (22.5 \times 78) + (77.5 \times 100) = 18\%$ c22.5

[c] $62 / (22.5 \times 62) + (77.5 \times 100) = 15\%$

[d] $22.5 \times d38 / (22.5 \times 38) + (77.5 \times 100) = 10\%$

assumed to be a progressively falling proportion of the consumption per capita in British India, for instance, 78 per cent in category II. These declining weights naturally implied import consumption levels lower than the population ratio.

Their declining importance made sense. But to assume that the states are relatively backward and then conduct the analysis on the basis of equality of consumption per capita in the category yielding the highest customs revenue, namely, category I, begs the question. Conspicuous consumption of the ruling classes might be one explanation. But the items of luxury were placed in the middle categories. The study recognized the difficulty, but argued that there were reasons to assume consumption per capita at the level of British India. The appeal was made to logic, illustrated by an example, and direct evidence from one state. In its implications, the logic was quite novel: a relatively backward area can actually end up importing more from abroad than its advanced partner so far as consumer goods are concerned. Taking the example of cotton piece goods, it was explained that British India had its own mill output as well as imports. Compared to imports, the British Indian mills had the advantage of insignificant transport costs in their neighbourhoods. As they approached the states borders, the edge began to be eroded.

> Thus in 1925–1926 the import of cotton piece goods was 1,563,713 yards, the Indian mill production was 1,954,461 yards, making a total of 3,518,174 yards. Now if we assume that instead of consuming 22[.5] per cent. of the mill-produced cotton goods the States because of their greater poverty consume only 18 per cent., but draw 60 per cent. of it from abroad, their consumption of imported cotton will then be 280,063 yards, or 24.3 per cent. of the total of imported cotton piece-goods. These figures are intended to be illustrative only, and it is not claimed that they represent the actual facts. It is here only our purpose to show that when an article is manufactured both in British India and abroad for import into India, even if the States consumption per head is demonstrably lower than that in British India, it may nevertheless happen that the States' proportion of the consumption of imported goods is as high or higher than the proportion that their population bears to the whole. (*The British Crown*, 1929, pp. 186–7)

In the state of Kashmir, where the excise duty on British Indian cotton piece goods and the duty on imported goods were rebated, the data collected for the purpose corroborated the analysis of the study. The import component was as high as 80 per cent (*The British Crown*, 1929, p. 186, *n.*1). On the whole, therefore, the assumption that the states' share was 22.5 per cent in category I does not seem to be unreasonable. Though Bagchi (1972, pp. 70–2) noted how little knowledge the Bombay mill owners possessed of the market in India beyond their neighbourhood, he doubted the neighbourhood hypothesis on the basis of the evidence that Bombay—the centre of Indian-owned cotton and textile mills—had larger competing imports compared to the other major ports, which were the centres of European-owned industries. He did not specifically deal with the states. The latter were generally situated away from the sea ports and main rail lines. It is, therefore, difficult wholly to dismiss the neighbourhood hypothesis in their context. While the study illustrated her case from Kashmir because of the availability of relevant data, the example is biased in that this state is the farthest from the sea as well as from the railways. At any rate, the objective was to emphasize that though the states, because of their relative poverty, might be consuming essential items at lower than the British Indian per capita levels, the imported component of their consumption was high enough to assume a share in total imports proportionate to their population. What Bagchi (1972, p. 11) called definite prejudice against Indian products in the case of finer varieties is quite likely to have existed in the states in a stronger way. The states' misgivings about Indian nationalists and the latter's impatience 'to make short work of them' [2] furnish some ground for this suspicion.

As opposed to the highest share for essential consumer goods, capital goods were assumed to claim the lowest share at 10 per cent. The study noticed two influences that tended to offset each other. The industrial backwardness of the states implied not only that machinery imports would be far less than 22.5 per cent of the total but that also they would be rising, reflecting the attempts to develop industry (The British Crown, 1929, p. 186). However, machinery imports could not have varied radically from the pattern of raw material imports. The study resorted to the data on the share of industrial output of selected items in the Industrial Census, 1921, to conclude that the share of the states in raw material imports would be less than 22.5 per cent. The figures in the census indicated the share of the states in selected industrial items to be in the range of 4–11 per cent. On this basis, it was assumed in the study that the raw material imports in the states would be no more than 15 per cent of the total.

The consumption of luxuries which the study reasonably enough put in the intermediate categories of 18 and 15 per cent could be expected to record higher proportions in the states due to the existence of conspicuous consumption by the leisure class and its demonstration effects.

However, a considerable proportion of this class was exempt from the payment of duty not only at their own borders but also at the British Indian ports of entry.[3] The analysis related to dutiable imports, so that the lower than expected percentage was justified.

Admittedly, these weights were arbitrary. Nevertheless, the discussion of them contains insights which suggest that while accuracy was precluded by the poverty of the states' statistics, the exercise was based on informed common sense, increasing thereby the chance of being loosely plausible than precisely wrong. Although category I broadly corresponds to essential consumption, and category IV to capital goods, as would be the case in later discussions of import structures, the intermediate categories are a mix of luxuries, consumer durables, raw materials and even food items. With the assumptions spelled out, the gross contribution of the states to total customs revenue was calculated by applying the percentages in row (2) to row (1) so as to obtain row (4), which added up to the total of Rs. 731 lakh in row (5). This total was corrected for collection cost and rebates to certain states to arrive at the net contribution of Rs. 706 lakh in part A of Table 11.2. To crosscheck that the error is one of underestimation and not overestimation, part B of Table 11.2 performs a straight calculation on import duties alone by using the population ratio.

The states did not have much interest in export duties as far as revenue contribution was concerned. It turns out that the net contribution estimated for the total customs revenue is less than the share in import duties on the basis of population, adjusted for collection cost. The comparative calculation confirms the conservative nature of the estimate of Rs. 706 lakh. As a ratio of net import duty receipts, it stands at 18 per cent, which is also the estimated share of the states in the total imports.[4]

Using the import duty data would have been more relevant, but the kind of breakdown presented in Table 11.1 was only available for customs as a whole.

Excise Duties

Excise duties were levied at central as well as provincial levels. The provincial excise was out of the purview of Butler Committee, and the yield of central excise 'at the present time is small' (*The British Crown*, 1929, p. 192). The discriminatory tariff had not been in position long enough to enter the import substitution stage where excises typically begin to replace tariffs to make up for the revenue loss in the protected industries. The most important excisable items were kerosene and motor spirit. Tax on

Table 11.2   Customs revenue: states' contribution and share

	Lakhs of rupees
A. *States' contribution to customs revenue*	
Total sea customs paid by states	731
Total customs revenue (import, export and other duties)	4738
Percentage of total paid by the states	15.4%
Total cost of collection and other charges	81
15.4% of cost	12.5
Net customs duties paid by the states	718
Deduct 77.5% of refunds paid to certain states[a]	12
Net contribution of the states to customs revenue	706
B. *States' share of customs revenue in proportion to population*	
Total import duties	3996
Gross share of states in proportion to population	899
Cost of collection[b]	15
Net share of states	884

Source: The British Crown (1929, p. 191)

[a]Certain states already receive a refund of a part of their contribution towards customs revenue. Under the Interportal Agreement, Cochin receives Rs. 1,00,000, and Travancore receives Rs.40,000, annually. Kashmir receives a rebate on goods imported in bond which in 1926 amounted to about Rs.14,00,000. Of these sums, 22.5 per cent have already been deducted from the states' contribution to customs, as they are included among the charges on customs revenue. We, must, therefore, deduct 77.5 per cent of Rs. 15,40,000 in order to obtain the net contribution of the states as a whole [footnote in original]

[b](Total import duties)/(Total customs revenue)(Total cost of collection)(Population ratio)

motor spirit had the well-known purpose of charging the users of publicly provided services, while kerosene was a case of inelastic demand. To estimate the states' share, the study assumed kerosene at 100 per cent of the consumption per capita in British India, being an item of common use, and motor spirit at 78 per cent, which was in line with the proportion of car imports in Table 11.1. An adjustment was made for the population of Kashmir, to whom excises were refunded. The results can be seen in Table 11.3 with total contribution estimated at Rs. 39 lakh.

Opium was another item of central excise, but great variations between states as to its use and internal production made an estimate of its contribution impossible. Only mention was made of the 'policy of the Government in regard to opium and the losses which have fallen upon the opium-growing states in their co-operation with that policy' (*The British Crown*, 1929, p. 194). The contribution to provincial excises was not estimated, being beyond the scope of the study.

Table 11.3 States' contribution to excises, 1926–1927

Items	Revenue (Rs lakhs)	States' share (per cent)	States' share (Rs lakhs)
Kerosene	104.7	21.5[a]	22.5
Motor spirit	96.4	17.6[a,b]	17.0
Total:	201.0	39.5	
States' share in cost of collection	–	–	0.6[c]
Net contribution of states			38.9

Source: *The British Crown* (1929, p. 193)
[a]After 1% adjustment for the population of Kashmir
[b]$21.5 \times 78/(21.5 \times 78) + (78.5 \times 100) = 17.6\%$
[c]Proportionate to the ratio of states' contribution to total collection

INCOME TAX

An estimate of the income tax contributed by the states was found to be impossible in the absence of 'detailed information from the Revenue Department' of British India. If the information had been made available, the estimation would have related to the refunds due the states' subjects in the event of concluding an agreement on the avoidance of double taxation similar to that between Britain and British India. Whether or not the states imposed an income tax, those of their subjects who earned incomes from investments made in British India before the promulgation of income tax there and spent in the states of their residence had had their capacity to pay states' indirect taxes reduced after the introduction of the British Indian income tax.

STATE MONOPOLIES

In the joint exercise of estimating the liabilities and contributions of the princely states by the Robinsons, the notes on the two main state monopolies—salt and railways—were prepared by Joan Robinson. [5]

Salt: The monopoly in salt, an item of common use with an inelastic demand, brought assured revenue to British India. Effectively, the government fixed the prices, and every buyer contributed to revenue squeezed out in the form of excise duty. The peoples of the states, 'with every pound of salt that they buy, make contribution to the central revenue', noted Joan Robinson. Estimating states' share in consumption did not present serious problems.

> There is no reason to suppose that the States consume less than their pro-portionate share of salt, since it is a commodity which the poorest must buy, and it is least needed in the wealthiest and most populous places, the large towns where there are almost no cattle. (*The British Crown*, 1929, p. 197)

Looking at the annual consumption figures for seven randomly selected states, she found that the average consumption stood at 12.2 lbs. It was close to the officially published figure of consumption per capita in British India. With the same per capita consumption, the revenue contribution of the states would be in proportion to their population ratio, that is, 22.5 per cent. In 1926–1927, the year of Joan Robinson's study, the total salt revenue was Rs. 583 lakh, 22.5 per cent of which worked out at Rs. 131 lakh. Deducting compensation of Rs. 38 lakh to salt-producing states, the net contribution came to Rs. 93 lakh (*The British Crown*, 1929, p. 198).

Railways: In British India, as noted in Chap. 10, the government grad-ually assumed the monopoly of railway services. After some difficult initial years, the railways started to generate a sizeable surplus. As the separation of railway budget from the ordinary budget became effective from the year preceding the year of Joan Robinson's inquiry, the contribution of railways to the general revenue was accounted for more clearly.

> This contribution comes from charging railway travellers, and people who consign goods by railway, more than the services have cost to provide. That is to say, it is in the nature of a tax paid by the consumers of railway services, either by travelling or consuming goods which have been carried. The inci-dence of the tax is therefore on travellers and consumers in the States as much as in British India. (*The British Crown*, 1929, pp. 202–3)

To estimate the states' contribution, it was necessary first to estimate their share of passenger and goods traffic on the 34,000 miles of railway under the British Indian control, out of a total mileage of 39,000. The difference was owned by the states, who had leased 2000 miles to the main lines and worked 3000 miles themselves. The average length of haul for foreign trade was longer for the states than British India as they were gen-erally farther away from the coast. Still, following the rule of erring in the direction of underestimation rather than overestimation, Joan Robinson did not allow the states a share in traffic equal to their share in population. Cautiously, she placed the railway use for the states at 85 per cent of the per capita use in British India. Given this weight, the contribution of the states came out to be 20 per cent of the total. [6] During the year of Joan Robinson's interest, 1926–1927, it implied that the states contributed Rs. 120 lakh out of the total railway contribution to the general budget of Rs. 601 lakh (*The British Crown*, 1929, pp. 203–4).

CURRENCY AND MINTS

The government of British India enjoyed a virtual monopoly of currency and mints, with only a handful of states coining their own rupees. They had given up the 'right of coinage' only 'with great reluctance' (*The British Crown*, 1929, p. 205) after the silver crisis of 1873–1893. As silver prices fell violently, the silver-based rupee depreciated from two shillings sterling to as low as a gold value of a little over one shilling. The monetary sovereignty of the states became a casualty to the measures to stabilize the rupee, the chief among them being a single monetary authority to control the supply of silver. There was a recurrence of the crisis at the beginning of World War I and for some years after; this time silver prices moved sharply upwards. In 1920, 'a misguided attempt to maintain exchange at the level to which inflation in Europe had raised it' led to serious losses to the government of British India (*The British Crown*, 1929, p. 207). The states were adversely affected by the rupee muddle. According to the study, it did not call for any compensation, as the states themselves would not have fared any better during this crisis due to the governments' general lack of understanding of monetary management. The study remarked: 'The control of currency is a difficult task at which no Governments of modern times have been conspicuously successful' (*The British Crown*, 1929, p. 207).[7]

This is not consistent with the analysis presented earlier, where the states were excluded from sharing the burden of budgetary deficits arising from currency troubles because they had no say in the framing of monetary policy. Here it is maintained that the states could not have been more efficient managers of money anyway. During a crisis, the currency profits may rise or fall; there may even be losses, as was the case at the start of World War I. It is not made clear why profits alone should be shared. Profits were, however, the norm, and the case for a fair share in them was presented as follows.

> Another service from the provision of which the Government make a profit is the supply of currency. The minting of rupees and small coins and the

printing of notes each yield a surplus measured by the difference between their respective nominal value and their costs of production. The surplus is used to build up a reserve, part of which is invested in income-yielding securities, and so contributes to revenue. (*The British Crown*, 1929, p. 205)

It was legitimate for the states to share the profits of currency and mints, which occurred when the value of rupee rose above the value of its silver content. Each rupee minted by the British Indian government created a profitable margin. Secondly, it was out of these profits that a gold standard reserve had been built up in Europe to support the rupee. Beyond a limit considered safe, the reserves were invested to earn interest, which accrued to the revenue budget. Thirdly, interest-bearing securities were held in currency note reserve, kept apart from the gold standard reserve.

The Butler Committee recommended some compensation to the states. But its main contention was that the profits of mints were not significant and that the paper currency profits related to the good credit rating of British India (*Report*, 1929, p. 47). The calculations in the study for the year of reference, given in Table 11.4, confirm low profits from metallic currency. But the committee glossed over the argument, made in the study, that the gold standard reserves had been piled up through the profits from metallic currency. The question regarding the credit of the government of British India went deeper. It had been argued before that, in the ultimate analysis, the credit of British India derived from the credit of England itself, making it possible for the former to borrow on relatively inexpensive terms (Morison, 1911, p. 239).

Table 11.4 Profits of currency and mints, 1926–1927

Items	Revenue (Rs. lakh)	States' share (per cent)	States' share (Rs. lakh)
Mint	7.1	–	–
Gold standard reserve	180.6[a]	–	–
Total:	187.7	22.5[b]	42.2
Currency note reserve	346.1	12.6[c]	43.6
Contribution of states			85.8

Source: The British Crown (1929, p. 209)

[a]In the original, this figure is misprinted as Rs. 194.8
[b]$22.5 \times 100/(22.5 \times 100) + (77.5 \times 100) = 22.5\%$
[c]$22.5 \times 50/(22.5 \times 50) + (77.5 \times 100) = 12.6\%$

An important implication is that indigenous rule such as that existing in the princely states would not have led to a situation where profits from paper currency arise. The argument ignores the fact that the credit of British India was in no small measure built on the basis of the all-India monetary union, to which the states had contributed by surrendering their coinage and currency rights. Moreover, the states stood behind British India when the latter declared a moratorium during World War I.[8] At any rate, the few states which continued to have their own currency, Hyderabad and Jaipur to name the most important, occupied the first and the fifth position among the states with respect to revenue. They made significant profits on currency. In an important way, the question of sharing currency profits of British India had arisen from the fact that 'those States who gave up their own currencies ... look with envy at the profits made by States who still had their own rupees in circulation' (*The British Crown*, 1929, p. 207).

In arriving at a basis to estimate the states' share in these profits, which are shown in Table 11.4, Joan Robinson revealed an understanding of the monetary features of an underdeveloped economy that would later become the starting point of the discussions of money and development.

Before an estimate could be attempted, an idea of the extent of the use of money in its important forms was needed. If the currencies of some states were taken into account, silver coins were the only item in the entire study the use of which in the states was expected to be somewhat higher than in British India. Their relative backwardness led to a preference for metallic money and to a lower velocity of circulation. In the words of the study,

> it is also necessary to allow for the fact that the use of silver is likely to be greater amongst the relatively poor and backward peoples of the States, and that the velocity of circulation of money is likely to be smaller among them than among the peoples of British India. In spite, therefore, of the smaller real wealth of the States, we may conclude that they make use of silver and token money to the same extent as the rest of India, or, allowing for Darbar currencies, slightly more than the rest of India. (*The British Crown*, 1929, p. 208)

The situation was different for paper money.

> In this the States cannot claim to be credited with a full share, for, as we have already said, their peoples prefer silver to paper. The habit of using cheques,

though it is beginning to develop in the industrial centres of British India, is not sufficiently advanced to have displaced the note circulation to a significant extent, and it is probable that notes are still used in British India to almost double the extent to which they are used in the States. (*The British Crown*, 1929, p. 208)

As a result of the above observations and the general approach to keep the estimate fairly conservative, the weight applied to mint and gold standard reserve profits, which we noted earlier were derived from silver coins, was 100 per cent of the use of silver and token money in British India and 50 per cent for the profits from paper currency. On this basis, the overall contribution of the states was estimated at Rs. 85.8 lakh, as can be seen in Table 11.4.

In the estimation procedures on the revenue side, we see a flavour of the applied economist that Austin Robinson would become in the future. We also see Joan Robinson attempting applied work in regard to salt monopoly and railways. The exercise covers one year. Considering that the study was carried out before they embarked on their proper academic careers at Cambridge, their work shows an impressive skill to analyse insufficient data to reach a plausible set of conclusions. The exercise also showed their early understanding of how policy can be influenced by keeping the sights low. For example, underestimation was preferred over overestimation. In the same vein, it seems, absolute measures were presented rather than relative shares.

NOTES

1. In the case of landlocked Mysore, with a level of development similar to British India, a calculation of total yield performed at British Indian customs rate on all rail-borne imports turned out to be a gross overestimate compared with the computation on per capita basis (Tirumalachar, 1929, p. 431).
2. Shah (1927, p. 524).
3. See *Report* (1929, p. 45).
4. No figures for the states' own import duties were given by the Robinsons. According to the Butler Committee, these stood at Rs. 450 lakh (*Report*, 1929, p. 43), 64 per cent of their estimated contribution to British Indian customs.
5. Aslanbeigui and Oakes (2009, p. 32, *n*.24).
6. $225 \times 85/(22.5 \times 85) + (77.5 \times 100) = 20\%$
7. See Coyajer (1929) for the details of the controversy on the exchange ratio.
8. See Shah (1927, p. 193) and Naik (1930, p. 308).

REFERENCES

PUBLISHED WORKS

Aslanbeigui, N., & Oakes, G. (2009). *The Provocative Joan Robinson: The Making of a Cambridge Economist.* Duke University Press.

Bagchi, A. K. (1972). *Private Investment in India 1900–39.* Cambridge University Press.

Coyajer, J. C. (1929). The Ratio Controversy in India: A Retrospect. *Asiatic Review, 25,* 405–412.

Morison, T. (1911). *Economic Transition in India.* John Murray.

Naik, D. A. (1930). The Indian States and Mints and Coinage. *Calcutta Review, 34,* 305–309.

Report of Indian States Committee 1928–29. (1929). H.M.'s Stationery Office.

Shah, K. T. (1927). *Sixty Years of Indian Finance.* P.S. King and Son.

The British Crown and the Indian States. (1929). P.S. King and Son.

Timmalachar, B. (1929). Fiscal Relations between the Indian States and the Government of India. *Indian Journal of Economics, 9,* 413–440.

The Drain, Backwardness and the State

CHAPTER 12

The Drain and Backwardness

In Part IV, we attempt an interpretation of the role the estimated resource transfer seems to play in *The British Crown* and Joan Robinson's views on development. This chapter dwells on the drain controversy and the reasons of backwardness, while the following chapter brings out the role of the state.

The analysis does not purport to explain backwardness in terms of resource transfers, as the early Indian drain theorists had done and as the surplus transfer theorists were to do later. Princely India was backward compared to British India because their relative political autonomy preserved their static economic organization longer than in British India. This did not prevent authors of *The British Crown* from making a case for the reversal of the transfer of resources to the Princely India in order to implement a development strategy which, like the pioneering development economists and what was subsequently dubbed the modernization paradigm, emphasized capital accumulation as the basic determinant of development.[1] There is an emphasis on the interdependent nature of development,[2] arising from a variety of external effects; the overall impact of the resource transfer exceeded the directly estimated financial effect.

© The Author(s), under exclusive license to Springer Nature 147
Switzerland AG 2022
P. Tahir, *Joan Robinson in Princely India*, Palgrave Studies in the
History of Economic Thought,
https://doi.org/10.1007/978-3-031-10905-8_12

THE DRAIN CONTROVERSY

Discussions of resource transfer were not new to India. The turn of the century had seen the onset of the famous drain controversy. Considering that the states were in some sense in a 'neo-colonial' relationship with the British power,[3] the interesting question is: Did the study for *The British Crown*, following the tradition of old,[4] or anticipating the latter-day, [5] drain theories hold the resource transfer as the principal cause of the relative backwardness of the states? No. It did not say that if Britain drained off Rs. 3000 lakh annually from India,[6] about one-third of it was contributed by the states and that it was the principal factor responsible for their backwardness.

In the old theories, the drain was an unrequited transfer in the form of export surplus, financed by the British Indian budget under the head of 'home charges'.[7] In the later theories of underdevelopment, surplus transfer took various forms—profit repatriation, secular deterioration of the terms of trade of primary products and unequal exchange. *The British Crown* did not specifically discuss the old drain theories.

Among the modern drain theorists, Joan Robinson never said anything about Frank. Baran was censured by her for counterfactuality. She denied that the real wage of the workers in the West was kept high by the exploitation of cheap labour in colonies and ex-colonies. It presumed a higher rate of profit in the colonies, redirecting investment towards the latter. As a result, the bargaining power of the Western workers would suffer, not increase. The route for gain by the Western workers, and not a significant one for that, was provided by favourable terms of trade of manufactures vis-à-vis foodstuffs and raw materials.[8] This mechanism benefited countries like Sweden as well, indicating that the link between higher real wage and colonial or imperialistic exploitation did not necessarily exist (Robinson, 1942, p. 39, *n*.2, 1948, pp. 142–3; 1955b, p. 24). When Emmanuel (1972) picked up the same thread to develop a sophisticated model of unequal exchange, Joan Robinson described it as 'formalistic Marxism'. An average hour of labour did command more purchasing power in the developed than in the underdeveloped countries, but this by no means explained the variation in the levels of development. Following Emmanuel's prescription to improve terms of trade by restricting output had, she argued, dangerous portents: it would only encourage substitution by synthetics, which largely caused the problem in the first place (Robinson 1973, pp. 457–9, 1979, p. 69).

Keeping the question of transfer of resources separate from the causes of backwardness is an insight Joan Robinson seems to have acquired from her work and experience in Princely India. It is important to remember that the insight was derived from the analysis of surplus transfer through taxation, not adverse internal or external terms of trade. British India and the Princely India constituted, for all practical purposes, a common currency bloc. There was, therefore, no exchange rate problem. The drain from Princely India to British India was thus different from the drain that was claimed to be taking place from Colonial India to Britain. This does not mean that Joan Robinson was confronted with a situation of apportionment of sharable taxes in a federal-provincial arrangement, as taxes were being collected without expenditure commitments. The princely states were neither fully independent countries nor members in a federation; there was no easy answer as to why the peoples of the states should bear the burden of taxes levied by the British Indian government. Underlying the analysis is the benefit principle of tax expenditures, whereby the liability to contribute to the exchequer is required to bear some relationship to the benefit received (Musgrave, 1959, pp. 63–73). The states were being taxed without benefiting from public spending by British India. No adjustment or redressal mechanism was provided; it was taxation without representation. Important similarities, nevertheless, remained. *The British Crown*, too, was dealing with a transfer that was unrequited. As the level of analysis was not the individuals but territories, it became a step closer to the old drain theories as well as the modern surplus transfer theories, all concerned with unilateral transfer of resources from one region to another. None had any role for the classes. In theory, the analysis in *The British Crown* is closer to Lipton's comparisons of taxes and expenditure benefits in the intersectoral context,[9] though the expenditure bias towards British India was much more pronounced than the urban bias in Lipton's case. Yet the object of the study was essentially different in that the most important determinant of backwardness was not stated to be the transfer of resources.

The transfer of resources became highly significant only after the imposition of a discriminatory tariff in the interwar period. True, some outflow had been taking place since the introduction of the salt monopoly, railways and direct tributes in the form of cessions of territory as well as money. Joan Robinson did mention how the salt monopoly left the resources of some states undeveloped. On the whole, however, the study did not place the causes of backwardness in the drain or surplus transfer.

There was at least one prominent case where heavy drain predated the rise of protective duties. A cash tribute of Rs. 35 lakh per annum was imposed on state of Mysore at the time of its rendition in 1881. Its burden was judged by the fact that this state alone paid one-third of the aggregate tribute realized from Princely India as a whole. Arguments about 'the drain of Mysore' were not uncommon. To quote but one contemporary author:

> That this is far too heavy a burden will be clearly seen when it is remembered that Mysore occupies less than five per cent of the total area of Indian States and that this heavy contribution comes from the pockets of only about 8 per cent of their population. (Timmalachar, 1929, pp. 425–9)

Later, a dependency framework too was fitted to the case. [10] However, these arguments are remarkable because of what they fail to say. What they fail to say is that the cash tribute, which as a proportion of state's own revenue stood at 32 per cent at the time of its imposition, declined to 10 per cent in 1924. If the absolute reduction of the tribute from 1927 is taken into account, the liability comes further down to about 7 per cent. In real terms, the burden would be even less. This shows a state making serious internal effort at resource mobilization. The strides it made in industry, agriculture and education, higher as well as compulsory primary, put it even ahead of British India in many respects.[11] Ergo, the state that was suffering the heaviest drain was also an outstanding example of development. It does not follow that development or underdevelopment is strongly correlated with drain. While the drain, if it makes empirical sense and it did in the case of Mysore as well as the states in general, cannot be denied as an unjust imposition, its connection with backwardness is not easily proved. In the framework pursued in *The British Crown*, the origins of backwardness lay elsewhere, as will be shown in the following paragraphs.

CAUSES OF BACKWARDNESS

The backwardness of the states was sometimes explained as follows.

> The Government of India took every opportunity afforded to them either by the minority or temporary embarrassments of rulers to force them into the economic life of British India. This process continued with such disastrous effects on the general prosperity of the population in the States

that they came to be considered backward areas, without realizing that their backwardness was due to the policy of economic aggression followed by the Government of India. (Keralaputra, 1929, p. 54)

This was the exact opposite of the argument in *The British Crown*. The states were backward, in terms of this study's analysis, because of their poor resource endowment, mainly agricultural as minerals were discovered later and, more important, the states which were doing better than others were those that were taking part in the economic life of British India. Economic backwardness is viewed as a pre-existing—in the case of British India, precolonial—condition that had persisted for a long time. The perception that it was so became acute as the British intervention unleashed the forces of 'growth and advance', the latter-day modernization. While these forces had been working their way forward for 'three generations in British India' (*The British Crown*, 1929, p. 138), the transmission of their impact to the Princely India was slow and unsteady. The search for the causes of this slowness resulted in the identification of some crucial characteristics of underdevelopment in the modernization paradigm.[12]

Historically, in the relative autonomy of the states, resulting either from geographical remoteness or poor endowments of resources to be exploited by the colonialists, lay the reasons for their relative backwardness. The exercise of quasi-sovereignty by these states served to perpetuate the old, pre-capitalist economic formation, based on self-sufficient villages, longer than in British India. To begin with, the states generally constituted a hinterland which the sea-power-dependent British considered more hazardous to conquer. In case the hazards could be overcome, the usually low fertility of the soil in the states affected adversely the profit motivation of what after all was a ruler-turned trading company. In any case, the distance from the sea acted as a deterrent 'to those who thought largely in terms of exports by sea'. The lower density of population relative to British India, indicating limited market opportunities, also worked against the opening up of the states (*The British Crown*, 1929, pp. 137–8). The results of poor accessibility and low density were summed up as follows.

> These two factors, the comparative isolation and the relative sparsity of population, apart from all other considerations, have made the States slower than British India to be affected by the changed economic conditions which have resulted from British occupation. *The continuity of their political forms has helped also the survival of their earlier economic organizations, and, viewed*

from the standpoint of Western industrialism, the states are more backward than British India [emphasis added]. (*The British Crown*, 1929, p. 138)

To show that the states were much 'less developed' in regard to 'industrial organization', *The British Crown* quoted figures from the industrial census of India for 1921 and set them against a notional share of 22.5 per cent on the basis of the population of the states. Table 12.1 gives this information.

In no industry did the states have a share exceeding even half of their proportion in population. (It was pointed out, though, that since the census was completed, iron and steel works had been started in Mysore.) Employing the use of telegraph services as an indicator of the emergence of groups of 'dealers and the business community in general', the study noticed that 'there are very few commercial centres of any importance within the States' (*The British Crown*, 1929, p. 178). Given the poor information collection system, it would have been impossible to estimate the share of industries in the states' own gross domestic output.

Corresponding to the sluggish pace of industrialization as well as commercialization, the states possessed financial and monetary features characteristic of underdeveloped economies. They had 'no considerable rich middle class' to apply the tax axe to 'and their banking system [was] in general less developed' (*The British Crown*, 1929, p. 143). As noted earlier, the use of money was chiefly in metallic form in preference to paper and credit money, marked by a low velocity of circulation.

Table 12.1 States' share in industrial output (1921)

Industry	% of Total for India
Cotton yarn	<6.0
Piece goods	7.7
Total value of goods woven in cotton mills	<4.0
Woollen goods	11.0
Coal	5.0
Other minerals	6.0
Iron and steel	0.0

Source: The British Crown (1929, pp. 184–5)

Geographical and commercial isolation played a critical role in keeping the states economically behind India. As the railroad construction started, the isolation of the states should at least have declined, if not ended, over time. This was not the case, as the railways were mainly designed for military and foreign trade purposes and only secondarily for internal trade, 'skirting or cutting briefly through the States' (*The British Crown*, 1929, p. 140). Some lines were forced on the states without much planning. For instance, the state of Hyderabad was left with 50 miles 'of railway leading nowhere' (*The British Crown*, 1929, p. 175). Others built with resources provided by the states were 'useful to the state concerned' (*The British Crown*, 1929, p. 174). Sometimes even commercially viable state railways did not necessarily imply their compatibility with the infrastructural requirements for the development of the state concerned. The state of Mysore provided a well-known example.

> Even when the lines financed by the various Darbars were successful they were not always those most suitable to the State in question, and they often contribute more to the general welfare of British India than to the particular State which provided the capital. For instance, it has been argued that industrial development in Mysore is handicapped by the fact that the railways in her territory do not follow the natural channels of trade. (*The British Crown*, 1929, p. 175)

On the whole, the external penetration of economic forces into the states was not strong enough to inject and institutionalize industrial development. The states lagged behind British India because (a) the motives for external forces in the form of economic incentives or the economic or strategic reasons for building up railways were weaker and (b) the preponderantly food economy of the village lacked in-built incentives to disturb itself. In this way, the Princely India was doubly drawn into backwardness: Not only that they were left alone; many were not unhappy to be left alone. True, foreign exogenous forces were not potent enough. But there was also in position in each of these territories a state which, in principle, could have embodied an 'urge to the break-up of the old village organization', as in the case of British India.[13] This did not happen generally for a host of reasons. Even if it could be assumed that the requisite transport links existed, 'a generation back the break-up of the village implied not the risks of specialization inside an Indian economic unity, but the additional dangers of an international trade' (*The British Crown*, 1929, p. 140). As was explained:

If, therefore, at first the States were slower to adopt new forms and to make industrialization their aim, they were in their own generation wise. The gains, even if they could have been calculated, were too small, and the risks too great to justify the break-up of the traditional village organization, even had available means of transport made it possible. (*The British Crown*, 1929, pp. 139–40)

Together with the immunity from outside influences and the self-preserving propensities of the overwhelming proportion of the population, the cultivators, biasing the village economic organization towards stagnation, the laissez-faire approach of the ruling princes could not but abet the continuance of a static socio-economic structure. The backwardness of the princely states retained somewhat their original condition so long as their economies hid behind the village cocoons, left more or less untouched by the British as well as their own archaic state structures. In a nutshell, the states were backward relative to British India, not due to surplus transfer but for reasons of geography, weak economic stimuli for the exogenous forces of modernization and the lack of political will on the rulers' part to encourage economic development. Their backwardness had historical roots, not in too much exploitation but too little. This is an insight that stayed with Joan Robinson in her later works on development. In the context of Sri Lanka, she had remarked:

Hitherto the trouble in the Ceylon [as the country then was called] economy has not been too much exploitation of labour but too little—the capitalists to employ labour force have not been forthcoming. (Robinson, 1959, p. 71)[14]

We now examine the way *The British Crown* envisaged that the ardour of development had started to enter the states and was forcing them to respond with appropriate policy action.

Economic Development: Problem and Policy

The function that was performed in the case of British India by the changes arising from British occupation was now being replicated in the princely states in the form of their economic occupation by British India. The mechanics of transition were the same; only it was harsher in the case of the Princely India because of the combined competitive offensive of

Lancashire, Bombay and Japan. Together they 'competed with the village weaver for custom' and so 'contributed to undermine the older system' (*The British Crown*, 1929, p. 141) under the free trade regime of the pre-war period. The existing structure of the states started to feel the shock waves coming in the wake of a money and exchange economy: 'whereas in British India much of the initial dislocation is gradually beginning to adjust itself, in many of the States the problem has only of late begun to arise, and the consequent changes are even now in progress'.

The industrial development of British India gathered momentum, and economic policies acquired sharper teeth, especially with the end of free trade and the introduction of discriminatory protection during the inter-war period. As a result, the states started to become conscious of the new limits on their areas of control placed by the policy requirements of the economic development of British India as well as learning to appreciate the problem of development and the necessity of producing a concerted and coordinated policy response. In some outstanding cases, the possibilities of an interventionist state too were being exploited.

The crucial question was: 'What are the political and economic consequences of this Industrial Revolution, which, beginning in British India, has now entered the Indian States?' The answer to this question contained the basic ingredients of the problem of and policy for economic development identified in the pioneering development economics after World War II. 'The chief political consequence' was 'growing interdependence', while the 'economic consequence' laid down the requirements for development (*The British Crown*, 1929, pp. 141–2). The two important consequences are considered in turn.

POLITICAL CONSEQUENCE: INTERDEPENDENT DEVELOPMENT

Interdependence referred to a number of developments originating in British India and affecting the states and inducing a political-economic response. The direct financial burden imposed by the resource transfer did not exhaust the full economic impact on the states. There were substantial externalities involved. The fact that benefits are internal as well as external has often been ignored in theories of surplus transfer (Kitching, 1982, p. 167). Besides making an estimate of the transfer of resources in apparent money terms, an attempt was made to deal with this question. In almost every source of transfer, external effects were mentioned. The effort seems to be focused more on external diseconomies than on economies. As the study put it, 'the excessive taxation to which they are subject is only one among a number of economic disabilities from which the States suffer' (*The British Crown*, 1929, p. 215). The analysis falls short of a proper accounting for external effects. External benefits were assumed to be mutual, an assumption that cannot be faulted. The states were no more liable for the external economies than British India. Since the externalities generated by the states services remained invariably uncompensated by British India, the study concluded that there was no reciprocal liability on the states. It is true that British India was shirking fiscal responsibility in the matter. However, the study overstates the princely states' case because the positive externalities generated by the states were not significant and the negative externalities imposed by British India were, in many cases, in the nature of creating pressures for development and thus supporting the general argument for interdependent development. Customs duties, internal taxes, currency and the common services charging monopoly prices were the important areas requiring policy coordination to avoid inflicting 'noticeable damage' or 'incidental hardships' (*The British Crown*, 1929, p. 192).[15] Further, 'economic interdependence must lead on to closer political working, since matters which were of little account, so long as internal trade was undeveloped, have now become of considerable moment' (*The British Crown*, 1929, p. 142). Elaborating further, it was stated.

> As economic interdependence grows, the States must join more and more with British India not only in the upheaval of a rapid change in economic organization, but also in the benefit of modern developments which in time will bring about readjustment. In those developments, such as railways, which are of necessity common to the two, they must unquestionably pay their fair share of expenses, but, in such cases as those of the railways and the Post Office, by the fact of this payment they become unwittingly involved in the fiscal system of British India, of which these concerns are profit-making enterprises. (*The British Crown*, 1929, p. 143)

Protection as Externality: Since World War I, significant changes had occurred in two areas.

> In the first place, the peoples of the States are becoming more and more dependent on imported goods. The old economy of the self-supporting village is fast breaking up, and as communications of every kind develop, the inhabitants of even the most remote parts of India are increasingly affected

by the results of her foreign trade. Secondly, the Government of India appear definitely to have abandoned the ideal of free trade. (*The British Crown*, 1929, p. 184)

The process was only beginning, however. 'Complete economic self-sufficiency' was considered impossible even for the larger states. Nor [was] the consumption per head of industrial products large'. The invasion of village industries by large-scale manufactures is seen as inevitable in the scheme of progress. Likewise, the fact of low per capita consumption of manufactures indicated that the 'individual States must therefore exchange goods much more freely than has been done in the past, both with each other and with British India' (*The British Crown*, 1929, p. 142). Their interest lay in the free movement of goods. Importing goods from British India also meant imports from other countries. It was in this context that the end of a free trade policy would adversely affect the states, interested as they would be in low prices rather than protection. After a review of the extremely low share of the states in the output of major industries, it was inferred 'that it is yet hardly time for the States to begin asking for protection, since they are still so preponderantly importers and consumers rather than producers of manufactured goods' (*The British Crown*, 1929, p. 185).

Historically, the states failed to foresee that the surrender of foreign policy in return for security against external threat would also in time mean the giving up of foreign economic policy without any return. 'As long as India was looked upon mainly as a market for British goods, import duties were out of question'. When the tariff was first imposed, it was kept as low as 5 per cent *ad valorem*. The 'injustice may have been theoretically as great, but the economic loss was small'. As British India replaced free trade by the tariff, first to tide over the pressures of World War I on the budgetary balance and then by following 'the policy of protection advocated by the Fiscal Commission in 1922', the states were inflicted by a fiscal burden not of their making. They felt 'both the sentimental attractions and the solid benefits of protection far less than the people of British India, for they are much less developed either in political views or in industrial organization' (*The British Crown*, 1929, pp. 184–5).

Protection was a key element in the pioneering development economics. The ideas in *The British Crown* outlined thus far seem to indicate, in the context of the Princely India, a rejection of protection. In the nature of the case,[16] the focus was on revenue, not protection, implying that the relative backwardness of the princely states imparted a general bias of the consumer towards free trade. Over and above the unrequited revenue contribution, the states found themselves protected, whether or not they needed it. These arose, in the main, from an externally determined tariff policy, but in no small measure from the dilemma of the states between 'the natural bias of the consumer towards free trade' and the 'wish to claim their share of protection' (*The British Crown*, 1929, p. 192). Here is how the contradiction between the consumer and producer biases in the formulation of commercial policy was dealt with.

> [W]hen the States, or some given State has no manufacture of [a] particular commodity and no intention of undertaking it, that State may not unreasonably plead that its interest lies solely in the price of the article, and it makes little or no difference to it whether the article is to be imported from abroad or from British India, that its loss through the customs, on cotton goods for instance, is spread not only over the goods which pay sea customs, but also over the piece goods manufactured in the protected mills of British India. (*The British Crown*, 1929, p. 187)

Being 'consumers rather than producers of industrial goods', the states had 'the natural bias of the consumers towards free trade'. With 'no say in the tariff policy', the states could neither enjoy the price benefits of free trade nor impose protection in particular cases of their interest (*The British Crown*, 1929, p. 192). A case in point was the situation in the state of Mysore. This state was the major grower of silk in the whole of India, but its industry was exposed to the Pacific competition, from Japan as well as China. Imposition of an import duty could help develop the local silk industry. Predominantly practised in the states, sericulture had no constituency in the policy-making process of British India. Likewise, it could develop local capacity for using its chrome and magnesium if it was allowed the benefit of an export duty. The state did not get the desired policy change from British India.

The fact that was not mentioned was that Mysore did not have its own import and export duties either.[17] In general, the states levied their own tariffs as well. As a matter of fact, the states never pursued a full free trade policy even in the heyday of the latter. Commercial and industrial backwardness ruled out income taxes; the British monopolization of salt and opium left little scope for commodity taxes; and a poor soil meant lower yield from land revenue. They had no choice but to hold on to customs as the major source of revenue (Haksar, 1928, p. 540). Neither side complained so long as the duties were low and non-protectionist. A one-time finance minister of British India described the whole of Indian sub-continent, on the basis of population, as the world's largest free trade area; the barriers erected by the states were of no consequence.

It is true that there are some minor and occasionally embarrassing customs barriers, due to the existence within the Indian sub-continent of numerous Indian States, small and great, some of which have retained the right to impose customs duties of their own. But these exceptions to freedom of trade can justifiably be ignored since in fact only Kashmir enjoys exemption from the general customs tariff of India, and the internal State customs duties are scarcely more than octroi duties. (Blackett, 1930, p. 314)

Be that as it may, the study had anticipated the rejection by Butler Committee of the counterclaim that the British Indian customs too were in the nature of transit duties. [18] The study stated.

Again, it might be urged that these duties are in effect transit duties, a form of taxation long familiar in India, but this plea would come ill from a Government whose aim has always been to abolish transit duties wherever they are found, and which is justly proud of the stimulus to Indian prosperity which has followed their abolition. (*The British Crown*, 1929, p. 183)

It was after the introduction of a discriminatory tariff by British India that the divergence of interests between the states and British India began to be seriously argued. Only a few years later, the same ex-finance minister was declaring, rather cynically, to have been 'very glad to escape from India' before facing up to the 'thorny problem of the rights and duties of the States of India with reference to the new Indian tariff and to the large revenue from customs which was being collected by the Indian Government at the ports, a proportion of which was necessarily paid, not by people of British India', but those of the states.[19] As we saw above, the contribution of the states to British customs was about one and a half times their own collection.

Protection thus was a negative externality imposed on the states by British India. Indeed, the effective protection for the states was higher, when their own import duties were also taken into account. Was it not a boon for their nascent industries, given that the states were on the whole largely agricultural, with not much industry? To take the view of the consumer made sense in the short run. But only a static view would suggest the continuation of this state of affairs. If the state of Mysore did not get the protection it needed for the silk industry, it benefited from the protection given to the sugar industry. Again, even in the case of sericulture, the lack of protection was forcing the industry to improve seed quality and methods to remain competitive (Kesavaiengar, 1930, p. 225). What is central to the case in *The British Crown* is the interdependent nature of development, be it a free trade or a protectionist regime. With the advent of the latter, economic interdependence was greatly intensified. While arguing the case for the states as consumers, the study did not overlook the possibilities and problems for the states as producers. In the situation of late industrialization in the states, it was observed:

> The Indian tariff, moreover, does not only cover consumable goods. Machinery and raw materials are taxed, though at a comparatively low rate, and the states which have come late into the field, find themselves in competition with factories in British India which were established before the duties on machinery were imposed, and whose capital charges are therefore on a lower scale. (*The British Crown*, 1929, p. 192)

The study ignored the possibility of acquiring improved technology by the late entrants, though. Nevertheless, the main point continues to be to emphasize not the blockages but the partaking of development opportunities. Although as consumers the states were affected not only by higher duty-paid imports but also by the higher prices of the protected output of British Indian mills, the study did not argue for an across-the-board refund.

This is no argument for a refund to the states of the customs rate on their whole importation of cotton goods, whether from British India or abroad. It does nevertheless show that in an economically interdependent area, whether or not in the strictest sense of the word a federation exists, there must be a great deal of give and take between different districts. No simple tax system can be uniformly fair (though that is not a sufficient reason for not endeavouring to make it as fair as possible), and the best that can be hoped is that the unfairness may to some extent cancel out. The states can reasonably claim that if one tax in its results, other than on revenue, is against their interests, those interests deserve favourable consideration in other matters (*The British Crown*, 1929, p. 187).

External Effects of Excises: Customs were not the only area where the states were burdened far in excess of the direct financial imposition. Central excise duties, particularly on salt, imposed significant external costs. In addition to the loss of revenue and control as a result of the British Indian monopolization of salt, there were indirect losses like lands becoming saline as a result of the forcible stoppage of salt extraction. Moreover, an important resource was not being permitted to develop. The note on salt monopoly was, as noted earlier, contributed by Joan Robinson.

> Not only do the salt-producing States suffer these indirect losses, and not only are their exchequers deprived of a source of revenue, but a part of their natural wealth remains undeveloped and their peoples often compelled to pay an unduly high price for salt which has been transported from a distance, or even imported from abroad, while a nearer and sometimes better supply remains unused. This is not only a disadvantage to the States concerned, but a loss of real wealth to the country as a whole. (*The British Crown*, 1929, p. 201)

The provincial excise policies imposed further injuries to the states. First, the British Indian provinces had acquired partial monopoly in certain drugs by banning the states producing them from export. 'So far as they are partly consumed by the inhabitants of the States, this must be regarded as an export tax, the burden of which the taxing authority is in a position to throw partly on a foreign consumer'. Secondly, the study regarded the excise duty on *charas*, imported overland from Central Asia, as a transit duty. 'It is as unjustifiable in principle that the burden of this tax should fall upon the people of the States as that the burden of customs duties should fall upon them' *(The British Crown*, 1929, pp. 194–5). Lastly, the states levying their own excise taxes were obliged to follow the policy of the neighbouring provinces, but the reverse was not allowed. The states had to fall in line with regard to not only rates and base but also the social objectives.

> Although the excise duties of British India yield a considerable revenue, their motive is partly social, and they are designed as much to check the consumption of liquor and drugs as to raise funds for the Provincial Governments. The duties, therefore, are imposed at a very high rate. But while the states are obliged to follow the moral views of the Provinces in their excise policy, the Mohammedan state of Bhopal, which was entirely prohibitionist, received no co-operation from the Provincial excise offices upon its borders, and was not even able to forbid the sale of liquor on the railway stations within its territory. (*The British Crown*, 1929, p. 196)

Railway-Generated External Economies: Railways provide the classic example of external economies. The critical issues related to the way the external economy argument was being presented and the monopoly pricing of common service. Joan Robinson, who authored the note on railways, understood that external economies were generated by the railway development, but objected to the one-sided approach of the British Indian policy makers in calculating the liability of the recipient. She had no quarrel with the argument but challenged a confusion.

> It has been argued that the existence of a railway confers benefits greater than can be measured by the yield of railway rates and the profits of railway companies, that a railway develops a territory, broadens markets, widens economic life and increases economic values, without taking a tithe of the increase as its toll, and that therefore the States are in reality liable for a contribution to the Central Government which provides them with transport. This argument is based on a confusion. It would be just as true to say that the railway from Dholpur to Agra, built with Gwalior money, yields a gain unmeasured by the profits of the G.I.P. [Great Indian Peninsula Railways], for which the central revenue should pay a tribute to Gwalior. (*The British Crown*, 1929, pp. 175–6)

What she criticizes is the asymmetry in applying the logic of the argument. While the states were held liable to contribute to the exchequer of British India for these external benefits, British India itself enjoyed a free ride in regard to the externalities generated by the state railways. While the lines operated by the states provided to the British Indian traffic the same services as were provided to the states traffic by the British Indian railways, Joan Robinson argued that these lines brought, in addition, 'profitable traffic to them which would not otherwise have been available'. For instance, the state of Indore was said to be given 'unusually favourable' terms by being allowed half of the profits on the state railway, built of course with a loan of Rs.100 lakh from the state. Even in this case, no allowance was made for the external benefit in the form of 'additional traffic which it brings to the main line' owned by British India (*The British Crown*, 1929, pp. 174–5).

'In the case of railways, as of excise, of customs, and of salt duty, the money payment is not the only burden of which the States complain'. The policy of the Railway Board was considered 'inimical' to the interests of the states (*The British Crown*, 1929, p. 204). In one case, a state spent enormous sums to electrify its collieries, only to find that they were 'unable to develop because the railway companies serving the Central Provinces have recently lowered the rates on coal coming from that district without allowing a similar concession to the coalfields' in the state concerned (*The British Crown*, 1929, p. 204). In the other case, the Gwalior state felt that its own railway managed by the companies did not get a 'fair share of traffic'. She elaborated as follows.

For instance, there are two possible routes between Howrah and Ahmedabad. Of these the shorter route, via Ujjain, lies partly over line owned by the Darbar. The company concerned fixes the minimum rates for goods traffic allowed by the Railway Board, upon the longer route, and maximum rates upon the shorter route, thus diverting traffic from the Darbar's lines. It would be possible to multiply instances of injustice suffered by the States at the hands of railway authorities, but here it is our purpose merely to point out that the States are treated by them as taxpayers, and yet denied the taxpayer's right to make his views respected. (*The British Crown*, 1929, p. 205)

In general, it was found that the situations of external economies requiring coordination were being disregarded by British India, so that the states could not fully reap the opportunities of interdependent development. In Joan Robinson's words,

it is often assumed that the railways belong to British India and ought to sell their services at a monopoly price to the States, who are regarded as purchasers. The same argument is often applied to defence, the postal services and other undertakings run in common. The confusion arises from the uncertainty that has hitherto cloaked the precise relations of the States to the Indian Empire. At one moment the British Government will sell services and goods to the States at monopoly prices, as if they were foreign countries, at another they will justify the imposition of taxes upon them and throw on to them the military responsibilities and economic policies as if they were ordinary districts, without any rights under treaties and agreements. They cannot claim the generous co-operation of the States in building railways for the sake of development and uniting the whole country and at the same time regard the States' share in that development as a benefit which they had no right to expect and for which they must unquestionably pay whatever price may be asked. (*The British Crown*, 1929, p. 176)

Tax Coordination and Capital Movements: Of crucial significance, in view of their backwardness, was the effect on capital movements in the presence of an income tax in British India. On top of the revenue effect, which *The British Crown* found hard to measure in the absence of data from British Indian income tax authorities, there were the disincentive effects. The principle of tax neutrality operated between British India and Britain through arrangements to avoid double taxation, but the same had not been considered necessary for the fiscal relations between the Princely India and British India. A copy of British income tax, the British Indian income tax was leviable on the incomes derived from the sources located on its territory, as well as the incomes of all persons resident in the territory. Such a system discourages capital movements, besides being unfair to individuals whose residence is different from the location of the sources of their incomes, if it prevails at both locations. To illustrate the argument, the study first took up the case of a British Indian subject with invested capital in a princely state. The best course for the state would be not to tax it.

> If there is an income tax, imposed before the investment was made, the effect will not be a burden on the individual investor, but enterprises in the State will have to offer a higher rate of interest than would otherwise be the case. This may retard development and lower the taxable capacity of the State's subjects.
>
> If the income tax was imposed after the investment was made there will be a burden upon the investor, which will take the form of a fall in the capital value of his investments, and the State will be benefited at his expense. It is open to the States to avoid this kind of injustice and this kind of discouragement to investment in their enterprises by exempting all foreign capital under their income tax schemes, but they not unnaturally feel that the concessions should not be upon one side alone. (*The British Crown*, 1929, pp. 210–1)

In the case of a state subject deriving all or part of income from British India, it was observed:

> If the investment was made before the tax was imposed or before any expectation of it had arisen, there will be a burden upon the States subject, and a diminution of his power to pay state taxes. As this type of investment in British India by subjects of States must be fairly common, the exchequers of the States are suffering a real loss and their citizens a considerable burden from this cause. The impediment to the free movement of capital is, however, even more important than the burden of the tax. (*The British Crown*, 1929, p. 211)

An arrangement for partial relief existed in that a state subject was allowed to deduct half of the income tax paid to the state of his origin from the liability of British Indian income tax. This was the reverse of what a British Indian citizen would get in Britain itself: he was allowed a refund of the tax paid in British India to the extent of 50 per cent of his liability in Britain. As the British Indian tax rate was half of the British rate, effectively the entire tax paid in British India was deductible in Britain. The state income taxes, wherever they existed, had rates lower than the British Indian income tax. The study argued that British India should treat the states in the same way as Britain treated British India for income tax purposes. While it would encourage capital movements for productive investment, a very important outcome would be the creation of strong incentives for all states to impose income tax, the very introduction of which has been considered an important step in the process of development. In short, the avoidance of double taxation would remove barriers to the movement of capital as well as goods, insofar as indirect taxes were replaced by direct taxes.

> Since the principle [between Britain and British India] has been admitted to be just, and since the system has worked satisfactorily, there seems no ground for withholding its full benefits from the States, and every reason to encourage, by granting it, the introduction of an income tax by any State which finds itself in a position to substitute that form of taxation for indirect taxes, which must always be an impediment to trade. (*The British Crown*, 1929, p. 212)

Economic Consequence: Catching Up

Economic interdependence resulting from direct fiscal impositions and external effects was the broad outcome of the centralization of the British power: the Indian subcontinent as a whole was becoming an economic community, with which was associated an 'ardour for development'.[20] The question was: How might the states respond? The answer in *The British Crown* was two-fold—a catching-up strategy of development and additional resource mobilization in the pursuit of this strategy. As in development economics and the modernization paradigm later, the argument was laid out in comparative terms, and the states own clock time was ignored.

Strategy of Development: Economic backwardness was conceived as the 'relative poverty of the States' and 'their earlier industrial backwardness', and the problem of development was reflected in their 'present efforts to catch up' (*The British Crown*, 1929, p. 186). The theme presages the concept of relative backwardness and linear development in the image of the developed countries, propounded by Gerschenkron (1962). Thus, in the states the 'problems of economic reconstruction' were 'in broad outlines the same as in British India'. The areas to catch up were not left vague. In the first place, the states needed to provide themselves with '[i]ncreased education, better sanitation and medical aid, the improvement of agriculture, the resuscitation and reorganization of handicrafts—assisted when necessary by modern mechanical improvements'. All of these required 'increased governmental revenue and expenditure'. Secondly, there was 'the imperative need for the means to finance the industrial reorganization' of the states (*The British Crown*, 1929, p. 142). The Princely India had to catch up by building up social and physical infrastructure and by encouraging industrial development; they had also to find the means to finance them. The basis for the states' case before the Butler Committee was to mobilize finance for capital accumulation.

Another important factor was the undesirable increase in the rate of growth of population.

> Moreover, a hundred years in which peace has been interrupted by only one or two brief and localized wars has led to an unprecedented increase in population, and this itself, in a country of hereditary employments and static organization, imposes unusual demands for material equipment if, even without raising it, the standard of living is merely to be maintained. (*The British Crown*, 1929, p. 143)

At the same time, it was on 'the provision of security' that the 'whole economic development of India in the nineteenth and twentieth centuries has depended'. In other words, it led to a climate of investment confidence by preventing 'the innumerable internal wars and organized raiding expeditions to which India was accustomed in the period preceding the establishment of the British power' (*The British Crown*, 1929, pp. 145–6). Chatterton, among others, had made a similar argument: 'Out of the chaotic conditions resulting from the disintegration of the Mughal Empire, law and order was re-established and private enterprise was afforded free scope' (1925, p. 715).

The provision of defence and internal security had a dual effect. On the one hand, as peace broke out, the Malthusian checks on population growth—war and famines—had been overcome. A higher investment would be required even to maintain the existing low living standard. Here lies the origin of Joan Robinson's unflinching view of population growth as a major obstacle to development. The Indian opinion has for the most part remained unconvinced of population growth as a major constraint on development during the British raj. [21] In her opinion, however, it had added significantly to the requirements of capital. On the other hand, the very factor mentioned here as responsible for population growth, that is, peace and security, also simultaneously created opportunities for safe investment. Population increased, but the investment prospects also improved. Static organization, in the sense of unchanged technique, would necessitate more of the same technique rather than greater output from an improved technique. Further stability was added to the static organization by the hereditary nature of employments. These self-employments were not geared to an increase in productivity per person or per unit of capital.

Bhagwati (1985, p. 229) has been critical of Joan Robinson for adhering to fixed coefficients or 'one-man-one-spade' technique merely to deny substitutability and thus take an ideological position against marginal productivity theory. We are concerned here with a period before she got involved in these controversies.[22] Moreover, one notices the beginnings of her theory of long-run development. *The British Crown* is pointing out the necessity of keeping a balance between the population growth and the pace of capital accumulation just to maintain per capita output. It is implied that the additions to the latter would require a larger effort to ensure a rate of accumulation higher than the population growth. These embryonic views link up with her later theory of long-run development in the following paragraph on situations of population growth running ahead of capital accumulation.

> The level of real wages corresponding to the required rate of accumulation may be lower than the tolerable minimum. In such a case it is impossible for accumulation to keep up with population growth and a surplus of labour develops, in the sense that there is not enough capital to employ all available labour. The surplus grows until Malthusian misery checks the growth of population. 'Underdeveloped economies' are those which have already got into arrears and have a surplus of labour relatively to the stock of capital goods. (Robinson, 1955a, p. 383) [23]

Not least important is her view of development having something to do with the standard of living, what the pioneering development economics would see as a sustained rise in per capita income. She was already departing from the prevailing concept of economic development coinciding with resource development.[24]

Resources for Capital Accumulation: If transfer of resources did not cause backwardness in framework of *The British Crown*, why were the states anxious to reverse the trend by their pleadings before the Butler Committee? The answer is that the states required more finance to accumulate capital. It is the internally arisen consciousness about development that led to demands for further resources.

The ability of the states to restructure their economies and reorganize industries, the key elements of the development strategy described in *The British Crown*, was seriously impaired by the existence of adverse financial arrangements, which left their hold on fiscal and monetary policies ephemeral. This was true of indirect taxation as well as state monopolies of British India. Joan Robinson treated the burden of monopoly prices of the state-regulated goods or services as no different from that of indirect taxes such as import duties and excises. Salt monopoly and railways were the most important, to whose profits the states made a substantial contribution.

> The Government already possesses in many districts, and is gradually acquiring in others, a monopoly of the railway services. The sales of monopoly products have long been recognized both in India and in other countries as a fruitful source of income for Governments. In India the salt duties are largely of that nature; in France, matches and tobacco have long been Government monopolies. While, strictly speaking, a monopoly price is different in nature from a tax, in practice the two converge. A tax imposed upon liquor by a Government is as dependent on the demand for liquor, and has the same effects in diminishing that demand, as an excessive monopoly price imposed by a producer. Between direct taxation and the extortions of a monopolist there is considerable difference, between indirect taxation and monopoly revenue very little. (*The British Crown*, 1929, pp. 201–2)

There is no length that the British did not go to in acquiring the salt monopoly, starting as far back as the beginning of their rule. [25] The states contributed a major share of the total output of India, but with no control over it. In recounting the process of takeover, Joan Robinson showed that the British had not exactly been the salt of the earth.

The treaties under which States agreed to refrain from the production of salt or by which they put their resources under the control of Government provide for certain forms of compensation. The terms granted to the different States vary considerably. Some received compensation for the transit duties which they had been accustomed to charge and which they were obliged to abandon, some received compensation for the price of the salt consumed by their subjects, some received compensation only for the transit duties, some received no compensation at all. Some were allowed to produce salt on condition it was not exported, some were induced to treat other excisable goods in the same way. Some were obliged to give up production altogether. In every case the convenience of the Government excise system was considered above everything, and in most compensation was inadequate and was fixed in an arbitrary way. (*The British Crown*, 1929, pp. 199–200)

A most important British Indian monopoly pertained to currency and mints. The points raised in this connection bear an interesting comparison with Keynes, the principal theorist on the subject of Indian currency and finance. *The British Crown* focused on the issue of profits from seigniorage on currency and mints. Keynes, 'usually the high-priest of iconoclasm', ended up on this important question, 'in the unaccustomed position of being wholly on the side of the angels!' (Chandavarkar, 1984, p. 774). He laid great stress on the point that the prevailing gold-exchange standard in India embodied a crucial ingredient for evolution towards an ideal currency—'the use of a cheap local currency artificially maintained at par with the international currency or standard of value' (Keynes, 1913, p. 36). In his memorandum on the setting up of a state bank in India for the Royal Commission on Indian finance and currency 1913–1914, he overlooked the advantage this cheap currency presented for development finance. Lionel Abrahams, a bureaucrat, admonished Keynes for the slip: 'What is the good of an economical currency if the fruits of economy are to be put in a sarcophagus? The economic error of India tends to be to hoard wealth instead of using it. It would be a calamity if the Government falls a victim to this error in its own action'.[26]

As opposed to Keynes, the whole point of the case for the states was to keep for them their legitimate share in the central resources, including seigniorage profits from currency and mints, for the purpose of utilizing them for capital accumulation. We may however note here that sharing profits of currency without sharing the concerns of its management, the situation obtaining in the case of the states, could be a factor in the relatively greater emphasis on profits. The princes, the notorious hoarders, were employing, through *The British Crown*, a dishoarding argument!

On top of the indirect taxes and monopolistic extractions was the direct burden of tributes, subsidies and cessions of income-generating territory. They were, however, free to levy their own indirect and direct taxes. This freedom was more apparent than real, assuming as it did a taxable capacity which was large enough to bear the burden of two tax systems.

> [I]t is important to remember that the imposition of this taxation lays upon the States a real burden far greater than can be measured by the actual sum which their peoples sacrifice. In the first place, it must react upon their whole fiscal system. The yield of any tax falls in an increasing ratio, the higher the taxation already imposed on the subjects who pay it. It follows that the yield of the Darbar's own taxes is diminished by this imposition, and the burden upon their peoples is all the greater because none of the proceeds are spent within the States. (*The British Crown*, 1929, pp. 213–4)

The point about falling tax yield for the states should be obvious.[27] Second, the British Indian customs threw 'the whole taxation system of the States into confusion'. An import duty charged at the ports of British India raised the prices not only of the imported goods in question but of import-competing goods as well, described in *The British Crown* as 'goods of the same class'. The payment of duty at the state borders subjected them to another round of taxation before reaching the consumers. An *ad valorem* state duty, being leviable on the base enlarged by the duty-paid or import equalizing British Indian prices, would have a higher effective rate. As prices in the states rose further, they would check the demand and deny them revenue they 'would otherwise have been able to collect' (*The British Crown*, 1929, p. 214). Third, and this is related to the second: 'even if the protective policy was just as useful or more useful to the States than it is to British India, that would be no reason for depriving the States of their share in the revenue which is incidentally raised' (*The British Crown*, 1929, p. 185). Here the interests of the states as consumers are being separated from their interests as potential producers.

In the ultimate analysis, all taxes are paid out of the global income. To the extent that indirect charges realized by British India took a big slice, the capacity to impose indirect taxes in the states was reduced. What *The British Crown* observed while considering alternatives sounds wholly modern.

The alternative exists of taxing incomes directly. This, while the obvious and most satisfactory course in a Western country is ill adapted to the Indian States. Agricultural income is already taxed by the land revenue. A taxable middle class hardly exists. The chief incomes large enough to pay income tax are those of the officials. These incomes are fixed at the figure which is required to attract men of the necessary ability into the service of the State, and the amount of taxation would naturally be taken into account by any man considering such service. To impose taxation on them would only result in having to raise their salaries. Until, therefore, a strong middle class has grown up in the States there is little scope for an income tax. (*The British Crown*, 1929, p. 214)

That agriculture is taxed by land revenue is an argument used even today against agricultural income tax in Pakistan. There is no doubt that land revenue is a direct tax, but as its name does not fail to suggest, it falls on land not income, lacking thus the elasticity characteristic of income taxes.[28] Not having a state income tax, though, was a strong incentive for attracting scarce administrative and professional personnel. It would also attract capital movements in favour of the states.

The indirect demands of the British Indian fiscal system on the states and the direct tribute payments depleted the states' resources for industrial and infrastructural development. *The British Crown* looked at the claims of the states before the Butler Committee as the search for resources to finance capital accumulation.

It is absolutely essential to the building up of a sound new industrial system that every anna [one-sixteenth of a rupee] which is available should be left in the States to assist in their reconstruction, and that the load of taxation, not only for internal purposes, where it may in many cases be devoted to uses which will be helpful to future development, but more especially for external purposes, should be reduced to a minimum.

It is this urgent need for capital which has led the Princes to review the payments made by them to central revenues and to examine the justice of the claims on which those payments are demanded. (*The British Crown*, 1929, p. 143)

The reference here is to the need of the states to build up social overheads and provide a fiscal incentive mix for development by ensuring lower tax burden within the states as well as the burden imposed by the fiscal system of British India. The aim seems to be a rational tax system to avoid, on the one hand, the erosion of incentives for work and attracting scarce skills and, on the other, to encourage investment. An end to the resource transfer was sought in the perspective of the states' requirements of capital accumulation, not as a policy of delinking their economies for illusory self-sufficiency. The focus of development was on internal factors, without losing sight of the interdependent economic structures of the two Indias.

The rapid economic and industrial changes occurring in British India were intensifying the interdependence between the economies of the Princely India and British India. As it raised the prospect of additional revenue, the princes were forced to demonstrate that their states possessed the capacity to implement economic development. At the same time, the growing interdependence created conditions for a cooperative political solution—a federation or a *Zollverein*. After the report of the Butler Committee came out in 1929, a negotiation process was set in motion to work out a political formula. Although Joan Robinson had left India by this time, there is evidence of her continued interest in an Indian *Zollverein*, facilitated by the fact that most of these negotiations took place in England. The political economy of an all-India *Zollverein* is discussed in Appendix 1.

To conclude: The transfer of resources was not in the nature of drain, and the old or the modern interpretations of drain linked to backwardness did not hold. It was not the principal factor responsible for the backwardness of the states. The question of transfer of resources was kept separate from the causes of backwardness. The transfer was an unjust imposition, but its connection with backwardness is not easily proved. The states were backward because of their poor resource endowment and weak integration with British India. Economic backwardness was a pre-existing, precolonial condition that had persisted in the shape of self-sufficient villages. It began to change in British India earlier than in Princely India due to the archaic ruling structures allowed by their quasi-autonomy. The analysis of resource transfer in *The British Crown* was based on the benefit principle of taxation. The states were being taxed without benefiting from public spending by British India. The presumption was that if these resources were made available to the states, they will be utilized for capital accumulation. Whether the state could play such a role in Princely India is the subject matter of Chap. 12.

NOTES

1. For an account of modernization paradigm, see Blomstrom and Hetme (1984, pp. 19–24).
2. After the report of the Butler Committee, political discussions started on constituting a federation and a *Zollverein* between the two Indias with a view to taking advantage of the potential for interdependent development. How this project came to grief is discussed in Appendix 1.
3. The states were among the few territories on the map of Asia during the interwar period which were not directly ruled by a colonial power. Though not fully independent like the Latin American republics, the states' publicists projected them as sounder than these republics, economically as well as politically (Papers, 1930, p. 142).
4. See Naoroji (1901) and Dutt (1904) for the case for and Morison (1911) for a rebuttal.
5. Baran (1957), Frank (1967) and Emmanuel (1972).
6. The amount was worked out by Shah (1927, p. 191).
7. There were some scathing criticisms of the drain theory by Indians as well. For instance, Broacha (1906, p. 43) stated: 'If you borrow 50,000 rupees at 6 per cent. to build chawls, that yield you a net rental of 4000 rupees per year, out of which you pay 3000 for interest, do you call that interest a drain on your resources? The drain is more than set off by the rental, and against an improving asset'. These were the utterings of a business leader. Significantly, the father of Indian economics, and without doubt the pioneer of Indian economic nationalism, Ranade, was among 'some notable exceptions' (Macpherson, 1972, p. 127), arguing against the drain theories. See Chandra (1965, pp. 122–3) for what Ranade had to say on the subject and an attempt to say that he (Ranade, 1906) did not say it.
8. An interesting coincidence is that she had to qualify her argument, both in 1948 and in 1973, by parenthetically noting the reversal of the terms of trade in favour of primary products (Robinson 1948, p. 142, 1973).
9. Lipton (1978, pp. 200, 211).
10. Hetme (1978).
11. See Chatterton (1925). Keralaputra (1929, p. 58) and Rao Sahib (1935).
12. See Bernstein (1971) for these characteristics.
13. The role of the state in princely India is discussed in the following chapter.
14. The better known quotation is from her *Economic Philosophy*: 'As we see nowadays in South-East Asia or the Caribbean, the misery of being exploited by capitalists is nothing compared to the misery of not being exploited at all' (Robinson, 1962, p. 46).

15. A League of Nations report in 1931 also pointed out the policy coordination between the states and British India as an intractable problem. See Lall (1941, p. 143).
16. The brief was to argue for a greater revenue share.
17. According to Butler Committee, the state of Mysore was 'the big exception' in this regard (*Report*, 1929, p. 42). It was the result of Mysore's special obligation to accept the advice of the Governor General of British India even on matters of taxes. See Thompson and Garratt (1934, p. 471). See also Tirumalachar (1929, p. 425) for the contention that it was Mysore's reluctance to doubly burden its people that was responsible for its free trade regime.
18. *Report* (1929, p. 42). Haksar (1928, p. 542) had wondered: 'Is it to be understood that the fact that the frontier crossed is a sea-board and not a land frontier metamorphoses a transit duty into a customs duty?'
19. See the discussion at the end in Rao Sahib (1935, p. 390).
20. The expression is taken from the unsigned introduction to *The British Crown* (1929, pp. xix–xx), presumably written jointly by K.N. Panikkar and Joan Robinson.
21. Bagchi (1972, pp. 22–23). It is true that population growth was not high 'by Japanese and other standards', but the available 'evidence does not fit easily with theories that postulate a decline from an already "subsistence" standard of living in 1858' (Macpherson, 1972, p. 135).
22. It was in '[t]rying to develop the long-period analysis sketched in [Robinson (1951) that she] had to come to terms with the Marshallian concept of substitution' (Robinson, 1974, p. xii). See also Harcourt (1984, p. 641).
23. Robinson (1955a) is the same paper that was circulated in mimeographed form at a workshop in Poona (India) in June 1955 under a different title—'Pure Theory of Development'. I am grateful to K.N. Prasad, who participated in the workshop, for sending me a copy of the paper bearing that title.
24. For various concepts of economic development, see Arndt (1972, 1981) and Meier (1984).
25. Haksar (1929) reproduces these arguments but with more details.
26. Quoted in Keynes (1971, pp. 214–5).
27. Assuming for simplification a single states tax rate, STR, and a base STB and denoting a hypothetical uniform tax rate for British India as BITR, the yield of the states tax, STY, will be given as follows: $STY = STR [STB (1-BITR)]$. Thus, the higher the BITR, the lower the STY; the states tax yield falls in an increasing ratio, given a higher pre-emption by the British Indian tax imposition.
28. See Bird (1974, pp. 133–5).

REFERENCES

PUBLISHED WORKS

Arndt, H. W. (1972). Development Economics Before 1945. In *J. Bhagwati and R.S.*

Bagchi, A. K. (1972). *Private Investment in India 1900–39.* Cambridge University Press.

Baran, P. (1957). *The Political Economy of Growth.* Monthly Review Press.

Bernstein, H. (1971). Modernization Theory and the Sociological Study of Development. *Journal of Development Studies, 7,* 141–160.

Bhagwati, J. N. (1985). *Wealth and Poverty.* Basil Blackwell.

Bird, R. M. (1974). *Taxing Agricultural Land in Developing Countries.* Harvard.

Blackett, B. P. (1930). The Economic Progress of India. *Journal of the Royal Society of Arts, 78,* 313–327.

Blomstrom, M., & Hattie, B. (1984). *Development Theory in Transition.* Zed Books.

Broacha, S. (1906). The "Poverty" of India. In *Speeches on Indian Economics.* Bombay Gazette Press.

Chandavarkar, A. G. (1984). Money and Credit, 1858–1947. In D. Kumar (Ed.), *The Cambridge Economic History of India* (Vol. 2). Bombay.

Chandra, B. (1965). Indian Nationalists and the Drain, 1880–1905. *Indian Economic and Social History Review, 2,* 101–144.

Chatterton, A. (1925). The Industrial Progress of the Mysore State. *Journal of the Royal Society of Arts, 63,* 714–737.

Dutt, R. C. (1904). *The Economic History of India* (Vol. 2). Burt Franklin Reprinted 1970.

Emmanuel, A. (1972). *Unequal Exchange: A Study of the Imperialism of Trade.* New Left Books.

Frank, A. G. (1967). *Capitalism and Underdevelopment in Latin America.* Monthly Review Press.

Gerschenkron, A. (1962). *Economic Backwardness in Historical Perspective.* Harvard University Press.

Haksar, K. N. (1928). Fiscal Inter-relation of Indian States and the Empire. *Asiatic Review, 24,* 539–543.

Haksar, K. N. (1929). The Salt Revenue and the Indian States. *Asiatic Review, 25,* 7–16.

Harcourt, G. C. (1984). Harcourt on Robinson. In *Contemporary Economists in Perspective* (Vol. 1, Part B). Jai Press.

Hetme, B. (1978). *The Political Economy of Indirect Rule: Mysore 1881-1947.* Curzon Press.

Keralaputra. (1929). The Internal States of India. *Annals of the American Academy of Political and Social Science, 145*(Part II), 45–58.

Kesavaiengar, B. T. (1930). The Development and the Resources of the Mysore State. *Asiatic Review, 26*, 218–227.

Keynes, J. M. (1913). *Indian Currency and Finance*. Macmillan.

Keynes, J. M. (1971) *The Collected Writings, Vol. 15*. E. Johnson. Macmillan.

Kitching, G. (1982). *Development and Underdevelopment*. Methuen.

Lall, S. (1941). Industrial Development in the Indian Provinces. *Journal of the Royal Society of Arts, 89*, 134–145.

Lipton, M. (1978). Transfer of Resources from Agriculture to Non-agricultural Activities: The Case of India. In J. F. J. Toye (Ed.), *Taxation and Economic Development*. Frank Cass.

Macpherson, W. J. (1972). Economic Development in India under the British Crown, 1858-1947. In A. J. Youngson (Ed.), *Economic Development in the Long Run*. George Allen and Unwin.

Meier, G. M. (1984). Introduction. In G. M. Meier & D. Seers (Eds.), *Pioneers in Development*. Oxford University Press.

Musgrave, R. A. (1959). *The Theory of Public Finance*. McGraw-Hill.

Naoroji, D. (1901). *Poverty and Un-British Rule in India*. Swan Sonnenschein.

Papers on Indian States Development. (1930). East and West Ltd.

Ranade, M. G. (1906). *Essays in Indian Economics* (2nd ed.). G.A. Natesan.

Rao Sahib, C. R. (1935). The Recent Industrial Progress of Mysore. *Journal of the Royal Society of Arts, 83*, 372–389.

Report of Indian States Committee 1928–29. (1929). H.M.'s Stationery Office.

Robinson, J. (1948). Marx and Keynes. In *Robinson (1951a)*.

Robinson, J. (1955b). *Marx, Marshall and Keynes*. Delhi School of Economics, Occasional Paper No.9.

Robinson, J. (1951). *Collected Economic Papers* (Vol. 1). Basil Blackwell.

Robinson, J. (1955a). A Theory of Long-run Development. *Economic Review, 6*(Tokyo), 382–385.

Robinson, J. (1959). Economic Possibilities of Ceylon. In *Papers by Visiting Economists*. National Planning Council.

Robinson, J. (1962). *Economic Philosophy*. C.A. Watts.

Robinson, J. (1973). 'Formalistic Marxism and Ecology without Classes,' Review of Emmanuel (1972). *Journal of Contemporary Asia, 3*, 457–461.

Robinson, J. (1974). Introduction. In J. Robinson (Ed.), *Selected Economic Writings*. Oxford University Press.

Robinson, J. (1979). *Aspects of Development and Underdevelopment*. Cambridge University Press.

Shah, K. T. (1927). *Sixty Years of Indian Finance*. P.S. King and Son.

The British Crown and the Indian States. (1929). P.S. King and Son.

Thompson, E., & Garratt, G. T. (1934). *Rise and Fulfilment of British Rule in India*. Macmillan.

Timmalachar, B. (1929). Fiscal Relations between the Indian States and the Government of India. *Indian Journal of Economics, 9*, 413–440.

CHAPTER 13

Role of the State

In this chapter, we deal with the question as to who would utilize the reverse flow of resources and how. The role of the state in Princely India is investigated, especially in somewhat progressive states. The rationale is provided not necessarily by market failure but by modernizing and imitative goals of some rulers and their ministers, who eschewed conservatism as an economic creed. Joan Robinson is known as a great advocate of an effective role of the state, socialist or other, in accelerating capital accumulation in the developing countries. We analyse the role of the state in Princely India to see whether there is a connection with this early experience. The case argued for the princely states by Joan Robinson was constructed around the need for capital and its utilization for enabling them to emerge out of industrial backwardness. The ardour for development, as noted earlier, resulted from the intensity of the contact with British India, the backwardness of the states having been the result of the slowness of this contact. Whether and by whom the consequent opportunities were to be taken up is the question addressed. The concern here is with the *dramatis personae* of capital accumulation. With the persistence of earlier, static economic organization, development had to be made to happen. A role was being assumed by the state. As there was no *the* princely state, the discussion of the role of the state in Princely India is problematic. For, there were a large number of them there, with extreme variations in size as well as the nature of the relationship with the British power.

© The Author(s), under exclusive license to Springer Nature Switzerland AG 2022
P. Tahir, *Joan Robinson in Princely India*, Palgrave Studies in the History of Economic Thought,
https://doi.org/10.1007/978-3-031-10905-8_13

STATE, BUT WHAT STATE?

It seems that the study carried for the princes and published in *The British Crown* left the question of the size variation aside, in a move likely to have been influenced by tactical considerations of presenting a united front.[1] This is how the individual sensitivities were dealt with to concentrate on an overall view.

> We have necessarily avoided embarking upon the still more complicated field of the particular rights and obligations of individual States. That topic lies wholly outside our present task save in so far as we have.....estimated and added up the military contributions of the individual States. (*The British Crown*, 1929, p. 215)

However, 71 per cent of the total area of Princely India, 66 per cent of population and an equal per cent of revenue was accounted for by 3–4 per cent of the states. In most discussions and analyses, the state's figuring prominently was never more than 12 or 13 in number, that is, even less than 3 per cent of the total number of the states. *The British Crown* was no exception. Therefore, the discussion in this chapter is confined to the states which satisfied a reasonable set of criteria.

More important than settling the actual number of the states was to define them politically. The status of the princely states was found without a parallel and, therefore, very hard to situate politically.[2] They were neither completely analogous to a federation of independent states nor analogous to 'the subject provinces of an Empire'; international law was 'of hardly any assistance at all' (*The British Crown*, 1929, p. 135). It was not a clear-cut case of the nation standing between the individual and the world, as List (1841) would have it. Broadly, the states were completely denied the conduct of foreign policy, and that included not only relations with countries outside the Indian subcontinent but also, for long, any contact with each other. Internally, they enjoyed a measure of autonomy. However, the internal autonomy was threatened by the extension of the role of the British Indian state in the economic sphere. British India, controlling all major sea ports, decided tariff policy for them, but the states, it appears, could have their own trade missions in London, as did the state of Mysore. The states had their own internal taxes, but a number of these were in effect mere surcharges on British Indian taxes.

This duplication and confusion of tax structures had attracted the attention of Marx. In his view the princes were 'the greatest obstacles to the Indian progress', and their states were organically weak. The time was the rule of 'John' Company.

> If you divide the revenue of a country between two governments, you are sure to cripple the resources of the one and the administration of both. Under the present system the native States succumb under the double incubus of their native Administration and the tributes and inordinate military establishments imposed upon them by the Company. The conditions under which they are allowed to retain their apparent independence are at the same time the conditions of a permanent decay, and of an utter inability of improvement. Organic weakness is the constitutional law of their existence, as of all existences living upon sufferance. (Marx, 1853, p. 198)

There is no doubt that the resources of the states had been crippled. During the time Marx was writing, their administration also left much to be desired. Contrary to British expectations, political discontent erupted in British India, not Princely India, starting with the uprising of 1857. The loyalty of the princes during these difficult times for their power convinced the British to change the existence-upon-sufferance status of the states. A halt was put to the policy of annexing princely states. As *The British Crown* stated, it was a shift 'from a policy of annexation on every pretext to the policy of preserving the States in existence whenever possible' (1929, p. 150). In 1881, the rendition of Mysore was found possible. A period of subordinate isolation followed, in which the British felt secure in the feeling that economic and sociopolitical development of British India relatively to Princely Indian states would keep the people in the former at bay. In their isolation, the states would be too backward either to pose any menace or be a model of native rule to which the people of British India might look up to. This theory proved naive. Just when some princes were beginning to shed what *The British Crown* described as their laissez-faire attitude towards development (1929, p. 141), the British announced their own laissez-faire approach vis-à-vis the states in 1909, with viceroy Minto giving official sanction to the rule of custom and putting breaks on the zeal for Westernization. For development in the image of Europe in British India was breeding political opposition and resistance, and the princely states had to be won over as allies against this.[3] The author of this policy was none other than Harcourt Butler, who later headed the committee for the purposes of which the Robinsons had prepared the economic case for the states.

STATE ACCUMULATION

Since this tilt towards the princes, the latter and quite a few others started to describe the states as 'Indian India'. In contrast to 'British' India, it was literally true, but the theme began to be propagated as a different view of life in the states. A visitor to 'Indian India', claimed a writer in *The Times*,

> will hear—and this everywhere the burden of conversation—of comparative prices, of little economies which mean so much to the lowly ones of the East. It is cheaper in the Indian States. They, too, pay taxes and get little in the way of roads and railways, school houses, and police stations. Irrigation is more primitive; life is less regulated; but life is happier and more Indian. (Lawrence, 1930, p. 147)

The burden of the study of Princely India seems to be that life cannot be happier just because it is Indian; modernization, through capital accumulation, is necessary. To begin with, the states had been slow in absorbing the impact of industrial advance in British India. But their real challenge came with the nationalist turn in British Indian industrial policy since World War I. So long as land revenue was the principal source of public receipts in both Indias, the overlap in the tax systems was not alarming. The agreements drawn up with the states had failed to envisage the end of free trade policy and the rising fiscal and economic role of the state in British India. They were contracts binding the states to a disarmed regime in return for British security.[4] That is why *The British Crown* found the argument that British Indian fiscal impositions were in the nature of a price for defence to be hollow. For all other expenditures, the states had no liability to contribute: they were supposed to fend for themselves through own tax effort.

The British Crown understood the problem in the following way, in the course of the analysis of the contribution of the states to the British Indian customs.

> If it be recognized that international relationships present no analogy relevant to this question, the *prima facie* case against these payments becomes

even stronger. It is clearly unjust to tax the whole of a nation or a confederacy and to exclude a particular part of it from participation in the revenue which that tax yields. If a motor tax was imposed on all owners throughout England and no share of the Road Fund spent in Yorkshire, the inhabitants of Yorkshire would certainly be justified in complaining. We are forced to return, therefore, to the plain question of what, in fact, consumers in the States contribute to the yield of customs, and what they receive in return. (1929, pp. 183–4)

The above is an interesting invocation of what has been described as contract theory of the state.[5] The objective of contract, according to the writers of enlightenment, was protection. Half of Adam Smith's first canon of taxation stressed contribution 'in proportion to revenue enjoyed under the protection of the state' (Smith, 1776). But the princely states, argued the study, had been guaranteed protection insurance under the treaties with the British, which also specified payments in kind and cash. The study showed these payments to be adequate to discharge defence liability. The main point, however, was not current adequacy but the fact that the payment had been settled already and any change required revision of the treaties and not fiscal impositions on the states for which British India had no jurisdiction.

This shifts the objective of contract to the other benefits of public spending, mainly developmental. Herein lay the whole difficulty. There was revenue contributed by the peoples of the states without any quid pro quo. It was also the result of the fact that British India had no jurisdiction to spend in the states; the revenue would have to be turned over to the states. At this point, the application of contract theory of the state encounters another difficulty. Could the states be supposed to have contracts whereby their peoples paid taxes for the benefits received, given that protection had already been granted by the British in return for payments provided in the treaties? The contract theory assumes that legitimation lies in the hands of the people. As a matter of fact, the British security assurance concerned the protection of princely rule[6]; the viewpoint of the peoples of the states was rarely heard. The British obligation to defend the princes underwrote their absolute rule. In one of the few writings airing the sentiments of the states' subjects, the princes were likened to the Stuarts, treating their own interests to be those of the states (Ramaiya, 1929, p. 505). Their rule could not be changed at the peoples' 'instance owing to the prowess and authority of the paramount power which is pledged to maintain an anachronic condition in the interests of a set of men who would have otherwise mended their manners and methods' (N.C.B., 1930, p. 139). Indian nationalists denounced 'the Princes as pampered and obsolete autocrats, an anomaly and a hindrance to a visionary, new, democratic India, who must kiss the rod or be swept away.[7] (Swept away they were immediately after the partition in 1947!)[8] While the government of British India made economic policies as if the states did not exist, the nationalists were even more strongly dismissive.[9] Hiding behind their terms of reference, the Butler Committee declined to hold hearings of the states' subjects.[10]

The nationalists doubted the Indianness of the states because the cry of Indian India was invariably coupled with the necessity of *Pax Britannica*.[11] A reviewer of *The British Crown* (1929) saw the whole work in similar light (Saunders, 1929, p. 541). In the course of a lecture in London, the Maharaja of Patiala, the chancellor of the Chamber of Princes that sponsored *The British Crown*, while denying any ill will towards the nationalists, threw a challenge of national development, but under the British Crown.

> We Princes, like all the greatest of the Nationalist leaders in British India, are firm believers in the value of the British connection. We do believe, however, that it is perfectly compatible with that connection that Indians should have greater power over the management of their own affairs than they possess today. We have not the slightest desire to thwart the progress of British India; indeed, we hope we shall run a friendly race with them along the lines of national development. (Patiala, 1928, p. 643)

In the discussion that followed, the Maharaja was reminded by some of his audience that it was the British power that had either created the states or saved them from total annihilation. Their emphasis on the British connection thus falls into perspective. Curiously, the connection expressed personal loyalty with the British Crown, which had long ceased to enjoy the divine right the princes claimed in their states. Haksar (1931, p. 346) went as far as to say that if the loyalty of the princes to the person of the British Crown was deemed 'unenlightened, then the Princes have every intention of remaining unenlightened'. This was the view of a close friend of Joan Robinson. Judging her by the company she kept will, however, be hazardous. Another of her friends made the remark that even some of the princes publicizing themselves to be enlightened while in Europe 'drop a few centuries when they return home' to resume their tyrannical rule and to 'mat the taxes which they wring out of their peasantry as if the money were their personal property' (Garratt, 1930, p. 785).

By these accounts the princely states were the bulwark of absolutist, conservative, pre-capitalistic dispensation, maintained by status rather than any notion of contract. Might not a British Indian obligation to share with the states' centralized tax revenue only fatten the personal purses of the princes rather than canalize them into development? To be sure, the case for the plough-back to the states of the revenues collected by British India from the peoples of the states without any benefits was well-argued. Even the critics of the princes' personal style of rule in the states were convinced of the need to harmonize economic and fiscal policies and the states' right to central revenues, especially customs.[12]

This is what the Robinsons' estimation exercise sought to demonstrate. Further, despite the constraints that the nature of the case may have imposed on the Robinsons, they seem to have been able to carefully distance their contribution from any impression of a plain plea of more for the princes. The study was building a case for the development of the states and its peoples rather than for the rulers of the states. In pushing the argument with relative freedom, they must have been helped by a number of favourable factors. At a time when the future of India as a dominion was under discussion, the princes could ill-afford to be seen as irresponsible rulers, oblivious of development requirements. At least the frontline members of the Chamber of Princes took a lead in prescribing privy purses and providing some participatory political arrangements for selected members of the public.

Before the issue of the sharing of resources and imperial burdens was decided, the contract theory of the state held in a peculiar way. The princely states could not tax their subjects for protection, as they provided none. For the princes, it removed the bias that the benefit principle of taxation imposed on the state in the nineteenth century to restrict public expenditure to the function of protection.[13] The developmental role was the only role left for the state in Princely India. With internal autonomy and absolute power over good or evil, it is hard to imagine that the indirect British rule was a serious constraint on development. Until the end of free trade, the indirect resource transfer problem had not assumed threatening proportions. Even as the import tariffs increased, causing a de facto erosion of resource base, there was no *de jure* bar on the states in Princely India to play developmental roles. If a significant number of them continued to be backward, the explanation lies in the attitude of the rulers themselves towards modernization. It has been stressed by Bagchi that the relative political autonomy of the states acted as a counter to what he perceives as the discrimination against the local capitalists in British India, despite the fiscal autonomy secured after World War I from Britain, rather than the economic incentives like free or cheap land, lower taxes and access to princely coffers.

> The effect of rule by the native princes may have been detrimental to ordinary people; but insofar as the native states provided a market and some capital for the development of Indian enterprise, the effect on industrial growth was positive. The political separateness of the native states from British India was more important for industrial growth than the semi-feudal structure of administration within many of those states, given the discrimination practiced against Indian businessmen under the imperial system. (Bagchi, 1972, p. 215)

That, however, was not the point of *The British Crown*. It was political separateness which had led to the backwardness of the states. Discrimination, in its analysis, existed against the states as fiscal units, but the extent to which they encouraged development was connected with the modernization goals absorbed by the princes trained by the British as well as the latter's inroads into the departmental structures of the states. For instance, the Mysore state boasted not only government departments patterned after British India but also quasi-representative institutions to have a semblance of popular participation. The British found their opportunity to penetrate the states especially during the minority administrations. While British education created among such princes autonomous aspirations, the virtual control of these states by the British put on the ground institutions and extensions of the central government departments which while expanding the economic domain of British India also sowed the seeds of change in Princely India. Here the laissez-faire attitude of the princes had begun to give way to interventionism. Some of the princes were also becoming, as Joan Robinson might have said, European enough to cherish progress with the aphorism: What was good for British India was good for Princely India.

Indeed, the state of Mysore, managed directly by a British commission for half a century and then turned over to its prince, was by far the economically most progressive state. This was consistent with the hypothesis in *The British Crown* that the relative backwardness of the states was related, in no small measure, to the preservation of the old economic organization in the absence of British intervention. Due to its history as an anti-British stronghold, Mysore was not left alone. It was kept under British control long enough for it to establish a state apparatus similar to British India. Unlike the other parts of India, local strongholds of big *zamindars* were not allowed to emerge. Small owner-operators dominated the scene (Manor, 1975, p. 34). The native rule continued to attract British administrators and professionals in the service of the state, as also the best local talent.

The states were fiscally far less autonomous of British India than British India was of Britain and monetarily not at all. And there was no reason for them not to welcome European investment, believed as they did in a strong British connection. If anything, the states would not discriminate between Indian and non-Indian capital. In regard to natural resources, the states were directing government finance in exploration, with a view to striking a better bargain with the outside capital for development on the basis of tested and proven reserves. They even set up an Indian States Business Group in Britain for disseminating economic and other information (Papers, 1930, pp. vi, 117–43). The experience of Mysore suggests that the states could raise funds in the international financial market, albeit under guarantees from British India (Hurd II, 1975b, p. 423). Similarly, the experience of Hyderabad's railway loan floatation in London in 1875 indicates how a state, under a dynamic prime minister, could jump over the hurdles placed by the officialdom in British India (Bawa, 1965).

In explaining the backwardness of the states, *The British Crown* had also emphasized geographical isolation; however, related but more important was the slow impact of the economic forces associated with British occupation. In other words, what Bagchi takes to be the reason for industrial growth, their relative independence, had been the reason for the preservation of their anachronistic economic organization which was antithetical to industrial development.[14] As suggested in the study, geographical isolation was of no consequence, once the contact with more progressive economic forces began to establish an industrial revolution. This was a theory radically different from the approaches such as Bagchi's (1972).

PRINCES AND DEVELOPMENT

The assessment of the attitude of the rulers of the states towards development was consistent with view of development and underdevelopment expressed in *The British Crown*.

> Their rulers were not necessarily conservative, though many of them were; they were not even necessarily apathetic. They simply did not happen to be Europeans, convinced without argument or experiment that whatever was best for Europe was best for India. Their attitude to the situation was that of *lassez-faire* [*sic*]. They neither particularly encouraged industrial developments nor expressly discouraged them. (1929, pp. 140–1)

First, the relative backwardness of the states was diagnosed mainly in terms of the slow and feeble economic impact on the states of the British ascendancy. Now it was suggested that the alternative for the rulers was to follow the modernizing British in British India. While the arguments for more capital went on, there is not enough evidence to suggest that the princes were actually restrained from implementing economic development goals as a matter of general policy. Hurd II (1975b) has claimed that from the very outset the British had placed restrictions on capital flows to the states. Although these restrictions were never fully observed in practice, capital was still shy to enter the states. Hurd was concerned with administrative restrictions, disregarding the effect of taxation. Especially since the introduction of income tax, capital movements were liable to be affected, as was stated in *The British Crown*, pointing out that it was in the states' hands to encourage capital inflow by avoiding disincentive effects. But the main case rested on poor resource endowment and lack of opportunities for economic exploitation. [15] Anyhow, with capital inflow being insignificant despite the reluctance of the British to enforce restrictions, Hurd fixed the responsibility on the British, who maintained the structures of the states by indirect rule. He goes further to make the peculiar contention that the British should have encouraged capital flows to the states and discouraged the princes from investing in British India (Hurd II, 1975b, pp. 420–4). For one thing, the semi-independent states viewed their credit-worthiness as far better than the independent Latin American republics, where British capital had moved in large amounts (Papers, 1930, p. 117). Yet capital inflow was not significant due mainly to the lack of profitable opportunities. And if the princes were inclined to invest in

British India, it involved a fundamental change of attitude from their notoriety as wealth-hoarders. (In a later study devoted to hoarding, Joan Robinson made no mention of the princes! [16])

The ruler of Gwalior was prominent among the financial backers of Tata Iron and Steel. He paid annual visits to Bombay and Calcutta to discuss the plans for the state with the industrialists and financial community.[17] Many states were regular investors in industries in British India.[18] It was not a one-way flow. Most states, in a more or less degree, were receptive to the Indian capitalists from British India. For instance, Gwalior, the state in which Joan Robinson was based, offered an attractive package of tax concessions, credit facilities, even gifts and special immunities from the state laws, not to speak of the virtual absence of labour legislation. The package was so attractive that the renowned *Marwaris*, the Birlas, shifted the site of a textile mill with an equity of Rs.18 lakh from the well-developed Delhi to Gwalior (Timberg, 1978, pp. 99, 171). However, the state was more active than private sector in industry, besides its role in providing infrastructure.

Kosambi provides an apt illustration of the argument in *The British Crown*, which is about learning and imitative applications associated with external contact, not indiscriminate approval of any external contact.[19] According to him, the contact with superior economic forces embodied in British capitalists had transformed 'even the most backward and degenerate of Indians, the feudal princelings, [into] shareholders on a large scale'. The same forces operated on *Marwaris* of the Rajputana states. They started as among the financial backers of the British in the latter's phase of expansion. The contact with a vigorous economic force turned them into expert futures traders (1946, pp. 394–5). *Marwaris'* migration response bears good testimony to the general argument in *The British Crown* that development-mindedness is related to the degree of contact with more progressive economic forces. It is also useful in understanding the inter-state variations in development levels. From the backward states of Rajputana, *Marwaris* migrated all over British India in search of economic opportunity. They also moved to the states of Princely India that offered them adequate incentives.

At any rate, the inadequate inflow of capital does suggest the need for vigorous efforts to mobilize internal resources. That is where giving the states their fiscal due, estimated by the Robinsons, becomes important. The significance of that did not arise from the failure of the princely states to mobilize revenue from the tax base under their control. Hurd assumes a low internal effort, based on an all-India average saving rate of 5 per cent in 1950–1951 (1975b, p. 420). An alternative view concluded that despite the lack of control over customs and excises and the requirement to pay tribute, the princely states did 'not seem to have taxed significantly less, and in some states incidence of taxation per head was considerably higher than in British India' (Kumar, 1984b, p. 927). Apart from the autocratic nature of the state making tax gathering, at times, as 'productive' as the hunting expeditions arranged by the princes for the visiting viceroys, higher tax incidence may have been justified by the higher spending on productive activity. The view in *The British Crown*, noted earlier, was that rising requirement of capital accumulation necessitated the retention of every *anna* within the states.

While the states competed with each other to attract Indian capital from British India as well as other states, there had not been any significant development of local bourgeoisies, leaving it for the state to pick up the slack. *Marwaris* had left their own states in Rajputana not only for their backwardness but for the apathy of those states towards development. A class of small capitalists was emerging in Travancore. Its prime minister observed: 'For better or worse, her body politic is essentially a bourgeoisie' (Watts, 1930, p. 725). Even here the presence of the state in the economy was massive. It possessed all 'the technical attributes of modernity—schools, roads, export crops, law courts, medical services, efficient bureaucracy'. [20]A visit to the state of Baroda was recommended to those raised on the stories about the 'unchanging East'. The state was active in banking and industry, apart from social services and infrastructure. [21] Indore started a state cotton textile mill in 1867 to capture the opportunity offered by the American Civil War, and the lead was followed by *Marwaris* in the private sector. A railway was also built. The Maharaja of this state was among the few Indians who subscribed to the share capital of the Indian railways in the earliest period, that is, up to 1875. [22]

In the widely acclaimed progressive state of Mysore, the state instituted a very impressive package of concessional policies for private investment. New crops were introduced, gold prospecting met with successful results, scientific education and research was encouraged, and the lack of coal was made good by the development of cheap hydroelectric power. As noted in *The British Crown*, an iron and steel mill had been established. All this activity was dominated by the state. In fact, the state became so active in its economic developmental role that its British director of industries looked back at it as 'an extremely good example of what might be termed 'state socialism.''[23]

Unlike the progressive states of Princely India, the nationalist opinion in British India had been indecisive and equivocal about the role of the state for a long time. Toye has chosen the attitude of a forward-looking prime minister of Mysore as a significant illustration of the nationalist disposition.

Another example of the nationalist disdain of state enterprise is the attitude of Sir M. Visvesvaraya. As Dewan of Mysore (1914–1918) and Chairman of the Bhadravati Ironworks (1923–1929), he established a major industrial enterprise in the state sector, and managed it with considerable success in adverse trading conditions. Yet when, in 1934, he came to write India's prototype development plan, despite its extreme emphasis on industrialization, the division of investment between private and public sectors was an issue left completely unresolved. He saw the role of the government as one of encouraging corporate and individual enterprise, advising India 'to proceed along the lines practised in such capitalist countries as France and the United States of America'. His later efforts aimed at promoting industry (vehicles and aircraft manufacturing schemes in the late 1930s) also centred on private sector. (Toye, 1981, pp. 29–30)

The reason given by Toye for this mixed-up policy is extremely relevant to the analysis pursued here.

The reason for this is that a state accumulation policy could only become attractive to nationalist sentiment once the *transfer of state apparatus to Indian control* [emphasis in original] was practically assured. (Toye, 1981, p. 30)

In Princely India, the state apparatus was under the control of the princes, so far as implementing a development policy was concerned. This control had been undermined since the government of British India opted for a policy of discriminatory protection. In other words, the extension of the role of the state in British India to the economic sphere impinged on the role of the princely states in their respective economies. It was to regain this lost control that provided the political basis for economic arguments in *The British Crown* for keeping the states' resources within the states. At the same time, the very loss of control brought in its train the pressures for further state accumulation. Sir M. Visvesvaraya had to have at his disposal the state apparatus of Mysore to follow a state accumulation policy, under both the pre-war free trade regime and the interwar protectionist regime.

At least in the progressive states like Mysore, serious attempts were being made to solve the Lewis problem—the transition from saving and investing 5–12 per cent of national income—albeit, through a policy of state accumulation, something which had eluded many independent Latin American countries (Lewis, 1954, p. 416; Griffin & Gurley, 1985, p. 1109). As noted above, the tax incidence in the major states was probably higher than in British India. It remains to outline their spending patterns. In her *magnum opus*, Joan Robinson identified a 'primitive state of stagnation', the description of which neatly fitted many princely states: 'What is lacking, primarily, is the idea of accumulation and a class of entrepreneurs to play according to the capitalist rules' (Robinson, 1956a, pp. 256–7). Mysore did build temples, symbolizing primitive stagnation; but more than that, it was investing in railways, dams, electrical works, light as well as heavy industry. The idea of accumulation had caught on, but the state had to play the capitalist. Table 13.1 portrays an impressive picture of fixed investment.

Coincidentally, the fixed capital formation of Rs. 1080 lakh is quite close to the Robinsons' estimate of resource transfer of Rs. 1044 lakhs from the states. While it is not quite legitimate to compare a single-year estimate of transfer from all states with a cumulative figure of investment of a single state, it does give an idea of the possibilities for state accumulation. There is evidence that Mysore regularly earmarked Rs. 70–100 lakh per annum to capital expenditure (Gopal, 1941). On an average, the proportions of revenue devoted by some states to social overhead capital

Table 13.1 Capital outlays on productive works in Mysore (as of 1 July 1924)

Investments	Lakhs of rupees
Mysore state railways worked by Madras and southern Mahratta railway company	190
Railways worked by the state	279
Electrical works	176
Krishna Raja Sagara dam on river Cauvery	217
Sandalwood oil factories	7
Iron works	191
Other works	2
Kolar gold fields water supply project	18
Total	1080

Source: Chatterton (1925, p. 736)

during 1901–1931 were phenomenal: 47 per cent in Cochin, 44 per cent in Bikaner, 38 per cent in Mysore and 25 per cent in Baroda, compared to 20–25 per cent in British India (Hurd II, 1975a, p. 175). At the time of the Robinsons' study, the states were beginning to industrialize, but their share in all-India output was insignificant. [24] Subsequently, although some caution is needed in interpretation as seasonality was considerable, the all-India figures for factory employment indicated a doubling of the share of the states during 1923–1938—from 8.7 per cent to 17.2 per cent (Morris, 1984, p. 644).

The state in the major princely states saved and invested significantly and regularly. In Joan Robinson's later work, the idea of a strong state as an organizer of rapid capital accumulation appears time and again. It is necessary to explore its possible connection with her work and experience in the autocratic states of Princely India. The strong state view does not connote those military or authoritarian regimes which, in effect, turn out to be weak in implementing development policies that hurt vested interests. It was the opposite of Myrdal's 'soft state'—a state which either fails to decide on policies because of its reluctance to impose costs or transfers this reluctance to implementation if policies are decided at all (Myrdal, 1968, pp. 66–7, 895–900). During the widespread development pessimism that followed Myrdal's study, Joan Robinson maintained that 'like a positive, China shows the lines of Myrdal's negative in reverse. Development is possible, but not in a 'soft state" (Robinson, 1968b, p. 389).[25]

No Marxist herself,[26] her support for socialist development derived from the perception, based on the Russian industrialization experience, 'that socialism is going to beat capitalism at its own game'—capital accumulation. This was because 'it is a far more powerful instrument than capitalism for extracting the investible surplus' in an underdeveloped economy. It was 'the quickest way to catch up on the technical achievements of the capitalist economies' (Robinson, 1957c, p. 98, 1957d, p. 158). Adler (1957, p. 63, *n*.12) ascribes to Joan Robinson the suggestion about the socialist state's 'ability to foresee the future *en gros*'. During her first visit to China, she observed: 'China seems to me to provide the final proof that Communism is not a stage beyond capitalism but a substitute for it' (Robinson, 1954, p. 8). Lord Kahn confirmed that the basic reason for her preference for the socialist strategy was the advantage of the state to decide the rate of accumulation at an appropriate level.[27]

A strong state, sharp emphasis on capital accumulation and a strategy to catch up were also the essential ingredients of Stalinism.[28] After the Poznan riots in Poland in 1956, the excesses of capital accumulation by the strong states had started to become known. She was quick to acknowledge that 'it has now become evident that some [socialist countries] have been over-doing it'. She recognized 'the excesses of Stalinism', but pointed out that 'its practical achievements cannot be denied' (Robinson 1957c, p. 97; 1957d, p. 159). The latter was said in a polemic with the Marxists. In the context of underdeveloped countries, she took an unequivocally anti-Stalinist stand. This is borne out by her critique of the choice of a surplus-maximizing technique, aptly described by Bent Hansen (1975, p. 403) as Stalin-Dobb-Sen technique. The critique bears full quotation.

> [I]t is often argued that by economizing labour per unit of output, orga-nized (more mechanized) industry is economizing wages, therefore econo-mizing consumption and yielding a large future investible surplus per unit of initial investment. This argument, when it is frankly stated, is hard-headed, not to say brutal. It means that the `abstinence' which corresponds to the saving out of profits which is made available for investment has to be borne by those who, under this policy, are left in unemployment and who, on the alternative policy, would be eating the wages. It is sometimes justified by appeal to the extreme hard-headedness of socialist policy, which enforces abstinence for the sake of accumulation. This argument has been weakened by the workers of Poznan, who demonstrated how hard-headedness may over-reach itself. (Robinson, 1956b, p. 9)

This criticism was made in regard to the second plan of India. Even in a socialist economy, assuming on its part full control and wise use of sur-plus, the technique had nothing to recommend itself before full employ-ment (Robinson, 1977).

The upshot of the above round-up of her later writing is that Joan Robinson considered a strong state essential for development, but the strength was not to be acquired by a Stalinist muscle.[29] Does this idea go back to her experience in Princely India? Marx, as noted earlier, had spo-ken of the princely states as organically weak, in the conditions of suffer-ance imposed on them by the British. If, despite these conditions, a group of them was able to record progress far ahead of the other states and sometimes above the standards of British India, there was something to be said for the structures of the states involved, making it probable at the same time that a student of the development of the states, which at the time Joan Robinson was, would be influenced by it. A number of states with enlightened princes had progressive and effective prime ministers like

Visvesvaraya,[30] mentioned by Toye (1981). Indeed, it was said of the state of Gwalior, where Joan Robinson was resident, and Baroda that there 'came to be just an occasional sign' of a Meiji regime: 'an authoritarian government, under skilled and forceful administrative command, leading the way' (Low, 1978, p. 378).

Under the blanket term 'India', many stories of long-term stagnation have been told. In all of these, there is no knowing, in terms of facts, what was the state of the economies of two-fifths of the subcontinent, especially its modernizing part. Meiji Japan and its dynamic 'mask[ed] considerable diversity'—the telescopic historians of Indian stagnation by-passed a lot more: 'Regional variations also make all-India generalization difficult. The native states, of which there were nearly six hundred in 1858, were themselves not homogeneous' (Macpherson, 1972, pp. 10–16, 1987, p. 131). Submerged under this macro picture were some forward-looking strong states. Joan Robinson's view of a progressive ruler was one who managed the economy like a European, brooking no obstacles in the way of modernization. Some states did show greater fiscal courage than British India, as well as the ability to take quick decisions and a capacity to implement projects. However, the analysis of the caste system presented earlier rules out Joan Robinson's acquiescence to the claim that it had nurtured in the states an 'elite fitted for highest achievement', out of which the 'rulers will draw the men who will collaborate with them in the execution of their schemes', and that the same elite which resisted Western industrialism in British India was used in the states for Western industrialization because respect for custom and tradition was also maintained under 'a traditionally established, consciously accepted, orderly hierarchy, ranging from the ruler through the upper classes down to the masses' (Papers, 1930, pp. 110–1). Caste, to her, was an obstacle to progress. Similarly, there is evidence of her awareness that the states did not necessarily have benevolent autocrats. Incompetence and corruption in what she had known to be the ruling oligarchies did not escape her attention.[31]

In short, a link does seem to exist between Joan Robinson's later view of a strong state, stripped of its Stalinist hard-headedness, and the earlier experience of a group of modernizing princely states which managed to somewhat overcome the corruption and anachronisms of the ruling oligarchies of the general body of the states. The co-author, Panikkar, who wrote the political part of *The British Crown* (1929), also showed the influence of the experience of Princely India in being caught up between the assertion that there was no going back to the oriental despotism of the states on the one hand and the apprehension, on the other, that the continuation of Gandhian political strategy after the Partition of India in 1947 had the effect of weakening the state (Panikkar, 1953, p. 499, 1962, p. 4). Joan Robinson's view of independent India brings out the link between a strong state and the problem of development even more clearly.

> In India democracy has been installed in advance. This has a two-sided effect, but both sides are inimical to quick development. On the one side, by the queer twists of latter-day political thought, democracy has become identified with respect for property, status and vested interests. Democracy in this sense draws the teeth of land reform, permits unearned luxury, retards the liberating shake-up in social relations, clogs the rationalists' struggle against hollowed nonsense. On the other side, democracy, in a more natural meaning of the word, demands a reduction in inequality, some elements of welfare state, attention to the standard of life of the workers; in short, to relax the stern process of squeezing out the surplus before it has fairly begun. (Robinson, 1957e, pp. 844–5)

Joan Robinson also noted the election of a communist party in the post-Partition state of Kerala. It could not exercise the full strength of a state because, as a provincial government, it had a limited scope. Kerala comprised the erstwhile princely states of Travancore and Cochin. These were maritime states which, along with Baroda, displayed during their princely existence, a number of characteristics that would make a Hong Kong, Singapore or Taiwan.

NOTES

1. This does not mean that such a front actually existed. Large states like Hyderabad pleaded their own case, while Gwalior, also a large state, led a large group of smaller states. The study by the Robinsons, however, was not confined to the group of states that commissioned it. It was a more general study of Princely India, though the concrete examples were chosen from the larger states.
2. A British constitutional writer concluded: 'Clearly the constitutional position of the Indian Princes is a question upon which widely differing views are strongly held, and there is no accepted criterion which can be applied to its solution' (Molson, 1931, p. 495). One strong opinion was that of the law expert on the Butler Committee (Holdsworth, 1930). An American analyst, however, argued that at least the major states were internally sovereign, 'bound only by treaty to a common central agency' (O' Rourke, 1931, p. 1028).

3. See Low (1978) and Copland (1982) for the changing British policy towards the states.
4. Often times it has happened in history that a country is defeated, disarmed to shear it of its hostile capability and, when joint defence burden becomes unbearable, asked to share this burden. The urgings on Japan and Germany to increase their defence spending fall in the same genre.
5. See Musgrave (1959, pp. 63–70, 1985, pp. 16–7).
6. Even in British India, special laws were enacted for the protection of the princes (Copland 1982, p. 249).
7. See Louis Dane's remarks in (The Indian States, 1929, p. 295).
8. See Menon (1956) and Bettelheim (1968, pp. 106–40).
9. For instance, a competent reviewer of the state of the Indian economy had to be reminded of the existence of the states by a discussant of the paper. See Premchand (1929) and the following discussion.
10. See *Memorandum* (1929).
11. See Rushbrook-Williams (1928, p. 396) and Patiala (1928).
12. See Ramaiya (1930).
13. Besides others, McCulloch advocated this bias. See Musgrave (1959, p. 68).
14. As for discrimination against local capitalists pointed out by Bagchi, *Marwaris'* learning-by-doing experience in jute trade and industry proved otherwise. See Timberg (1978, pp. 38, 97) and Morris (1984, pp. 570–1, 615–6).
15. Jeffrey (1978, p. 26) makes a similar point while criticizing Hurd (1975b).
16. Robinson (1938).
17. See Bull and Haksar (1926), Haksar (1930) and Morris (1984, p. 591). Macpherson (1972, p. 181) mentions a sum of £400,000 as the contribution of the Maharaja Scindia of Gwalior to the working capital of Tata Iron and Steel.
18. When the Commission on Indian Currency and Finance asked a leading Bombay broker handling funds from princely states the following specific question: 'Have you found any great disposition on their part to invest in industrial enterprises lately? Have they been getting increasingly disposed to invest in industrial enterprises?' the reply was in affirmative. The sum mentioned in a single transaction handled by the same agent was Rs.100 lakh (Royal Commission, 1926, p. 251).
19. See Toye (1983, pp. 100–1) for a critique of a modern variation of this old theme.
20. Jeffrey (1978, pp. 136–7, 144–5). Travancore state had later become part of Kerala in the partitioned India, where the communists secured an electoral victory (Question 1957, pp. 427–8). In a letter to me, K.N. Raj informed that Joan Robinson visited the state every year from 1972 until her death in 1983.

21. Thompson and Gamut (1934, p. 652), Hardiman (1978).
22. Timberg (1978, p. 216). Besides the Maharaja Holker of Indore, the investors included the Nizam of Hyderabad and the Maharaja of Patiala (Macpherson, 1972, pp. 164–5).
23. See Chatterton (1925), Rao Sahib (1935, p. 392).
24. Table 12.1.
25. See also Robinson (1968c).
26. She told Indian readers: 'The orthodox academic economists in U.S.A. labelled me as a Marxist so as to defend their pupils from paying attention to what I wrote while the orthodox Marxists were very much annoyed that I should treat Marx in analytical terms at all' (Robinson, 1974, p. xi).
27. Interview with the author.
28. Indeed, Stalin and Joan Robinson have been quoted together with similarly interpretable message (Dalton, 1974, p. 114).
29. There is room for debate on Joan Robinson's view of the state and development in China, where she thinks a strong state was able to avoid Stalinist excesses. See Tahir (2019).
30. See Iyengar (1941, p. 683).
31. Harry M. Bull's letter to Joan Robinson, 26 January 1947. JVR Collection, King's Modern Archives.

References

Unpublished Material

Harry M. Bull's letter to Joan Robinson. (1947, January 26). JVR Collection, King's Modern Archives.

Published Works

Adler, S. (1957). *The Chinese Economy*. Routledge and Kegan Paul.
Bagchi, A. K. (1972). *Private Investment in India 1900–39*. Cambridge University Press.
Bawa, V. S. (1965). Salar Jang and the Nizam's State Railway. *Indian Economic and Social History Review, 2,* 305–340.
Bettelheim, C. (1968). *India Independent*. Macgibbon and Kee.
Bull, H. M., & Haksar, K. N. (1926). *Madhavrao Scindia of Gwalior*. Alijah Darbar Press.
Chatterton, A. (1925). The Industrial Progress of the Mysore State. *Journal of the Royal Society of Arts, 63,* 714–737.
Copland, I. (1982). *The British Raj and the Indian States*. Orient Longman.

Dalton, G. (1965). History, Politics and Economic Development in Liberia. *Journal of Economic History, 25*, 569–591.

Dalton, G. (1974). *Economic Systems and Society*. Penguin.

Garratt, G. T. (1930). Indian India. *Asia, 30*, 783–789, 804–805. (U.S.)

Gopal, M. H. (1941). Public Expenditure in Mysore—A Review. *Indian Journal of Economics, 21*, 594–604.

Griffin, K., & Gurley, J. (1985). Radical Analyses of Imperialism, the Third World, and the Transition to Socialism: A Survey Article. *Journal of Economic Literature, 23*, 1089–1143.

Haksar, K. N. (1930). Economic Development in Gwalior State. *Asiatic Review, 26*, 150–157.

Haksar, K. N. (1931). Mahatma Gandhi and the Indian States. *Spectator, 147*, 346.

Hansen, B. (1975). Review of R. Findlay, International Trade and Development Theory. *Journal of Development Economics, 1*, 403–404.

Hardiman, D. (1978). The Structure of a "Progressive" State. In R. Jeffrey (Ed.), *People, Princes and Paramount Power*. Oxford University Press.

Holdsworth, W. (1930). The Indian States and India. *Law Quarterly Review, 46*, 417–445.

Hurd, J., II. (1975a). The Economic Consequences of the Indirect Rule in India. *Indian Economic and Social History Review, 12*, 169–181.

Hurd, J., II. (1975b). The Influence of British Policy and Industrial Development in the Princely States of India—1890–1933. *Indian Economic and Social History Review, 12*, 409–424.

Iyengar, S. K. (1941). "British" and "Indian" Finance. *Indian Journal of Economics, 21*, 830–870.

Jeffrey, R. (Ed.). (1978). *People, Princes and Paramount Power*. Oxford University Press.

Journal of Contemporary Asia. (1983). Editorial. *13*, 3–6.

Kosambi, D. D. (1946). The Bourgeios Comes of Age in India. *Science and Society, 10*, 392–398.

Kumar, D. (Ed.). (1984b). The Fiscal System. In *Kumar (1984a)*.

Lawrence, W. R. (1930). The Indian States. In *India*. The Times Publishing Company.

Lewis, W. A. (1954). Economic Development with Unlimited Supplies of Labour. *Manchester School of Economic and Social Studies, 22*, 139–191.

List, F. (1841) *The National System of Political Economy*. Longman and Green, Reprinted 1885.

Low, D. A. (1978). Laissez-faire and Traditional Rulership in Princely India. In *Jeffrey (1978)*.

Macpherson, W. J. (1972). Economic Development in India under the British Crown, 1858–1947. In A. J. Youngson (Ed.), *Economic Development in the Long Run*. George Allen and Unwin.

Macpherson, W. J. (1987). *The Economic Development of Japan, c.1868–1941.* Macmillan.

Manor, J. (1975). 'Princely Mysore Before the Storm. *Modern Asian Studies,* 9, 31–58.

Marx, K. (1853). The Russo-Turkish Difficulty—The East India Question. In K. Marx, & F. Engels (Eds.), (1979) *Collected Works* (Vol. 12). Lawrence and Wishart.

Memorandum of the Indian States People. (1929). Arya Bhushan Press.

Menon, V. P. (1956). *The Story of the Integration of the Indian States.* Longmans, Green.

Molson, A. H. E. (1931). The Constitutional Position of the Indian States -II. *Asiatic Review, 27,* 487–495.

Morris, M. D. (1984). The Growth of Large-Scale Industry to 1947. In *Kumar (1984).*

Musgrave, R. A. (1959). *The Theory of Public Finance.* McGraw-Hill.

Musgrave, R. A. (1985). A Brief History of Fiscal Doctrine. In A. J. Auerbach & M. Feldstein (Eds.), *Handbook of Public Economics* (Vol. 1). North-Holland.

Myrdal, G. (1968). *Asian Drama* (Vol. 1–3). Allen Lane.

N.C.B. (1930). Review of P.L. Chudgar. *Calcutta Review, 36,* 139.

O'Rourke, V. A. (1931). The Sovereignty of the Native Indian States. *American Political Science Review, 25,* 1022–1028.

Panikkar, K. M. (1953). *Asia and the Western Dominance.* Allen and Unwin.

Panikkar, K. M. (1962). *In Defence of Liberalism.* Asia Publishing House.

Papers on Indian States Development. (1930). East and West Ltd.

Patiala, Maharaja of. (1928). The Indian States and the Crown. *Asiatic Review, 24,* 628–647.

Premchand, K. (1929). The Economic Position in India. *Asiatic Review, 25,* 682–703.

Question Mark over Kerala. (1957). *Economic Weekly, 9,* 427–428.

Ramaiya, A. (1929). The Point of View of the Indian States' Subjects. *Contemporary Review, 135,* 505–508.

Ramaiya, A. (1930). The Indian States and British India: Their Financial Relations. *Empire Review, 51,* 208–211.

Rao Sahib, C. R. (1935). The Recent Industrial Progress of Mysore. *Journal of the Royal Society of Arts, 83,* 372–389.

Robinson, J. (1957c). Notes on the Theory of Economic Development. In *Robinson (1960a).*

Robinson, J. (1957d). What Remains of Marxism. In *Robinson (1965).*

Robinson, J. (1977). Employment and the Choice of Technique. In *K.S.*

Robinson, J. (1938). The Concept of Hoarding. *Economic Journal, 48,* 231–236.

Robinson, J. (1954). *Letters from a Visitor to China.* Students' Bookshops.

Robinson, J. (1956a). *The Accumulation of Capital* (1st. ed.). Macmillan.

Robinson, J. (1956b). Unemployment and the Second Plan. *Capital,* 7–9.

Robinson, J. (1957e). 'The Indian Mixture,' Review of M. Zinkin. *Development for free Asia, New Statesman and Nation, 54,* 844–845.

Robinson, J. (1968b). 'The Poverty of Nations,' Review of G. Myrdal, Asian Drama. *Cambridge Quarterly, 3,* 381–389.

Robinson, J. (1968c). 'The Poverty of Nations,' Review of G. Myrdal. *Asian Drama, Listener, 80*(509–510), 17.

Robinson, J. (1974). Introduction. In J. Robinson (Ed.), *Selected Economic Writings.* Oxford University Press.

Royal Commission on Indian Currency and Finance. (1926). *Minutes of Evidence Taken in India* (Vol. 4). H.M.'s Stationery Office.

Rushbrook-Williams, L. F. (1928). Joint Action Among the Indian Princes. *Asiatic Review, 24,* 390–396.

Saunders, A. L. (1929). Review of *The British Crown and the Indian States. Asiatic Review, 25,* 540–541.

Smith, A. (1776). *An Inquiry into the Nature and Causes of the Wealth of Nations.* George Routledge and Sons. Reprinted 1890.

Tahir, P. (2019). *Making Sense of Joan Robinson on China.* Palgrave Macmillan.

The British Crown and the Indian States. (1929). P.S. King and Son.

Thompson, E., & Garratt, G. T. (1934). *Rise and Fulfilment of British Rule in India.* Macmillan.

Timberg, T. A. (1978). *The Marwaris: From Traders to Industrialists.* Vikas.

Toye, J. (1981). *Public Expenditure and Indian Development Policy 1960–1970.* Cambridge University Press.

Toye, J. (1983). The Disparaging of Development Economics. *Journal of Development Studies, 20,* 87–107.

Watts, M. E. (1930). Travancore-III: Economic Conditions, Trade and Commerce. *Asiatic Review, 26,* 725–740.

CHAPTER 14

Conclusion

This book, *Joan Robinson in Princely India*, is about her early activities and work in the field she had chosen during her undergraduate days at Cambridge, that is, economics. After completing the Economics Tripos from Girton College in 1925, she got married to Austin Robinson, her teacher who held a temporary faculty assignment. In 1926, the couple left for India. The colonial India was divided into British India and Princely India. While British India was directly ruled by the British Crown, Princely India consisted of a large number of quasi-autonomous states ruled by local princes. One of the relatively larger princely states, Gwalior, was looking for a tutor for its minor prince. Joan Robinson's aristocratic background came in handy in getting her husband appointed to this position.

I

Life in Gwalior was not just the enjoyment of a tax-free income or the conveniences of being close to royalty. Court intrigues, rivalries and jealousies took their own toll. Tutoring a minor Maharaja, whose conduct is overseen by two mothers and a residency council including the British and the state bureaucracies, was not an ordinary pupil-teacher relationship. This kept Austin Robinson extremely busy. Not cut out for the life of an idler, Joan Robinson started to visit a local educational institution to give occasional lessons in economics.

P. Tahir, *Joan Robinson in Princely India*, Palgrave Studies in the History of Economic Thought, https://doi.org/10.1007/978-3-031-10905-8_14

The political and economic relations between the British India and the states of Princely India were a matter of frequent debate. In December 1927, a committee headed by Harcourt Butler with W.S. Holdsworth and S.C. Peel as members was appointed to inquire into these issues. Specifically, the terms of reference were two-fold. There was a political part to report on the relationship between the Paramount Power and the states of Princely India. More relevant to us, there was a financial and economic part to inquire into the relations between British India and Princely India.

There existed a Chamber of Princes and its Standing Committee to collectively represent the case of the princely states, but it did not have a proper secretariat and professional support. Joan Robinson and K.N. Haksar, the foreign secretary of Gwalior state, had developed a close contact as both shared an interest in the issues of poverty and back-wardness in India. The contact was confirmed by Austin Robinson. Haksar was appointed the director of the Special Organization of the Chamber of Princes created as secretariat. He assisted Sir Leslie Scott, the counsel for the princes. Before the Butler Committee held its first meeting in New Delhi in January 1928, Haksar was brainstorming the economic and financial issues with Joan Robinson. Together, they attended the meeting in New Delhi. The unpublished papers of the Robinsons show that Joan Robinson went to London with the delegation presenting the final case of the princes before the Committee. Haksar is on record having stated that she had done more for the princes than any other European. The record also shows that she continued to be consulted on the economic issues of the princely states even after the submission of the report by the Butler Committee in February 1929. These included Peel Subcommittee on federal finance and a financial enquiry committee in 1932.

In 1929, the case of the princes was published in book form under the title of *The British Crown and the Indian States*. As it was meant to be a report, the cover mentioned sponsoring body of the princes, without naming any specific contributors. The introduction to the book made 'it clear that the following pages are not the work of a single hand' (xxvii). The subtitle, 'An Outline Sketch Drawn Up on Behalf of the Standing Committee of the Chamber of Princes', made it absolutely clear that it was not the work of an individual. It was completed 'By the Directorate of the

Chamber's Special Organisation'. As noted above, Haksar, Joan Robinson's close contact, was the director of Chamber's Special Organisation. It is obvious that two worked together in reading, editing and finalizing various contributions.

This book never found a mention in any of Joan Robinson's writing. There is no reference to it either in her unpublished material collected by King's College Library. Similarly, the extensive works of Austin Robinson contain not a single reference to the book. The collections of his unpublished material at the Marshall Library of Economics and Churchill College Cambridge include manuscripts related to the issues before the Butler Committee, but nothing in regard to its publication. It is safe to conclude that the Robinsons were completely unaware of the publication of *The British Crown and the Indian States*.

In 1986, when I was researching the early career and works of Joan Robinson for my doctoral dissertation at Cambridge, I came across the autobiography of K.M. Panikkar. Like Joan Robinson, he assisted Haksar in preparing the case of the princes before the Butler Committee. Panikkar made a categoric claim that he wrote the early historical section and that the second part dealing with finance was written by Joan Robinson. According to him, Leslie Scott had argued the case before the Butler Committee on the basis of his and Joan Robinson's work.

With this information given by a co-author and a person who was part of the whole process of finalizing the princes' case, I went ahead to write two essays of my dissertation on Joan Robinson's early work, based on the second part of *The British Crown and the Indian States*. Panikkar had first published his autobiography in his native language, Malayalam, in 1954. Obviously, it did not reach the Western readers. It was translated into English in 1977 and reprinted with corrections in 1979. Still, the claim about Joan Robinson remained unnoticed. It came to light, it seems, just around the submission of my dissertation in 1988. At that time, Austin Robinson contended that he, and not Joan Robinson, was the major contributor to the second part of *The British Crown and the Indian States*.

My claim rested on the evidence of a person present on the spot, K.M. Panikkar. His attribution to Joan Robinson has never been challenged. Indeed, the claim had not been challenged till the writing of this book. Panikkar died in 1963. Austin Robinson was not only present on the spot but also alive in 1988. A lot of the work fell in the domain of applied economics, a specialization of Austin Robinson. Joan Robinson had no taste for applied or quantitative analysis. Hence, the two essays attributing sole authorship to Joan Robinson in my dissertation were dropped. However, due to her active involvement in the preparation of the draft and the presentation of the final case, it can be concluded that this was her earliest encounter with the issues and reality of poverty and backwardness, transfer of resources, state monopolies, taxation and public spending. It should not be surprising if there was a reflection of this exposure in her later work on development and underdevelopment.

Subsequently, when Austin Robinson Papers became available at the Marshall Library of Economics, it was discovered that there were a few sections on which Joan Robinson was working specifically. Box 75 (7/1/11914–1992) of Section Seven titled 'Geography Based Career Part 1 India' contains 'undated preface and sections on Customs Revenue and salt production by JVR for draft on Princely States'. There is also 'preface with JVR corrections including attribution to EAGR' (7/1/10 c1927–1928). A folder 'Papers on India' includes 'typescript speech text on Indian States with some JVR corrections' (7/1/11 c1929–1931).

In a letter to Austin Robinson, Joan Robinson talked about 'our note' that became a 'mangled remnant' in the presentation before the Butler Committee (10/3/28, eagr/Box 8/2/1/13/26–32). In another letter to Austin Robinson, Joan Robinson informed that she had added notes on salt and railways to the princes' case presented before the Butler Committee. She was, however, not happy with the results (11/13/28, eagr/Box 8/2/1/13/78–81).

In short, these papers suggest four attributions to Joan Robinson. First, there was an 'undated preface' and a 'preface with JVR corrections including attribution to EAGR'. It seems a preface was jointly written by the Robinsons. Secondly, a 'typescript speech text on Indian States with some JVR corrections' is mentioned. Thirdly, Joan Robinson spoke of 'our note' reduced to a 'mangled remnant'. Fourthly, there is a section on customs revenue. Fifthly, there are references to a section on salt production and a 'note on salt'. Finally, Joan Robinson 'added' a note on railways.

The following table compares the list of sections in the archival manuscripts and the contents appearing in *The British Crown and the Indian States*.

Archival Manuscripts and Published Sections

Archival manuscripts[a]	Published sections[b]
	Introductory
I. Economic Development of States	XXII. Some General Considerations
II. Liabilities of States	XXIII. The Liability of the States in Regard to Defence
III. Contributions to Defence	XXIV. The Contractual Aspect
IV. Treaties	XXV. Defence and Armed Forces. I
V. Payment for Defence	XXVI. Defence and Armed Forces. II
VI. Debt Service and Political Department	XXVII. The Question of Debt
VII. Communications	XXVIII. Communications
VIII. Post Office	XXIX. Posts and Telegraphs
IX. Miscellaneous Services	XXX. Public Works
Another series of drafts	
VII. Contributions of the States in Customs	XXXI Customs and Tariffs
VIII Excise	XXXII. Excise Duties
IX Salt	XXXIII. The Salt Monopoly
X. Railways	XXXIV. Railways
XI Currency and Mint	XXXV. Currency and Mints
XII Income Tax	XXXVI. Income Tax
XIV. Summary of Liabilities and Contributions	XXXVII. Summary of Conclusions
XVII. Recommendations (about refunding customs duties to states)	Appendix II. Payments for Defence
	(1) Territories Ceded
	(2) Lump Sum Payments
	(3) Subsidies
	(4) Tributes

[a]Austin Robinson Papers Box 75 (7/1/10 c1927–1928)

[b] *The British Crown and the Indian States* (1929)

The two columns in the table match but not entirely. There was no preface and no attributions. A 'General Foreword' was written by the foreign minister of the Patiala state, L.F. Rushbrook Williams, for both Part I and Part II. As can be seen, Part II comprised of an introduction, 15 sections and summary of conclusions. Appendix II dealt with 'Payments for Defence'.

The 'Introductory' note gives an overview. The objective is to analyse the economic relationship between British India and Princely India, a territory that did not fit any available political configuration. It is made difficult by the paucity of data. Care is exercised in using whatever information is there to highlight the nature of the problem. In particular, the fiscal relations are examined in 'a conspectus of fact and law' to see if one side is paying more than it should and the needed adjustment. It was also an attempt at 'preparation of the site' for a future constitutional change in India. (One possible solution being discussed, Zollverein, is given in Appendix 1.) It seems someone reduced 'our note' to a 'mangled remnant' while putting together the material for the preface and the 'typescript speech' on Indian States.

From the unpublished material, it is clear that the notes on salt and railways were prepared by Joan Robinson. These are reproduced as Appendices 2 and 3. The section on customs revenue attributed to her seems to have been incorporated in the 'Summary of Conclusions', as the main section on 'Customs and Tariffs' has an unambiguous stamp of Austin Robinson.

The byline was 'The Directorate of the Chamber's Special Organisation'. The Chamber, of course, was the Chamber of Princes. By self-admission that has not been contradicted so far, 'PART L. A Consideration of the Evolution Political Relationship Between the Crown and the States' was written by K.M. Panikkar. Panikkar attributed 'PART II. An Examination of Some Aspects of the Fiscal Questions at Issue Between the States and the Government of India' solely to Joan Robinson. However, Austin Robinson Papers at the Marshall Library of Economics suggest that most of the sections and the basic applied work were contributed by Austin Robinson. Joan Robinson oversaw the process and reviewed and edited Austin Robinson's contributions in the light of the presentational requirements of the Directorate of the Chamber's Special Organisation, besides making specific contributions on state monopolies, namely, salt and railways. All said and done, the experience in Princely India laid the origins of Joan Robinson's interest in the problems of underdevelopment and development.

II

In this background, it is interesting to juxtapose Joan Robinson's early exposure to the problems of underdevelopment and development in the Princely India and her later contributions to the economics of development. Throughout, an effort is made to place the analysis and ideas of Joan Robinson in the perspective of the development notions prevailing at the time of the writing of *The British Crown and the Indian States* as well as the perspective of pioneering development economics.

According to Robert Clower:

Though it is true that Joan Robinson commented on various aspects of our work in Liberia, those comments were rather casual and I have no way of recalling them now. I can't remember her commenting directly or indirectly on the constraints imposed on Liberian development by 'the lack of advantages of imperialistic conquest'.[1]

Liberia provides a hole in the explanations of development or underdevelopment in terms of the absence or presence of a colonial history. As a co-author of Clower observed: 'For those who are impressed by the favourite myth of African political leaders—that before European colonization, Africa must have enjoyed some sort of golden age, because its present economic and social problems are the evil legacy of wicked European colonialism—an examination of Liberia is instructive' (Dalton, 1965, p. 572). The message that Clower's provocative remark seeks to convey is that Joan Robinson who, as he continued in the same letter, 'was greatly impressed by the "spirit" of revolution that prevailed in places like Cuba and China' could not be expected to comment on an economy which in many ways indicated that colonial exploitation would perhaps have shaped the course of development for the better.

A most important conclusion of the discussion so far is that in the case of the princely states, *The British Crown* emphatically placed the causes of backwardness in being left alone in their anachronistic socio-economic organization by the British occupation forces. Their earlier economic forms, according to the study by the Robinsons, lasted longer, therefore, than in British India. As a theme, the necessity of exploitation for development—any kind of development—was to be a critical element in Joan Robinson's view of development in later writings. Exploitation, it may be noted, in Joan Robinson's works was the 'unkindest cut' that a society must suffer in order to produce a surplus for productive investment.

The British let the princely enclaves survive for the limited opportunities for economic exploitation while at the same time pulling out their military teeth through effective disarmament. External economic influences were thus weak. Any internal dynamic was precluded by the self-sufficient village system. The princes were too conservative to disturb this low-level equilibrium. In general, the states were the enclaves of tradition and custom surrounded by British India, showing no early signs of dualistic development that was taking roots in the latter.

Despite a policy of no more annexation, there were three escape routes from the enclave story. First, and the most powerful, was the temporary replacement of the indirect rule by direct rule either under minority administrations or under the pretext of misrule by a prince. What were later termed as progressive states had, in most cases, been under these administrations at one point or the other. These states were forced to accept, during these periods, what Clower described as the 'advantages of imperialistic conquest' in the above-quoted letter and specified in the Liberian study as 'the tangible benefits of roads and schools [and] the more important but less tangible benefits of trained administrators and a civil service ethic of efficient and honest performance' (Clower et al., 1966, p. 10). Add to this the improved revenue collection system and the education of the princes to Europeanize them and the main elements of external penetration through this route started shaping into progressive prototypes such as Mysore and Baroda states. A sharp contrast was presented by Udaipur (Mewar), a state that satisfied the population and the area criteria of a major state. It had a long record of resistance to external penetration. It was also thoroughly backward (Ray, 1978).

This is not to say that all external influences led to development in the states. The second possible escape route to the enclave story, the salt monopoly of British India, caused difficulties for the development of the states. Salt taxation had the longest history of economic penetration in the states, almost independently of the changing political policy of the British towards them. An otherwise laissez-faire government chose to control and manufacture, without hesitation, a significant proportion of the output of as common an item of consumption as salt. It was also notorious because of the excesses committed. A defence is possible for its having the features of a poll tax in an otherwise undertaxed India.[2] For the states it was more than that: it distorted the development of their salt resources, besides emitting negative externalities by turning large fertile tracts into wastelands. The two major salt lake states, Jaipur and Jodhpur (Marwar), were not mentioned among the progressive states despite satisfying all three criteria of the major states. Indeed, they lost the *Marwari* entrepreneurs in large numbers to British India and other states. In this case, the external influence was not on the state structures but on a class of merchants that had come into early contact with the British during the latter's expansionist phase.

The third escape route was the development of transport and communications, mainly railways. Whatever the predominant objective of the railway development, there is no doubt that the interests of British India heavily outweighed those of the states, as did the interests of the paramount power vis-à-vis British India. The states received only the parts that were necessary for the development of main lines, not in any case adequate to start the process of de-isolating them in a significant way.

The origins of backwardness were traced to the sluggish or late arrival of the social and economic influences of the British ascent, depending on the intensity of this contact through the escape routes suggested above. This was the era of free international trade, the consequences of which must now be examined. *The British Crown* considered the contradiction between the village crafts and modern manufactures absolutely crucial. Just as it had to be resolved during England's transition to industrial revolution, and just as it was being resolved in the British Indian transition, so would it have to be resolved in the states' transition. The forces of transition in the princely states towards a money and exchange economy were also the same, as were the mechanics.

There were initial difficulties in the way of this transition. For one thing, the states had their import duty structures intact even during the free trade era. In general, the duties were not high enough to discourage imports. The important explanation for the late arrival of cheap imports was the physical and geographical isolation. In the earlier stages, it was quite rational for the states in Princely India not to intervene to disturb the village economy. It would have exposed it at once to the world economy, with no intervening stage of an internal Indian trade, as the rail links served this purpose inadequately. In making a transition from the village economy, they could not rely on their low-pitched tariffs for easing its pressures. Overtime, the internal rail links improved somewhat, in important cases at the instance of the more progressive states that themselves invested heavily in railways. They embraced industrialization objectives and took a lead in introducing new crops. The dualistic development began to be imitated in the princely states. However, the states were constrained by the fact that they faced the combined competitive onslaught of Britain, British India and Japan, and the decisions about tariff policy were not in their hands. Indeed, the industrial development of British India started to make a strong impact on the states after the former introduced a discriminatory tariff during the interwar period.

After laying out this historical background, the study for *The British Crown* followed the route of a development economist. A development economist is a person concerned with the development of an underdeveloped state. This begs the question of what is development and which economics provides a relevant suffix to it. Part of the answer lies in the historical assessment of the backwardness of the states. They were backward relative to British India, which itself was backward relative to Britain. The states were more backward than British India because the industrial change in the latter was making a delayed entry into the former.

This had important political and economic consequences. Politically, railways, international trade as well as the gradual development of internal trade of the Indian subcontinent, tariff and excise and income tax policies of British India bearing directly on the economies of the states—all these were creating conditions for interdependent development. The states were forced to seek coordinated action at political level, not only with British India but also with each other. An autarkic solution was not even hinted at. In order to develop, the states had to come out of their isolation, not reinforce it by a policy of self-sufficiency. As Toye would put it: development 'process does not occur exclusively inside' a state or group of states (1987, pp. 18–19).

Economically, the princely states had to tread the path trodden by British India—industrial development, reorganization of agriculture, improved education and health and the construction of infrastructure. In essence, the content of development was coextensive with industrialization. Same was the case with the pioneering development economics later. Much has been written since against this lopsidedness, but 'industrialism is what most countries in the Third World aspire to', and the standards of living in industrial economies continue to be examples of what is, 'in principle, possible'.[3] In her later work, Joan Robinson continued to maintain that development was 'rightly identified with industrialization'. More significantly, 'Once the industrial revolution has happened anywhere in the world, the situation for all the rest is radically changed'. Its consequences would be 'followed elsewhere when the political situation allows' (Robinson & Eatwell, 1973, p. 323). As a matter of approach, Joan Robinson had 'always taken the view that [development] is essentially a political question' (Robinson, 1974, p. xi).

The political question before the states of Princely India was that the implementation of the industrialization strategy required resources in addition to what the states could muster themselves. The need for additional capital arose as the states, having been backward relatively to British India for over a century, were now feeling the pressure for change and wanted something done about it. Backwardness as a concept was understood much in the way the pioneering development economics would later interpret underdevelopment; it referred, in the main, to slower pace of industrialization. While the leading states did not seem to have fared any worse than British India in terms of resource mobilization, the new requirements of the states' development could not be met while the major source of revenue since the end of free trade, sea customs, left them high and dry. Moreover, the rise of population after a century of peace added to the requirements of capital equipment even to maintain the existing low standard of living.

This was the sense of development in *The British Crown*. Regarding the question of what kind of 'economics' should be suffixed to 'development'—to make it development economics—it is only necessary to look at some of the concepts employed or underlying the analysis, as also their context: Division of labour, specialization, risk, laissez-faire, standard theory of public finance, especially the benefit principle, equivalence of indirect taxation and state monopolization, income tax effects on capital movements, velocity of circulation of money, protection and external economies. This is nothing but the stock-in-trade of economics as taught anywhere at the time of her writing and also nowadays. The difference is that all these concepts were the elements in the formulation of a development policy for underdeveloped structures, which context necessitated an allowance for local peculiarities. The difference between the states of underdevelopment and development was one of degree, not kind. Development economics is the art of capturing these peculiarities.[4]

Additional resources were required for development, and the case to secure them from British India was based on economic analysis in such a way that the time and place were not glossed over, though not always with success. The main case for the states' right to claim a share in the British Indian revenues was provided by sea customs. The case prepared by Austin Robinson for this purpose was unmatched either in detail or analytical sense by any studies carried out before or in the decade after this study.[5] Though crude by today's standards, it was the first-ever attempt, in an underdeveloped context, to conduct a disaggregated analysis of the import structure and use it as a base for revenue claims of contributing units. The peculiar context of the princely states posed difficult problems. Due to their backwardness and meagre local production base, their interest was that of a consumer. At the same time, the urge to industrialize opposed the potential producer interest to the consumer bias. They were states within a state, contributing to customs revenue like the provinces of the latter but denied a share in it or public spending, for which purpose they were considered foreign territories. A discriminatory tariff existed for the states as an externality, available in steel, while the states might need it in silk, hence the emphasis on the interdependent nature of development and the need for policy coordination. Similar cooperation in the case of income tax, argued Austin Robinson, would rationalize capital movements as well as encourage the states to introduce this modern fiscal instrument.

Railways have always occupied a prominent position in the discussions of external effects. Joan Robinson's analysis was no exception. So far as the British Indian railways charged directly for the use of the service provided, the benefit was internalized, with no room for dispute. The problem arose when external benefits such as development of territories and markets, improvement of economic life and the raising of economic values were brought into consideration. She conceded the existence of these benefits, but stressed that to hold the states liable to pay for these benefits assumed that all railways were owned by British India. Operated directly by them or leased to the British Indian railways, the states had a considerable mileage of their own. Her case rested on the presumption that the external benefits of railways amounted to mutual backscratching. In the process, the case for the states was overstated. It would be hard to believe that the 13 per cent of the railway mileage belonging to the states could fully reciprocate the external benefits of the 87 per cent of the track under British Indian ownership. Similarly, the greater average length of haul from the states for sea-borne foreign trade as compared with British India implied not only a greater liability to pay as Joan Robinson suggested but also the beginning of the end of their isolation, which she had identified as among the important causes of their backwardness. The total benefit exceeded the internalized benefit of the service provided and charged for, despite mileage discontinuities. Among the external disbenefits, she counted non-participation in the railway tariff policy. This was true, but an example given in support does not seem appropriate. A certain destination could be reached by two routes, a shorter route passing partly through Gwalior state via its line leased to the main line and a longer British Indian route. Tariff for the shorter route was fixed higher than the longer route. She found it to be unjust and an attempt to divert traffic away from the state lines. Her criticism seems to ignore demand considerations operating on the shorter route or a policy of decongestion. That is not the case. What she ignores is a peculiarity of railways in India. It is these peculiarities that a development economist has to watch out and account for. The discriminatory rates had more to do with the irrationality of operating all railway systems as independent organizations for the purpose of tariff and the resulting mileage discontinuities.[6]

With external benefits assumed to be mutually cancelled, the railway service was easy to conceptualize as a publicly provided private service. Her insistence that there was little difference between an indirect tax and monopolistic extortions thus falls in place. Railway fares were in the nature of an indirect tax designed to raise revenue for the British Indian state. A price exceeding marginal cost was charged, yielding a profit that was used as a contribution to the revenue budget of the government of British India. The states' subjects paid in excess of the cost of service provided and, therefore, had a right to a share in it.[7]

Joan Robinson devoted most of her arguments to the sharing of profits. In their early phase, railways had been running losses, and their guaranteed return of 5 per cent had to be secured through the contribution from the British Indian budget (Macpherson, 1955, p. 186). In this regard, she maintained that a study like hers covering that period would show that the states were sharing the burden of losses. This is no fudging, if a global view is taken. Salt revenue, involving a poll tax on the states' subjects and a forcible takeover of an important resource of the states by British India, could be construed as their contribution to the railway losses. The railways were not a perfect example of a state monopoly imposing the burden of an indirect tax,[8] as Joan Robinson's case for the neutralization of externalities is not convincing. Salt, however, provides the classic case of mobilizing resources through state monopoly, with the states' right to have a share in the excise duty realized from it.

In monetary matters, the peculiar characteristics of backwardness noticed in *The British Crown* were the metallic currency preference and its lower velocity of circulation, as well as a meagre density of financial intermediaries. Unlike Keynes, the study was against hoarding the currency profits. The states were shown to have a rightful share in these profits and, as far as they were concerned, they formed part of the additional resources sought from British India for capital accumulation. A useful insight related to the reduction of the taxable capacity of the states as a result of resource pre-emption by the British Indian taxes. Unlike the modem development economists, however, the study did not favour an agricultural income tax. It was a clever strategy, though, to keep the states' taxes low enough to achieve incentive effects and turn on the British Indian tap for revenue objectives.

The British Crown took a global view of the transfer of resources from the princely states to British India, as against the common practice of setting off the high rise of customs revenue against the proliferating defence burden.[9] In so doing, *The British Crown was* a study that was the brainchild not merely of a development economist; it became an applied development economic investigation. Not only the economic concepts were extended to the context of development, an attempt was also made to prepare plausible and meaningful estimates. Harcourt was puzzled by Joan Robinson's lack of interest in applied or empirical work.[10] During the sojourn to Princely India, she had an early exposure to applied work in the field of development. As for her lack of interest in empirical work, the puzzle continues to hold.

The British Crown contended that the states were not liable to contribute to the defence burden through the fiscal system because under the arrangements for disarming them, the British had specified the tributes and the territories to defray these costs. It made alternative estimates to demonstrate that the states were shouldering their burden of defence under these arrangements. According to one, these contributions by the states would support one-third of the strength of the British Indian army, more than their population proportion. Another estimate worked out the liability of the states under the assumption of a federation. This amount stood at about one-third of the resources being transferred through the fiscal system. In principle, however, the states had been disarmed in return for security guarantees. Therefore, the study estimated a net transfer of resources from the states. It is the estimate of the states' contributions to the customs duties that shows the attributes of a latter-day development economist. The classification of commodities into categories similar to essentials, luxuries and intermediate and capital goods is one; allowing them weights to reflect the relative backwardness of the states is another, and working in an environment where the only undistorted data are those that do not exist is yet another.

What is conspicuous by the absence is a general explanation of the backwardness of the states in terms of the surplus transfer. This is even more surprising in a country known for its drain controversies. An obvious reason is the fact that the resource outflow had become significantly high only after the introduction of discriminatory tariff by British India following World War I. More important was the irony that the princely state of Mysore's fame was not only for the crushing burden of tribute imposed on it but also as the most progressive state of the Indian subcontinent, British

India not excluded. The correlation between backwardness or drain was not clear. What was clear was that the slowness of the contact with the more modern imperial forces prolonged the life of pre-capitalist formations in the states.

The purpose of estimating resource transfer was not to blame backwardness on it but to seek its reversal to finance capital accumulation in the states. These were the crude beginnings of Joan Robinson's later theory of long-run economic growth. Also traceable here is her later view of a strong state as a vehicle for rapid acceleration of capital accumulation. While all princely states were authoritarian, only a handful translated authority into an effective capacity to make policies and implement projects. The states could not grant themselves protection or line up external finance without approaching officialdom in Delhi or London. But internal finance and low own taxation were the first steps required for dynamic leaderships in the more progressive states to overcome the external hurdle. These states invariably had gone through the first escape route mentioned above. These leaders were not conservative believers in laissez-faire. They had acquired European ideals of progress and 'convinced without argument or experiment that whatever was best for Europe was best for' their states. A number of these rulers were not natives of their own states, nor were some better known prime ministers. Others had administration installed by the British during the minority period, which considered modernization to be their major task. These states embodied what has been described as a 'state bias' (Nolan & White, 1984, p. 77), acting in their own defined interests of industrialization and capital accumulation. With no wars to fight, some of the princes were running a development race. The case in *The British Crown* contributed to the hope of making additional resources available for this race.

Before the pioneering of modern development economics after World War II, 'economic development' was the province of historians. In the case of India, two leading historians were women, Knowles (1925) and Anstey (1929). Their prime concern was British India. If the arguments of the preceding chapters and the evidence presented are broadly accepted, then an important conclusion is obvious. It was also a woman, Joan Robinson, who focused on Princely India, which was neglected by Knowles and Anstey. The fact that the states in Princely India were backward relative even to British India gave Joan Robinson an opportunity not only to look at the historical roots of underdevelopment or backwardness but also to attempt to apply analytical concepts learned at the Marshall-dominated

Cambridge to these issues, as well as to formulate, along with Austin Robinson, a policy-oriented view of ways to overcome it. This brought her closer to the spirit of the pioneering development economics. She noticed that the assumptions of the received theory did not capture the Indian reality, the two most important examples being the international division of labour and the peasant rationality. After returning to Cambridge, she was to conclude that the conventional wisdom reflected even Western reality imperfectly. Still not satisfied, she continued to investigate the defects in orthodox theory until she discovered that it was mainly the notion of equilibrium, and not merely its other worldly assumptions, that rendered orthodox theory useless. And not only in developed economies. It was 'inappropriate' in the context of economic development as well (Robinson, 1963, p. 300). This was only a short step from a structuralist view. However, we find her criticizing the work of Chenery and others. According to her, the interesting questions revolve around

> a discussion of how far the differences between countries can be accounted for by different natural endowments, how much by the character of labour force, how much by past history, how much by the intentions of current policies, and how much by the relative success in carrying them out. (Robinson, 1980, p. 132)

The last-mentioned questions of policy intentions and ability to carry them out hit the nail on the head. To put her idea of progress in the Princely India study of the 1920s in schematic terms, development was coextensive with European industrialization, which required capital formation to counteract the effect of growth of population. As the states were too poor to mobilize adequate resources, a case was prepared to keep within the states the resources being transferred to British India. A point of enormous contemporary significance is that the backwardness was blamed not on the externally manipulated resource transfer but on the internally preserved structure of the static village economy. The transfer of resources became significant only after the end of the free trade. Underdevelopment was a pre-existing condition, perpetuated by the laissez-faire attitude of the conservative rulers of the princely states. Surplus transfer or unequal exchange never appealed to her as the major determinants of backwardness. The reason was that such theories taught the 'Southern intellectuals … to moan about injustice instead of showing workers and peasants the cause of their misery' (Robinson, 1978, pp. 383–4).

The two well-known presumptions in Joan Robinson's later work on development are thus noticeable in her earliest confrontation with the problem of poverty and backwardness. These relate to the emphasis on fixed capital, referring essentially to the creation of industrial assets and supportive infrastructure, and the role of the state. Compared to the modern usage of underdevelopment, the term backwardness was not vague in suggesting what was involved in outgrowing it. Development was like a ladder: British India had to catch up with Europe, and the Princely India had to catch up with British India. A Gerschenkron-type[11] view was implicit here. The farther down the ladder a country was, the greater the role for the state accumulation.

In the end, we must take a look at the nature and social circumstances of Joan Robinson's Princely India connection. The foregoing analysis indicates a concern for the political economy of an Indian *Zollverein*. It does not seem to have been a regrettable necessity of an 'upper middle-class English family' background (Harcourt, 1979, p. 663) nor, if you will, a Cambridge education.[12] Her interest in the problems of Princely India seems nothing like the pastime of a social class fellow. Purely in terms of economic analysis, the existence of a great number of internally autonomous states surrounded by a de facto unitary economic state of the size of British India must have presented a challenge to Joan Robinson's 'incisive mind' (Harcourt, 1984, p. 640). It held out the prospects of investigating economies of scale, externalities and other benefits of a large economy. These were among the issues she focused on after returning from India. It was, in fact, the earliest opportunity to analyse *Zollverein*-type possibilities in a backward economy. The complex fiscal dimension, with an utterly wanting statistical base of the princely states of the 1920s, was by no means a task for an analyst with no taste for challenge. The most important dimension of the challenge was the requirement to apply economic theory in a developmental context, a task lacking any precedence worthy of note.

During 1927–1932, the period in which Joan Robinson was intimately connected with the issues of an Indian *Zollverein*, none of the parties with stakes in the future of India could have imagined that within a decade and a half would take place the Partition of India and the end of the British *raj*.[13] A federation keeping the British connection and an all-India *Zollverein* seemed the best that could be hoped for by way of economic and political advance. The focus was on finding practical ways to overcome the obstacles to development in this direction. There were serious economic problems to be sorted out before an arrangement acceptable to the princes could be worked out, so as to elicit their willing cooperation for the federal project and an economic *Zollverein*. Joan Robinson's contribution must be seen in the light of these efforts to preserve an Indian economic community. The nationalists, as noted above, would not hesitate to make short work of the princes. So, for Joan Robinson to work from the side of Princely India on the *Zollverein* project and to maintain a nationalist stance at the same time would be contradictory.

Yet this very position has been suggested. Marcuzzo (1985, p. 6) quotes from an obituary in an unspecified issue of the *Economic and Political Weekly* to the effect that Joan Robinson 'attracted the grave displeasure of the authorities by her support and friendship with (sic) the leaders of the movement for Indian independence'. As was pointed out above, it was not yet clear then whether or not there was an independence movement. Even the Nehru Committee of 1928 stood for a dominion status, which 'will be as much the King's Government as the present Government of India'.[14] At any rate, no issue of that journal since Joan Robinson's death on 3 August 1983 contains the obituary from which Marcuzzo gleans these observations. The journal did publish one (A.M., 1983), but it does not even touch upon the subject. In her correspondence, one sees Gandhi and other names named and the *Harijans* and the Hindu-Muslim issues discussed, but there is no hint of a significant rapport with the nationalist leadership. After Joan Robinson's death, Narasimhan (1983, p. 217) mentioned Joan Robinson's association with Sarojini Naidu, a nationalist activist. In Garratt's correspondence with her, we find details of what is known as the Meerut case against the Indian communists.[15] However, this does not provide an adequate basis from which to deduce an active interest in the Indian nationalist movement. Rather, the connection was with Princely India, through an interest excited by the challenge of development in an extremely complex sociopolitical environment.

NOTES

1. Letter to the author, 10 March 1987. The reference to the work in Liberia is Clower et al. (1966).
2. Shah (1927, pp. 249–56), Kumar (1984b, p. 928).
3. Bell (1987, p. 818). This is from the new Palgrave. The old edition, available during Joan Robinson's undergraduate days, described the following as one sense of evolution or development: 'the growth of new forms of

industrial organization, keeping pace with new wants, new powers of science over nature, and ne political relations'. The article went on to conclude: 'The conception of economics as a body of doctrines of universal validity or absolute truth is now discredited; but the conception of 'economic categories' as a permanent basis of further development has gained ground' (Palgrave's, 1925, p. 573). The concept of industrial organization was not confined to business firms. Morison's recommended text at Cambridge was about the industrial organization of a province in India. See Morison (1906) and Cambridge (1922, p. 391). *The British Crown* characterized the princely states, in comparison with British India, as 'much less developed either in political views or in industrial organization' (1929, p. 184).

4. On the meaning of development economics and its continued relevance, see Toye (1984, p. 6).

5. See Appendix 1 for later official studies.

6. See Tiwari (1940, pp. 71–2).

7. For an elaboration of the equivalence between an indirect tax and a state monopoly, see Shoup (1969, pp. 285 8).

8. Ramaiya (1930, p. 209) maintained that the railways were only getting a modest return on vast sums of capital invested. The states' subjects were charged for the service provided and not taxed in anyway. However, the railways were making a significant contribution to the British Indian budget. An allowance for the externalities was the real problem, dismissed by Joan Robinson as mutually cancelling, while Ramaiya completely disregarded it. It may be noted that the states were not allowed to impose company tax on railways operating on their territories (Khan, 1937, p. 127).

9. See Appendix 1 for such theories.

10. Harcourt (1984, p. 652).

11. Gerschenkron (1952).

12. Joan Robinson's upper-class relatives were present even in India. For instance, the governor of Sind province, L. Graham, was married to an aunt. See his letter of 8 January 1931 in the JVR Collection, King's Modern Archives, which touches on the Round Table Conference. Narasimhan gives further details about Joan Robinson's class background and connections in India. 'Both her father and her grandfather were generals', and 'there were already family connections on both sides with India. On her side, there were Civil Service connections'. But it would be simplistic to conclude about a person who would soon be labelled by *The Economist* (1949, p. 95) as 'being at once an economist of standing' and 'a socialist' that her interest in the issues before the Butler Committee and beyond was a mere reflection of leisure-class affinities. Narasimhan has a

telling way of bearing this out: 'Connections like these produce their own pressures. One can only draw attention to the sheer weight of the burden of consciousness on a more than usually intelligent, growing girl. One heard from her happy stories of riding and walking, but one also sensed a consciousness of the reaches of power and human fallibility. Most important of all, though, is something she used to say in a voice of outraged dismissal, 'You know, there was an "us" and a "them"' (Narasimhan, 1983, pp. 215–7).

13. See Copland (1982, p. 313).
14. Quoted in Menon (1956, p. 25).
15. G.T. Garratt's letter to Joan Robinson, 2 July 1931. There is some evidence also of the interest she showed in events on the eve of the Partition. See Harry M. Bull's pessimistic letter to Joan Robinson, 26 June 1947. JVR Collection, King's Modern Archives.

REFERENCES

UNPUBLISHED MATERIAL

G.T. Garratt's letter to Joan Robinson. (1931, July 2). JVR Collection, King's Modern Archives.
Harry M. Bull's letter to Joan Robinson. (1947, June 26). JVR Collection, King's Modern Archives.
L. Graham's letter to Joan Robinson. (1931, January 8). JVR Collection, King's Modern Archives.
Robert Clower's letters to the author. (1987, March 10, April 8).

PUBLISHED WORKS

A.M. (1983). Obituary: The One Who Said Boo. *Economic and Political Weekly*, *18*, 1461–1462.
Anstey, V. (1929). *The Economic Development of India*. Longmans and Green.
Bell, C. (1987). Development Economics. In J. Eatwell, M. Milgate, & P. Newman (Eds.), *The New Palgrave: A Dictionary of Economics* (Vol. 1). Macmillan.
Cambridge, University of. (1922). *The Student's Handbook*. Cambridge University Press.
Clower, R. W., Dalton, G., et al. (1966). *Growth without Development: An Economic Survey of Liberia*. Northwestern University Press.
Copland, I. (1982). *The British Raj and the Indian States*. Orient Longman.

Dalton, G. (1965). History, Politics and Economic Development in Liberia. *Journal of Economic History, 25,* 569–591.

Gerschenkron, A. (1952). *Economic Backwardness in Historical Perspective.* Harvard University Press.

Harcourt, G. C. (1979). Robinson, Joan. In H. W. Spiegel & W. J. Samuels (Eds.), *International Encyclopaedia of the Social Sciences, Bibliographical Supplement* (Vol. 18). The Free Press.

Harcourt, G. C. (1984). Harcourt on Robinson. In *Contemporary Economists in Perspective* (Vol. 1, Part B). Jai Press.

Khan, M. M. (1937). *Federal Finance.* Robert Hale.

Knowles, L. C. A. (1925). *The Economic Development of the British Overseas Empire.* George Routledge.

Kumar, D. (Ed.). (1984b). The Fiscal System. In *D. Kumar (1984a).*

Macpherson, W. J. (1955). Investment in Indian Railways, 1845–1875. *Economic History Review, 8,* 177–186.

Marcuzzo, M. C. (1985). *Joan Violet Robinson.* Universita Degali Studi, Dipartimento di Economia Politica. Mimeo.

Menon, V. P. (1956). *The Story of the Integration of the Indian States.* Longmans, Green.

Morison, T. (1906). *The Industrial Organization of an Indian Province.* John Murray.

Narasimhan, S. (1983). Joan Robinson: In the Radical Vein a Laywoman's Homage. *Cambridge Journal of Economics, 7,* 213–219.

Nolan, P., & White, G. (1984). Urban Bias, Rural Bias or State Bias? Urban-Rural Relations in Post-Revolutionary China. *Journal of Development Studies, 20,* 52–81.

Palgrave's Dictionary of Political Economy, Vol. 1. (1925). Macmillan.

Ramaiya, A. (1930). The Indian States and British India: Their Financial Relations. *Empire Review, 51,* 208–211.

Ray, R. K. (1978). Mewar. The Breakdown of the Princely Order. In *Jeffrey (1978).*

Robinson, J. (1963). Review of G. Maynard. Economic Development and the Price Level. *Economic Journal, 73,* 299–300.

Robinson, J. (1974). Introduction. In J. Robinson (Ed.), *Selected Economic Writings.* Oxford University Press.

Robinson, J. (1978). 'Formalism Versus Dogma,' Review of I. Steedman, *Marx after Sraffa. Journal of Contemporary Asia, 8,* 381–384.

Robinson, J. (1980). Review of H. Chenery. Structural Change and Development Policy. *Journal of Developing Areas, 15,* 131–132.

Robinson, J., & Eatwell, J. (1973). *An Introduction to Modern Economics.* McGraw-Hill.

Shah, K. T. (1927). *Sixty Years of Indian Finance.* P.S. King and Son.

Shoup, C. S. (1969). *Public Finance.* Weidenfeld and Nicolson.

The British Crown and the Indian States. (1929). P.S. King and Son.

The Economist. (1949). 156, 95.

Tiwari, R. D. (1940). *Railway Rates Policy.* New Book Company.

Toye, J. (1984). *A Defence of Development Economics.* University College.

Toye, J. (1987). *Dilemmas of Development: Reflections on the Counter-revolution in Development Theory and Practice.* Basel Blackwell.

Appendix 1: Beyond the Butler Report: The Political Economy of an Indian *Zollverein*

It may be recalled that one of the alternative estimates of defence liability worked out in *The British Crown and the Indian States* assumed a federal structure. This was not merely one way of looking at the problem. An important objective of the study was to identify the difficulties in the way of economic unity and initiate attempts towards their resolution.

> [I]f any new constitutional machinery is to be set up by which the economic unity of India may be made a reality and the states be asked of their own free will to come into such an arrangement, federal or other, it is absolutely vital to know exactly what the economic foundations are upon which to build. The object of this note is to make some contribution towards the preparation of the site. (*The British Crown*, 1929, p. 137)

A beginning had been made, but more remained to be done to firm up details. The Robinsons admitted the limits of their knowledge. With a view to making further progress on the economic and technical matters, the setting up of an expert committee was suggested.

> Our main purpose in this survey has been to show that in our opinion the peoples of Indian States are at present subjected to a considerable burden of taxation for which they receive no return and for which there can be no justification. The difficulties which we have met in examining this state of affairs have, however, made it clear that an authoritative estimate of the

© The Author(s), under exclusive license to Springer Nature Switzerland AG 2022
P. Tahir, *Joan Robinson in Princely India*, Palgrave Studies in the History of Economic Thought,
https://doi.org/10.1007/978-3-031-10905-8

actual amount of the burden can only be made by somebody with powers and with knowledge far greater than our own ....

As regards procedure, we have urged that, after the Indian States Committee have reported, and the principles recommended by them have been considered and settled in consultation with the Princes, the expert body we recommend should be set up in order that it may, upon the basis of the principles so agreed, pronounce with authority upon the figures which we have discussed. (*The British Crown*, 1929, p. 215)

The Butler Committee accepted this suggestion.

The questions involved are very intricate...We recommend that an expert body should be appointed to enquire into (1) the reasonable claims of the state or group of states to a share in the customs revenue, and (2) the adequacy of their contributions to imperial burdens. The question of a *Zollverein* would come at once before such a body. The terms of reference would be discussed with the Princes, who would, of course, be represented on the enquiring body. In the result a financial settlement would be made between the Imperial Government and the state or group of states on the basis of settlements made in the past between the Imperial and Provincial Governments. Such a procedure would no doubt take time. Much new ground will have to be broken. (*Report*, 1929, p. 44)

Thus the Butler Committee agreed with the Robinsons' proposal that the question of economic community be investigated further to find out its costs and benefits, but failed to enunciate any guiding principles. An article by 'E.A.J. Robinson'[1] reviewed the post-Butler Committee situation as follows.

The economic issue was in a sense an appendage of the political. The treaties of the States appeared to guarantee them defence, while limiting their external sovereignty. Since central revenues are raised mainly by customs duties and spent mainly on defence, the States claimed that their subjects were in fact being taxed to provide a service which was already guaranteed to them by their treaties, and for which many of them had already paid by tributes or cessions of territory. The committee turned over the whole of this economic case to a new machinery which they wished to have set up, without laying down any guiding principle on the main point at issue.

The outlook for future was viewed thus.

An opportunity offers itself now for the beginnings of co-operation. The Butler Committee has recommended a *Zollverein*, wherein the States shall abolish their internal customs barriers, receiving in exchange a share of maritime customs. It is to be hoped that both the Government and the States will do everything in their power to achieve this, and make it the beginning of closer working. Whatever happens, it would be disastrous if a first attempt at cooperation were allowed to break down through hard bargaining on the part of the Government, where strict justice admitted a smaller share than would justify a State in giving up a valuable source of revenue. A longer view would suggest that, just as in the case of Germany, time will extinguish all temporary losses in a greater volume of trade, and in closer harmony between the States and British India, and that a few thousand rupees are well spent if they can lay the foundation of a federation. (Robinson, E.A.J., 1929, p. 393)

These warnings went unheeded, and the federal project as well as a negotiated *Zollverein* failed to materialize. The government of British India indulged in hard bargaining on giving up every *anna*, while the princes failed to grasp the ultimate gains from trade and development.

The proposed expert body was never set up, as the Butler Committee report was rejected by the princes as well as the nationalists. For instance, a nationalist commentator saw the economic and financial findings of the Butler Committee as of 'less far-reaching importance' (Das,1929, p. 22). The committee themselves seemed to agree. While the chairman and the lawyer member chose to write on the political and constitutional issues after the submission of the report (Butler, 1930; Holdsworth, 1930), the economist member—Sidney Peel—never found the subject fit for his further consideration. The economic issue, as was pointed out by 'E.A.J. Robinson', was merely an appendage to the political.

There was a strong reaction from the nationalist politicians. The Nehru Committee report condemned it as an attempt to create an Ulster in India,[2] while it disappointed the princes' hopes of getting a suitable settlement of their revenue claims. All was not lost for the states as they had scored a strategic point in that the Butler Committee legitimized their position that the states obligations to the British Crown could not be transferred to a future British Indian legislature without their consent. For their part, the British succeeded in their attempt to present Princely India as a force apart from the Muslim League and the Congress parties and an ally which supported the British connection in no uncertain terms.

From the Butler Committee, the arena shifted to the Round Table Conference, with a full contingent of the princes represented as a third force. The Layton report on federal finance, which formed part of the report by the boycotted Simon Commission regarding the constitutional reform, came out in the year after the Butler report and just before the first session of the Round Table Conference in November 1930. The Layton report was the first professional and technical vindication of the main economic points raised in the Robinsons' study: the states were burdened with indirect taxes, particularly customs, the burden of the latter being proportionate to the states consumption of imports; their own taxes had to be lower than they would otherwise be; and that tariff protection for the generally backward states was not as beneficial as it was for British India. More important, a share in tax revenue was only a part of the problem.

Progress in the direction of a federation would also require policy coordination, not only with British India but also with the provinces. However, while the Butler report had spoken of compensating the states for these contributions, to be determined by the expert body proposed in it, the Layton report adopted a view of contributions and liabilities embodied in a federal project. As an illustration of the problem, the Butler report assumption of the states' consumption of imports being two-thirds of the consumption per capita in British India, which allowed the states 16 per cent of the imports as their share, was used to argue that contribution to customs corresponding to this share was less than the defence liability of the states on the basis of population (Layton, 1930, pp. 270–3, 279). If the contributions to customs had dramatically increased during the interwar period as compared with the pre-war period, defence spending had risen even more, leaving the states in arrears.

The Robinsons, as was seen above, also had the federal project in view, with assumptions that were more realistic than those of Layton. The overall share of the states in the consumption of imports, estimated by a rational breakdown of imports rather than an across-the-board percentage used by Layton, was placed higher at 18 per cent. Further, a downward adjustment of the defence expenditure was required to allow for the significant component of internal security, as the states would have no interest in it as members of a federation. Further still, tributes, subsidies for the defence establishments and the revenues from the ceded territories would also have to be adjusted.

That this was the brief for the states at the Round Table Conference is evident from the stand taken by Haksar at the first session. Haksar, it may be recalled, was in close touch with Joan Robinson on these issues. He was an important member of the states' delegation and a member of the Peel[3] subcommittee on federal finance, set up in the second session. Although federal finance was not discussed in the first session, he repeated the basic argument in *The British Crown* (1929) and urged the federal structure subcommittee 'to explore this question of the financial contribution of the States' (Indian Round Table, 1931, p. 10).

Haksar believed that no European at any time had done more for the princes than Joan Robinson.[4] She had returned to England in the summer of 1928, where the three sessions of the Round Table Conference were held in the early 1930s. Her correspondence during this period confirms her involvement. She had continued to brief the states on the presentation of their case.[5] By raising hopes that the federal project, of which an Indian *Zollverein* was the important economic manifestation, would yield net economic and financial gains, she had contributed her bit to the future development of India. The economic arguments in *The British Crown* were instrumental in bringing home the benefits of federation to those who had hitherto been more concerned with personal privileges and seen customs and currency problems as ceremonial issues of sovereignty rather than the gut issues of economic policy to be thrashed out by negotiation. With the princes, it appears, the immediate revenue gains were more important than the long-term economic advantages of a *Zollverein*. Their position hardened, as noted before, when the government of British India started fighting for each rupee of the prospective loss of revenue.

The first session was a lacklustre affair, having been boycotted by the Congress party. The issues of federal finance and *Zollverein* came up for discussion in the second session of the Round Table Conference, held during September–December 1931. In June 1931, Joan Robinson had been warned about the exploratory discussions going on between the states and the government of British India and the amount of hard work awaiting her.[6] In a memorandum prepared for the conference, the government of British India made three points of note. First, it conceded that the feudal tributes extracted from over 200 states would have no place in a federation, but their end must be phased out over a long enough period. In the transitional period, the tributes were to be renamed cash contributions. Secondly, the problem of ceded territories was recognized, but it was held to be of concern to no more than three to four states. Thirdly, it was conceded that 47 states maintained troops satisfying British Indian standards at a cost of Rs. 250 lakh. The alternatives were either to reduce the defence expenditure correspondingly or to declare the claim on this account inadmissible on the ground that the maintenance of these troops was not obligatory. In sum, the approach of British India was to stand its ground; 'the position hitherto has not been one in which on balance the Indian States have contributed more than what is a fair equivalent for the benefits which they have received' (Indian Round Table, 1932b, Appendix I, pp. 501–3). Haksar was referring to this approach when he stated before the federal structure committee the position of the princes: 'Indeed, it has been said that, if the position were examined, it could only lead to the discovery that the states were not pulling their weight'. With the force of the Robinsons' analysis behind him, he strongly argued for an enquiry into the claims. The Maharaja of Bikaner made it clear that there was no question of joining the federation without first knowing the liabilities and obligations (Indian Round Table, 1932b, pp. 155, 94).

The discussion was taking place in the context of the report of the federal finance subcommittee, the so-called Peel report. It laid down the principle that the units should have similar sharing of federal burdens and that the special claims arising from tributes, territories and the cost of the states' forces be handed over to an enquiry body (Indian Round Table, 1932a, pp. 46–50). It is interesting to know that both Gandhi and Jinnah felt that the states had a right to know beforehand what the federal project involved, though Gandhi would rather have the Peel subcommittee rework a formula acceptable to the states than to set up a future enquiry (Indian Round Table, 1932b, pp. 191–3). Both the princes and the government of British India, however, were dead set on a future enquiry body, the princes believing that it would uphold their claims and the government of British India convinced that the net outcome would only place the states in arrears. The nationalist cause had been taken over by the government of British India.[7] After the Butler report and just before the first session of the Round Table Conference, the British officialdom in India had become active in preparing their counter-case.[8] A special committee was set up, which produced a first volume in 1930 and the second in 1932. This committee had no qualms about phasing out tributes and changing their name, but emphasized the optional nature of the states' forces. A new feature was the finding that the ceded territories, once all federal claims were allowed for, yielded either none or insignificant revenue surpluses over provincial spending (India, 1930–1932).

Eventually, the much-debated enquiry body was set up, called the Davidson committee (Indian States Enquiry, 1932). In its report, this committee bore out the Robinsons' contention that tributes and ceded territories were nothing but different ways of paying for the British protection. With a consensus on the phasing out of the tributes, there was no escape from settling the question of territories. It had, however, been easy to agree to phase out what the Robinsons described as bad bargains, that is, tributes. But the territories had turned out to be a bargain. The Robinsons had mentioned the case of Berar, a territory which was yielding in revenue far more than the amount envisaged in the original agreement, indeed, even higher than the rapidly rising rate of defence cost. Interestingly, this lucrative territory was specifically excluded from the terms of reference of the Davidson committee. As for the other territories, the committee decided that the net revenue at the time of cession should be set off against the defence liability of the states after they join the federation. In other words, they were treated as if they too were bad bargains like the cash tributes.

For foregoing a revenue claim of over a thousand lakh rupees estimated by the Robinsons in *The British Crown*, the states were offered a settlement of about Rs. 50 lakh.[9] So far as the princes were concerned, this is the point where the federal project began to fizzle out. There was a hint of truth in the sarcasm of the arch states' buster, Menon, when he remarked that with the end of 'any hope that rulers could gain any financial profit by joining the federation', the federal project became a dead horse.[10] The leading princes never returned in person to the third session of the Round Table Conference. Panikkar discussed the prospects of the conference with Joan Robinson in an optimistic tone.[11] Around this time, Joan Robinson was fully involved in finishing up her 'nightmare', a reference to *The Economics of Imperfect Competition*.[12] She had taken a plunge into 'high theory'[13] and would not return to the theme of development until 1943.

As for the *Zollverein*, not one but two—India and Pakistan—were set up in less than two decades. In the process, the princely states disappeared as political entities. With them also disappeared any serious interest in their study. Small wonder, an Indian economist claimed after Partition that the 'method, manner and suddenness of the revolutionary change in the political structure of India manufactured by the iron hand of the Deputy Prime Minister [Sardar Patel, in charge of the Ministry of States] far exceeds the achievement of the iron Chancellor of Germany of the eighties of the last century' (Kibe, 1951, p. 399). The more important among these 'anachronisms', destined for extinction, had, just before that event, per capita total revenue, tax revenue, total expenditure and social expenditure much above the erstwhile provinces of British India (Sarma, 1951, p. 395). What is even more noteworthy is the fact, revealed officially at the time of the integration of the states with India after Partition, that the important states like Mysore, Travancore and Cochin would lose many times more revenue to the federation than the latter would spend in them (India, 1950).

The 'Cambridge school' of historians sought to change the focus of inquiry from the sterile, Congress-inspired question of how 'the British came to leave' to 'how they managed to stay so long'. The result was many studies of princely states. But the school admits study of capitalism and economic development within individual states did not get attention.[14] For research in this direction, *The British Crown* is an important source. Applying dependency framework to the princely states runs into serious problems. The case of Mysore enables comparisons of direct British rule, indirect British rule and the freedom from British rule. In a dependency analysis of Mysore, Hettne (1978, p. 377) sees economic development taking place with more autonomy since 1910 under indirect rule, but does not quite know where to put the blame for the reverse economic gear after 1947—on colonialism that existed no more or on independence? The neocolonial argument will be even more problematic. Who is the neo-colonialist in the case of Mysore?

References

Unpublished Material

G.T. Garratt's letter to Joan Robinson. (1931a, April 13). JVR Collection, King's Modem Archives.

G.T. Garratt's letter to Joan Robinson. (1931b, July 25). JVR Collection, King's Modern Archives.

G.T. Garratt's letter to Joan Robinson. (1932, November 26). JVR Collection, King's Modern Archives.

Harry M. Bull's letter to Joan Robinson. (1931, June 7). JVR Collection, King's Modem Archives.

KN. Haksar's letter to Joan Robinson. (1932, October 11). JVR Collection, King's Modem Archives.

K.N. Haksar's letter to Joan Robinson. (1933, March 9). JVR Collection, King's Modem Archives.

L. Graham's letter. (1931, January 8). JVR Collection, King's Modern Archives.
Joan Robinson's letter to Keynes. (1932, April 9).

Published Works

Butler, H. (1930). The Indian States and the Crown. In *India. The Times* Publishing Company.
Copland, I. (1982) *The British Raj and the Indian States.* Orient Longman.
Das, T. (1929). Report of the Indian States Committee. *Calcutta Review, 33,* 21–31.
Hettne, B. (1978). *The Political Economy of Indirect Rule: Mysore 1881–1947.* Curzon Press.
Holdsworth, W. (1930). The Indian States and India. *Law Quarterly Review, 46,* 417–45.
India, Government of. (1929). *The Indian States.* Central Publication Branch.
India, Government of. (1930–1932). *Special Committee on Economic and Financial Relations Between British India and Indian States* (Vols. 1, 2). Foreign and Political Department.
India, Government of. (1950). *Indian States Finance Enquiry Committee Report.*
Indian Round Table Conference. (1931). *Proceedings of Sub-committees, November 1930–January 1931.* H.M.'s Stationery Office.
Indian Round Table Conference. (1932a). Proceedings, September–December 1931. H.M.'s Stationery Office.
Indian Round Table Conference. (1932b). *Proceedings of Federal Structure Committee, September–December 1931.* H.M.'s Stationery Office.
Indian States Enquiry Committee (Financial), The Report of. (1932). H.M.'s Stationery Office.
Jeffrey, R. (Ed.). (1978). *People, Princes and Paramount Power.* Oxford University Press. *Journal of Contemporary Asia* (1983). Editorial. 13, 3–6.
Keynes, J. M. (1973). *The Collected Writings, Vol. 13, Part I* (D. Moggridge, Ed.). Macmillan.
Kibe, M. V. (1951). The Financial Implications of the Integration of States. *Indian Journal of Economics, 31,* 397–400.
Layton, W. (1930). The Problem of Indian States. In *Report of the Indian Statutory Commission* (Vol. 2). H.M.'s Stationery Office.

Menon, V. P. (1956) *The Story of the Integration of the Indian States.* Longmans, Green.

Report of Indian States Committee 1928–29. (1929). H.M.'s Stationery Office.

Robinson, E. A. J. (1929). The Indian States. *Nation and Athenaeum,* 45, 392–393.

Robinson, J. (1933). *The Economics of Imperfect Competition.* Macmillan.

Sarma, N. A. (1951). The Financial Implications of the Integration of States. *Indian Journal of Economics, 31,* 389–396.

Shackle, G. L. S. (1962). *The Years of High Theory.* Cambridge University Press.

The British Crown and the Indian States. (1929). P.S. King and Son.

Toye, J. (1981). *Public Expenditure and Indian Development Policy 1960–1970.* Cambridge University Press.

Appendix 2

XXXIII: The Salt Monopoly

The Government of India derives some Rs 6 crores of revenue from the taxation of salt. Some of this is raised by means of customs duties on salt entering the country; some by an excise duty on salt manufactured locally, part of which is mined, part taken from lakes and part from the sea; and some by the sale of salt produced in government works. In effect the government fixed the price of salt, and every purchaser of salt is contributing to revenue.

The taxation of salt dates from the early days of British rule in India, and since a large part of the salt consumed in India comes from Rajputana, it was necessary for the taxing authority to draw a customs line across India, which was maintained at great expense both of trouble and of money. In 1870 Lord Mayo initiated a fresh policy by negotiating a treaty with the states of Jodhpur and Jaipur by which the Sambhar Lake was leased to the government, and by later agreements all other important sources for the supply of salt came under Government control, and the customs line was abolished.

But the methods by which the Government of India acquired the monopoly of salt are not our immediate concern. It is the states regarded as consumers rather than as producers of salt that we must consider. Their peoples, with every pound of salt that they buy, make a contribution to the

© The Author(s), under exclusive license to Springer Nature Switzerland AG 2022
P. Tahir, *Joan Robinson in Princely India*, Palgrave Studies in the History of Economic Thought,
https://doi.org/10.1007/978-3-031-10905-8

central revenue, and it is the amount of that contribution which we are concerned to discover.

There is no reason to suppose that the states consume less than their proportionate share of salt, since it is a commodity which the poorest must buy and it is least needed in the wealthiest and most populous places, the large towns where there are almost no cattle.

Rough estimates can be made of the amount of salt consumed in certain states. The figures of the annual consumption of seven states, taken at random, which cover a population of some 8 million, show an average of 12'2 lbs. per head. The returns published in the Statistical Abstract for British India show that the average consumption for all India is 12'3 lbs. per head. These calculations are not accurate enough for a difference of 0'1 lb. to have any significance, and we may safely assume that the average consumption in the states is roughly the same as in the rest of India.

The states, therefore, can fairly claim that they contribute a share of the salt revenue proportionate to their population. During the last five years, the salt revenue has varied between five and six crores of rupees, of which 22 per cent is something over Rs. I crore. From this it is necessary to deduct the compensation which is paid to certain salt-producing states to the amount of some 40 lakhs.

Net salt revenue after paying charges and capital outlay

		22.5% of net revenue	Less compensation
	Lakhs Rs.	Lakhs Rs.	Lakhs Rs.
1924–1925	6.49	1.46	1.10
1925–1926	5.41	1.21	81
1926–1927	5.83	1.31	93
1927–1928 (Revised estimate)	5.89	1.33	94
1928–1929 (Budget)	6.14	1.38	99

Source: *The British Crown and the Indian States* (1929, Section XXXIII, pp. 197–201)

One or two of the salt-producing states are allowed a certain quantity of salt free of duty, and to this extent the above calculation is inaccurate. [15] But this privilege is only one of the concessions by which they were induced to give up the revenue which they had formerly made from salt and to turn their productive resources over to the control of the British authorities, so that if they had not been compensated in this way, it would have been necessary to compensate them in some other way. If the states which merely consume salt can justly be credited with the amount of the tax that their subjects pay, the states which formerly owned salt works, and which are already exempted from the tax, can claim to be credited with something more. We therefore do not exclude the population (which amounts to 3 million) of the states which enjoy this concession from the general calculation, and we conclude that the states' populations bear the burden of some 90 lakhs of rupees taxation which they contribute to the salt revenue.

Besides the direct burden of the tax, there are various disadvantages to the states from this payment. The whole control of salt revenue is taken out of their hands, and they are unable to influence the policy of the government in regard to the price which they choose to charge for salt. An illustration of this is afforded by the fact that pressure was brought to bear upon the states in whose territory salt is produced, and which are allowed a certain quantity for their own consumption, to raise the price of salt to their own peoples at the time when an increase in the rates of the salt tax happened to suit the needs of the British Indian budget. A dispute over this point with Jodhpur lingered on until it was brought to an end by an improvement in the British Indian financial position which made it possible for the tax to be lowered again, but the states which have no source of supply within their own borders were unable to protest against the rise in the price of salt.

The states in which salt is found suffer, besides the payment which all must make, various special disadvantages.

The treaties under which states agreed to refrain from the production of salt or by which they put their resources under the control of the government provide for certain forms of compensation. The terms granted to the different states vary considerably. Some received compensation for the transit duties which they had been accustomed to charge and which they were obliged to abandon, some received compensation for the price of the salt consumed by their subjects, some received compensation only for transit duties, and some received no compensation at all. Some were allowed to produce salt on condition it was not exported, and some were induced to treat other excisable goods in the same way. Some were obliged to give up production altogether. In every case the convenience of the government excise system was considered above everything, and in most compensation was inadequate and was fixed in an arbitrary way. Sir John Strachey, the Finance Minister of the time, advanced the argument that the states were also compensated by 'the removal from April 1st, 1878, of the duties formerly levied on all sugar exported across the customs line from our own territories, which fell mainly upon the people of the Native States of Rajputana'. But he did not explain how the removal of export duties on a commodity of which the Rajputana states had their own sources of supply could be a benefit to them, nor did he mention that the benefit of the abolition of the duty must in any case have been far greater to the British Indian exporters. That such contentions were made at the time suggests that a doubt lurked in the government's mind as to the justice of the arrangement, but no change has been made in it up to the present day.

It is not only the states which suffer from the fact that the government drove so hard a bargain with them.

In some states sources of supply are available, the use of which is prohibited, and certain Darbars are even required to destroy natural salt which occurs in the ground without the necessity of human effort. Several states which formerly produced salt from brine wells find that since the salt workings have been stopped the land grows saline and unfit for cultivation. Sir Michael O'Dwyer, when he was Settlement Commissioner (1897–1900), wrote of a part of Bharatpur State:

> This was a great seat of salt manufacture and was one of the most busy and prosperous parts of the State, but it has now a forlorn and depressed appearance, with large areas of land lying waste or deserted owing to bad soil, bad water, want of hands and the inroads of wild cattle. ... Since the abolition of the salt trade population has become sparse and the jungle has speedily encroached upon cultivation. ... The village sites have a forlorn and desolate appearance aggravated by the belts of dismal farrash trees which alone thrive in the ungenerous soil.

Colonel Brockman, who was in Bharatpur in 1905, writes:

> The continual abstraction of water from Katcha wells, dug for the purpose of drawing lime water from the salt-bearing strata, annually removed from the soil tons of lime which now, owing to the suspension of salt manufacture in the State, remains in the soil, and contaminates the water with enormous quantities, chiefly of chloride of sodium, which accounts for its brackish nature.

Not only do the salt-producing states suffer these indirect losses, and not only are their exchequers deprived of a source of revenue, but a part of their natural wealth remains undeveloped, and their peoples are often compelled to pay an unduly high price for salt which has been transported from a distance, or even imported from abroad, while a nearer and sometimes better supply remains unused. This is not only a disadvantage to the states concerned but a loss of real wealth to the country as a whole.

Appendix 3

XXXIV: Railways

We have hitherto been considering the contributions made by the states to central revenues as the result of taxation. There is a further group of contributions which is represented by their share in the profits of the profit-making enterprises of the government. The government already possess in many districts, and is gradually acquiring in others, a monopoly of the railway services. The sales of monopoly products have long been recognized both in India and in other countries as a fruitful source of income for governments. In India the salt duties are largely of that nature; in France, matches and tobacco have long been government monopolies. While, strictly speaking, a monopoly price is different in nature from a tax, in practice the two converge. A tax imposed upon liquor by a government is as dependent on the demand for liquor and has the same effects in diminishing that demand, as an excessive monopoly price imposed by a producer. Between direct taxation and the extortions of a monopolist, there is considerable difference and between indirect taxation and monopoly revenue very little.

The history of Indian railways has been a chequered one. For many years they failed to produce a sufficient surplus above their running expenses to pay in full the interest on the capital sunk in their originally rather extravagant construction. In the last few years, they have come into

P. Tahir, *Joan Robinson in Princely India*, Palgrave Studies in the History of Economic Thought, https://doi.org/10.1007/978-3-031-10905-8

their own as a sound profit-making concern of the government. The separation of the railway budget from the general budget has made it much easier than it was to distinguish the profits and losses attributable to the railways, and the present system of accounting specifically separates the part of profits which is retained in the railway reserve fund, to balance good and bad years and build up a general reserve for the railway finances, from that part which is transferred as a contribution from railway to general revenues. The table on next page shows the financial results of working in the two last available years.

The figure with which we are at the moment concerned is that of the contribution from railways to general revenues. This contribution comes from charging railway travellers and people who consign goods by railway, more than the services have cost to provide. That is to say, it is in the nature of a tax paid by the consumers of railway services, either by travelling or consuming goods which have been carried. The incidence of the tax is therefore on travellers and consumers in the states as much as in British India. To make an accurate estimate of the incidence, it would be necessary to know exactly to what extent the inhabitants or the states do, in fact, consume the services or the railway companies which contribute to the government balance, that is, those railways which are owned by the state or in which it has an interest as a guarantor. This includes directly and indirectly (for a guaranteed minimum profit goes to the main line operating company in the case of those of the state-owned railways worked by a main line) some 34,000 miles out of the 39,000 miles of railway in the country. It is true that the Darbars own and work some 3000 miles of line of their own, apart from lines leased to main lines, and to some extent these lines must provide for local travellers the services which in British India are provided for such people by the state-owned lines. On the other hand, these bring profitable traffic to them which would not otherwise have been available. Furthermore, the average length of haul for export and import goods from an India state to a seaport is probably greater than from British Indian districts, since the latter lie for the most part nearer the coast.

If we take the share of the states in the traffic to be in proportion to population, their share of the contribution to revenue would be (in 1926–1927) 22.5 per cent of Rs. 6,01,13,000, or about Rs. 135 lakhs. It is possible that this would be an overestimate, and for the purpose of our calculations, we will take the figure of Rs. 120 lakhs which would result from an average use of the railways by the peoples of the states, 85 per cent of the average in British India.

In the case of railways, as of excise, of customs and of salt duty, the money payment is not the only burden of which the states complain. They feel that the policy of the Railway Board is often inimical to their interests and that the decisions of the railway officials carry more weight with the government than protests from a state which feels itself unfairly treated.

The Rewa Darbar, for instance, find that their collieries which they have lately electrified at considerable cost are unable to develop because the railway companies serving the Central Provinces have recently lowered the rates on coal coming from that district without allowing a similar concession to the coalfields in Rewa. There may be some good reason for this action, but if so it should at least be made clear to the Darbar. Again, the Gwalior state suffers from the fact that the lines which are owned by the Darbar, but managed by the companies, do not receive their fair share of traffic. For instance, there are two possible routes between Howrah and Ahmedabad. Of these the shorter route, via Ujjain, lies partly over line owned by the Darbar. The company concerned fixes the minimum rates for goods traffic allowed by the Railway Board, upon the longer route, and the maximum rates upon the shorter route, thus diverting traffic from the Darbar's lines. It would be possible to multiply instances of injustice suffered by the states at the hands of railway authorities, but here it is our purpose merely to point out that the states are treated by them as taxpayers and yet denied the taxpayer's right to make his views respected.

Financial results of railways (figures in thousands)

	1925–1926 Rs.	1926–1927 Rs
(1) (a) Gross earnings	9,97,000	9,90,398
(b) Surplus profits from subsidized companies	3507	3972
(c) Interest and depreciation and reserve fund	5377	6392
(e) Other miscellaneous railway receipts	66	475
	10,05,950	10,01,137
(2) (a) Working expenses excluding depreciation	5,57,508	5,35,114
(b) Depreciation	1,06,688	1,08,858
(c) Surplus profits paid to companies	17,742	16,656
(d) Land and subsidies to companies	438	521
(e) Interest	3,48,112	2,58,670
(f) Miscellaneous railway expenditure	2628	6552
	9,13,116	9,26,271
(3) Net gain	92,834	74,966
(4) (a) Contribution from railway to general revenues	54,904	60,113
(b) Surplus railway revenue transferred to railway reserve fund	37,930	14,855
	92,834	74,966

Source: *The British Crown and the Indian States* (1929, Section XXXIV, 201–5)

NOTES

1. 'E.A.J. Robinson' is obviously a pseudonym combining the initials 'E.A.' of E.A.G. Robinson and 'J.' of Joan Robinson.
2. See Menon (1956, pp. 24–5).
3. Lord Peel, not to be confused with Sir Sidney Peel, the economist member of the Butler Committee.
4. G.T. Garratt's letter to Joan Robinson, 13 April, 1931a. JVR Collection, King's Modem Archives.
5. See KN. Haksar's letters to Joan Robinson during 1931–1935, especially the letter dated 11 October 1932; G.T. Garratt's letter, 26 November 1932; L. Graham's letter, 8 January 1931. JVR Collection, King's Modern Archives.
6. Harry M. Bull's letter to Joan Robinson, 7 June 1931. JVR Collection, King's Modem Archives.
7. This was not the first time that, at least in matters economic, the British officialdom in India had looked more national than the nationalist opinion. See Toye (1981, p. 29).
8. India (1929) presented the otherwise useful information on the states in a manner that highlighted their bewildering diversity, with no attempt even to provide column totals, as if to announce before any negotiation that Princely India did not add up!
9. This was computed on the basis of the revenues from the territories at the time of cessions and waiver of tributes in excess of 5 per cent of the revenue in the respective states, given in the Davidson report (Indian States Enquiry, 1932, pp. 35, 64–5).
10. Menon (1956, p. 31). It may be noted that Menon was part of the officialdom in British India, often acting as more national than the nationalists.
11. K.N. Haksar's letter to Joan Robinson, 9 March 1933. JVR Collection, King's Modem Archives.
12. Joan Robinson's letter to Keynes 9 April 1932 (Keynes, 1973, p. 269). It must be this book (Robinson, 1933) which Garratt had thought she would write after returning from India, whose esoteric nature would make quantum mechanics look a lighter reading! Letter from G.T. Garratt to Joan Robinson, 25 July 1931b. JVR Collection, King's Modern Archives.
13. Shackle (1962).
14. See Jeffrey (1978, pp. 1, 26). Copland (1982, p. xi) mentions, among others, John Gallagher. Gordon Johnson and Anil Seal as members of this school.
15. Certain states are allowed to produce salt for their own consumption; but the amount thus produced is negligible. Kashmir is only allowed a rebate on salt imported from overseas, and in practice she imports almost no salt in this way.

REFERENCES

UNPUBLISHED MATERIAL

JOAN ROBINSON'S CORRESPONDENCE

Charles Gifford's letter to Joan Robinson. (1932, November 2). JVR Collection, King's Modem Archives.

G.F. Shove's letter to Joan Robinson. (1932, October 19). JVR Collection, King's Modem Archives.

G.T. Garratt's letters to Joan Robinson. (1931–1937). Especially those dated 13 April, 1931; 2 July, 1931; 25 July,1931; 3 August, 1932; 27 September, 1932; 26 November, 1932; 27 July, 1936. JVR Collection, King's Modem Archives.

Harry M. Bull's letters to Joan Robinson. (1931–1951). Particularly the letter dated 26 January, 1947. JVR Collection. King's Modem Archives.

J.M. Keynes' letter to Joan Robinson. (1942, August 20). Keynes' Papers, King's College Library.

K.N. Haksar's letters to Joan Robinson. (1931–1935). Especially those dated 13 April, 1931; 11 October, 1932; 9 March, 1933. JVR Collection, King's Modem Archives.

L. Graham's letter to Joan Robinson. (1931, January 8). JVR Collection, King's Modem Archives.

© The Author(s), under exclusive license to Springer Nature
Switzerland AG 2022
P. Tahir, *Joan Robinson in Princely India*, Palgrave Studies in the
History of Economic Thought,
https://doi.org/10.1007/978-3-031-10905-8

Other Unpublished Material in JVR Collection

JVRC. iii/5.3. King's Modem Archives.
JVRC. viii/Ayres. King's Modem Archives.

The Papers of Sir Austin Robinson

GBR/0014/ROBN. Churchill Archives Centre.
Marshall Library. Austin Robinson Papers. https://www.marshall.econ.cam.ac.
   uk/system/files/documents/robinson
EAGR 7/1/2/23. n.d. Austin Robinson Papers, Marshall Library, University of
   Cambridge.
EAGR 7/1/2/41. n.d. Austin Robinson Papers, Marshall Library, University of
   Cambridge.
EAGR 7/1/2/46. n.d. Austin Robinson Papers, Marshall Library, University of
   Cambridge.
EAGR 8/2/1/13/13–16. n.d. Austin Robinson Papers, Marshall Library,
   University of Cambridge.
EAGR, 8/2/1/13/17–21. n.d.. Austin Robinson Papers, Marshall Library,
   University of Cambridge.
EAGR, 8/2/1/13/26–32. n.d. Austin Robinson Papers, Marshall Library,
   University of Cambridge.
EAGR, 8/2/1/13/78–81. n.d. Austin Robinson Papers, Marshall Library,
   University of Cambridge.
EAGR, 7/1/1 1914–1992. n.d. Austin Robinson Papers, Marshall Library,
   University of Cambridge.
Marshall Library. (2016). Faculty of Economics, University of Cambridge. http://
   marshlib.blogspot.com/2016/11/austin-robinsons-indian-sojourn.html
Marshall Library. (2018). Faculty of Economics, University of Cambridge. http://
   marshlib.blogspot.com/2018/

Author's Correspondence

Austin Robinson's letter to the author. (1986, June 18).
K.N. Raj's letter to the author. (1986, July 11).
K.N. Prasad's letter to the author. (1986, September 29).
Sol Adler's letter to the author. (1986, November 30).
Carl Riskin's letter to the author. (1987, February 3).
Sukhamoy Chakravarty's letter to the author. (1987, July 13)
Robert Clower's letters to the author. (1987, March 10, April 8).
William Brown's letters to the author. (1988, May 4, 6).

INTERVIEWS

Lord Kahn.
Ronald Berger.
Sukhamoy Chakravarty.
Gamni Correa.
Ajit Singh.

DISSERTATIONS/MANUSCRIPTS

Keen, C. (2003). *The Power Behind the Throne: Relations Between the British and the Indian States 1870–1909*. Thesis submitted for the degree of Ph.D. at the School of Oriental and African Studies, University of London.

Khan, M. A. W. (1935). *The Financial Problems of Indian States under Federation*. University of London.

Shrivastava, H. K. (1970). *A Critical Examination of the Relation of Paramount Power with the Gwalior State*. Vilcram University.

Tahir, P. (1988). *Some Aspects of Development and Underdevelopment: Critical Perspectives on the Early Contributions of Joan Robinson*. Unpublished.

Tahir, P. (1990). *Some Aspects of Development and Underdevelopment: Critical Perspectives on Joan Robinson*. Dissertation submitted for the degree of Ph.D. in Economics, Faculty of Economics and Politics, University of Cambridge.

Turner, M. S. (1986). *Joan Robinson and the Americans*. Manuscript.

OFFICIAL RECORDS

India Office Library. IOR v/26/272/2–3.

PUBLISHED WORKS

A.M. (1983). Obituary: The One Who Said Boo. *Economic and Political Weekly, 18*, 1461–1462.

Adler, S. (1957). *The Chinese Economy*. Routledge and Kegan Paul.

Amdekar, S., & Singh, A. (2017). Cambridge and Development Economics. In R. A. Cord (Ed.), *The Palgrave Companion to Cambridge Economics*. Palgrave Macmillan.

Anstey, V. (1929). *The Economic Development of India*. Longmans and Green.

Arndt, H. W. (1972). Development Economics Before 1945. In J. Bhagwati & R. S. Eckaus (Eds.), *Development and Planning: Essays in Honour of Paul Rosenstein-Rodan*. George Allen and Unwin.

Arndt, H. W. (1981). Economic Development: A Semantic History. *Economic Development and Cultural Change, 29,* 457–466.

Ashton, S. R. (1982). *British Policy Towards the Indian States, 1905–1939.* Curzon Press London.

Aslanbeigui, N., & Oakes, G. (2009). *The Provocative Joan Robinson: The Making of a Cambridge Economist.* Duke University Press.

Ayres, C. E. (1944). *The Theory of Economic Progress.* University of North Carolina Press.

Bagchi, A. K. (1972). *Private Investment in India 1900–39.* Cambridge University Press.

Baran, P. (1957). *The Political Economy of Growth.* Monthly Review Press.

Bardhan, P. (1986). Marxist Ideas in Development Economics: An Evaluation. In J. Roemer (Ed.), *Analytical Marxism.* Cambridge University Press.

Bawa, V. S. (1965). Salar Jang and the Nizam's State Railway. *Indian Economic and Social History Review, 2,* 305–340.

Bell, C. (1987). Development Economics. In J. Eatwell, M. Milgate, & P. Newman (Eds.), *The New Palgrave: A Dictionary of Economics* (Vol. 1). Macmillan.

Bernstein, H. (1971). Modernization Theory and the Sociological Study of Development. *Journal of Development Studies, 7,* 141–160.

Bettelheim, C. (1968). *India Independent.* Macgibbon and Kee.

Bhagwati, J. N. (1985). *Wealth and Poverty.* Basil Blackwell.

Bird, R. M. (1974). *Taxing Agricultural Land in Developing Countries.* Harvard University Press.

Blackett, B. P. (1930). The Economic Progress of India. *Journal of the Royal Society of Arts, 78,* 313–327.

Blomstrom, M., & Hattie, B. (1984). *Development Theory in Transition.* Zed Books.

Brahmananda, P. R. (1983). Joan Robinson, 1904(sic.)-1983. *Indian Economic Journal, 31,* 1–24.

Brebner, J. B. (1931). Book note on *The British Crown and the Indian States. Political Science Quarterly, 46,* 315–316.

Brenner, R. (1977). The Origins of Capitalist Development: A Critique of neo-Smithian Marxism. *New Left Review, 104,* 25–92.

Broacha, S. (1906). 'The "Poverty" of India. In *Speeches on Indian Economics.* Bombay Gazette Press.

Bull, H. M., & Haksar, K. N. (1926). *Madhavrao Scindia of Gwalior.* Alijah Darbar Press.

Business Week. (1975, October 20).

Butler, H. (1930). The Indian States and the Crown. In *India. The Times* Publishing Company.

Cairncross, A. (1993). *Austin Robinson: The Life of an Economic Adviser.* Palgrave Macmillan.

Cambridge, University of. (1922). *The Student's Handbook*. Cambridge University Press.

Chakravarty, S. (1983). Joan Robinson: An Appreciation. *Economic and Political Weekly, 18*, 1712–1716.

Chandavarkar, A. G. (1984). Money and Credit, 1858–1947. In D. Kumar (Ed.), *The Cambridge Economic History of India* (Vol. 2). Orient Longman.

Chandra, B. (1965). Indian Nationalists and the Drain, 1880–1905. *Indian Economic and Social History Review, 2*, 101–144.

Chatterton, A. (1925). The Industrial Progress of the Mysore State. *Journal of the Royal Society of Arts, 63*, 714–737.

Clark, C. (1984). Development Economics: The Early Years. In *Meier and Seers (1984)*.

Clower, R. W., et al. (1966). *Growth Without Development: An Economic Survey of Liberia*. Northwestern University Press.

Copland, I. (1982). *The British Raj and the Indian States*. Orient Longman.

Copland, I. (1997). *The Princes of India in the Endgame of Empire, 1917–1947*. Cambridge University Press.

Coyajer, J. C. (1929). The Ratio Controversy in India: A Retrospect. *Asiatic Review, 25*, 405–412.

Cunningham, W. (1892). The Perversion of Economic History. *Economic Journal, 2*, 491–506.

Dalton, G. (1965). 'History, Politics and Economic Development in Liberia. *Journal of Economic History, 25*, 569–591.

Dalton, G. (1974). *Economic Systems and Society*. Penguin.

Das, T. (1929). Report of the Indian States Committee. *Calcutta Review, 33*, 21–31.

Dutt, R. C. (1904). *The Economic History of India* (Vol. 2). Burt Franklin Reprinted 1970.

Emmanuel, A. (1972). *Unequal Exchange: A Study of the Imperialism of Trade*. New Left Books.

Findlay, R. (1975). Review of *International Trade and Development Theory* by B. Hansen. *Journal of Development Economics, 1*, 403–404.

Frank, A. G. (1967). *Capitalism and Underdevelopment in Latin America*. Monthly Review Press.

Furtado, C. (1973). The Concept of External Dependence in the Study of Underdevelopment. In C. K. Wilber (Ed.), *The Political Economy of Development and Underdevelopment* (pp. 118–123). Random House.

Garratt, G. T. (1930). Indian India. *Asia, 30*, 783–789, 804–805. (U.S.).

Garratt, G. T. (1932). The Indian Industrial Worker. *Economic Journal, 42*, 399–406.

Gerschenkron, A. (1952). *Economic Backwardness in Historical Perspective*. Harvard University Press.

Gopal, M. H. (1941). Public Expenditure in Mysore—A Review. *Indian Journal of Economics, 21,* 594–604.

Graham, H., & Harcourt, G. C. (2020). Keynesian Uncertainty: The Great Divide between Joan Robinson and Paul Samuelson in their Correspondence and Public Exchange. In R. Cord, R. Anderson, & W. Barnett (Eds.), *Paul Samuelson. Remaking Economics: Eminent Post-War Economists* (pp. 375–419). Palgrave Macmillan.

Griffin, K., & Gurley, J. (1985). Radical Analyses of Imperialism, the Third World, and the Transition to Socialism: A Survey Article. *Journal of Economic Literature, 23,* 1089–1143.

Guillebaud, C. W. (Ed.). (1961). *Marshall's Principles of Economics* (Vol. 2). Macmillan.

Habib, I. (1963). *The Agrarian System of Mughal India.* Asia Publishing House.

Haksar, K. N. (1928). Fiscal Inter-relation of Indian States and the Empire. *Asiatic Review, 24,* 539–543.

Haksar, K. N. (1929). The Salt Revenue and the Indian States. *Asiatic Review, 25,* 7–16.

Haksar, K. N. (1930). Economic Development in Gwalior State. *Asiatic Review, 26,* 150–157.

Haksar, K. N. (1931). Mahatma Gandhi and the Indian States. *Spectator, 147,* 346.

Haksar, K. N., & Panikkar, K. M. (1930). *Federal India.* Martin Hopkinson.

Hamilton, A. (1791). *Report on Manufactures.* U.S. Government Printing Office, 1913.

Hansen, B. (1975). Review of R. Findlay. *International Trade and Development Theory, in Journal of Development Economics, 1,* 403–404.

Harcourt, G. C. (1979). Robinson, Joan. In H. W. Spiegel & W. J. Samuels (Eds.), *International Encyclopaedia of the Social Sciences, Bibliographical Supplement* (Vol. 18). The Free Press.

Harcourt, G. C. (1984). Harcourt on Robinson. In *Contemporary Economists in Perspective* (Vol. 1, Part B). Jai Press.

Harcourt, G. C. (1986). On the Influence of Piero Sraffa on the Contributions of Joan Robinson to Economic Theory. *Economic Journal, 96*(Supplement), 96–108.

Harcourt, G. C., & Kerr, P. (2009). *Joan Robinson.* Palgrave Macmillan.

Hardiman, D. (1978). The Structure of a "Progressive" State. In R. Jeffrey (Ed.), *People, Princes and Paramount Power.* Oxford University Press.

Heston, A. (1984). National Income. In D. Kumar (Ed.), *The Cambridge Economic History of India* (Vol. 2). Bombay.

Hettne, B. (1978). *The Political Economy of Indirect Rule: Mysore 1881–1947.* Curzon Press.

Hirschman, A. O. (1981). *Essays in Trespassing.* Cambridge University Press.

Hobsbawm, E. (Ed.). (1964). *Karl Marx: Pre-capitalist Economic Formations.* Lawrence and Wishart.

Holdsworth, W. (1930). The Indian States and India. *Law Quarterly Review, 46*, 417–445.

Hurd, J., II. (1975a). The Economic Consequences of the Indirect Rule in India. *Indian Economic and Social History Review, 12*, 169–181.

Hurd, J., II. (1975b). The Influence of British Policy and Industrial Development in the Princely States of India—1890–1933. *Indian Economic and Social History Review, 12*, 409–424.

Hutchison, T. W. (1953). *A Review of Economic Doctrines 1870–1929*. Clarenden Press.

India. London: The Times Publishing Company.

India, Government of. (1918). *Report of the Indian Industrial Commission 1916–18*. Central Publications Branch.

India, Government of. (1922) *Report of the Indian Fiscal Commission 1921–22*.

India, Government of. (1925). *Report of the Indian Economic Enquiry Committee*. Central Publications Branch.

India, Government of. (1929). *The Indian States*. Central Publication Branch.

India, Government of. (1930–1932). *Special Committee on Economic and Financial Relations between British India and Indian States* (Vols. 1, 2). Foreign and Political Department.

India, Government of. (1932). *The Origin, Rise and Consolidation of the Indian States: A British Assessment 1929*. B.R. Publishing. Reprint 1975.

India, Government of. (1950). *Indian States Finance Enquiry Committee Report*.

Indian Finance Year Book. (1932). *Annual Supplement of Indian Finance*. Central Publications Branch.

Indian Round Table Conference. (1931). *Proceedings of Sub-committees, November 1930–January 1931*. H.M.'s Stationery Office.

Indian Round Table Conference. (1932a). *Proceedings, September–December 1931*. H.M.'s Stationery Office.

Indian Round Table Conference. (1932b). *Proceedings of Federal Structure Committee, September–December 1931*. H.M.'s Stationery Office.

Indian States Enquiry Committee (Financial), The Report of. (1932). H.M.'s Stationery Office.

Iyengar, S. K. (1941). "British" and "Indian" Finance. *Indian Journal of Economics, 21*, 830–870.

Jeffrey, R. (Ed.). (1978). *People, Princes and Paramount Power*. Oxford University Press.

Journal of Contemporary Asia. (1983). Editorial. *13*, 3–6.

Kalecki, M. (1938). Review of Die Nationalen Produktivkraefte and der Aussenhandel by M. Manoilesco. *Economic Journal, 48*, 708–711.

Keralaputra. (1929). The Internal States of India. *Annals of the American Academy of Political and Social Science, 145*(Part II), 45–58.

Kesavaiengar, B. T. (1930). The Development and the Resources of the Mysore State. *Asiatic Review, 26,* 218–227.

Keynes, J. M. (1911). Review of T. Morison. *The Economic Transition in India. Economic Journal, 21,* 426–431.

Keynes, J. M. (1913). *Indian Currency and Finance.* Macmillan.

Keynes, J. M. (1936). *The General Theory of Employment, Interest and Money.* Macmillan.

Keynes, J. M. (1971) *The Collected Writings, Vol. 15* (E. Johnson, Ed.). Macmillan.

Keynes, J. M. (1973). *The Collected Writings, Vol. 13, Part I* (D. Moggridge, Ed.). Macmillan.

Keynes, J. M. (1981). *The Collected Writings, Vol. 19, Part II* (D. Moggridge, Ed.). Macmillan.

Keynes, J. M. (1983). *The Collected Writings, Vol. 12* (D. Moggridge, Ed.). Macmillan.

Khan, M. M. (1937). *Federal Finance.* Robert Hale.

Kibe, M. V. (1951). The Financial Implications of the Integration of States. *Indian Journal of Economics, 31,* 397–400.

Kidwai, R. (2021). *The House of Scindias: A Saga of Power, Politics and Intrigue.* Roli Books.

Kitching, G. (1982). *Development and Underdevelopment.* Methuen.

Knowles, L. C. A. (1925). *The Economic Development of the British Overseas Empire.* George Routledge.

Kosambi, D. D. (1946). The Bourgeios Comes of Age in India. *Science and Society, 10,* 392–398.

Kumar, D. (Ed.). (1984a). *The Cambridge Economic History of India* (Vol. 2). Orient Longman.

Kumar, D. (Ed.). (1984b). The Fiscal System. In *D. Kumar (1984a).*

Lall, S. (1941). Industrial Development in the Indian Provinces. *Journal of the Royal Society of Arts, 89,* 134–145.

Lawrence, W. R. (1930). The Indian States. In *India.* The Times Publishing Company.

Layton, W. (1930). The Problem of Indian States. In *Report of the Indian Statutory Commission* (Vol. 2). H.M.'s Stationery Office.

Lewis, W. A. (1954). Economic Development with Unlimited Supplies of Labour. *Manchester School of Economic and Social Studies, 22,* 139–191.

Lewis, W. A. (1955). *The Theory of Economic Growth.* George Allen and Unwin.

Lewis, W. A. (1970). *Tropical Development 1880–1913.* George Allen and Unwin.

Lidman, R., & Domrese, R. I. (1970). India. In *Lewis (1970).*

Lipton, M. (1978). Transfer of Resources from Agriculture to Non-agricultural Activities: The Case of India. In J. F. J. Toye (Ed.), *Taxation and Economic Development.* Frank Cass.

List, F. (1841). *The National System of Political Economy*. Longman and Green, Reprinted 1885.

Little, I. M. D. (1982). *Economic Development*. Basic Books.

Little, I. M. D., Scitovsky, T., & Scott, M. (1970). *Industry and Trade in Some Developing Countries*. Oxford University Press.

Low, D. A. (1978). Laissez-faire and Traditional Rulership in Princely India. In *Jeffrey (1978)*.

Luxemberg, R. (1913). *The Accumulation of Capital*. Routledge and Kegan Paul. Reprinted 1951.

Macpherson, W. J. (1955). Investment in Indian Railways, 1845–1875. *Economic History Review, 8*, 177–186.

Macpherson, W. J. (1972). Economic Development in India under the British Crown, 1858–1947. In A. J. Youngson (Ed.), *Economic Development in the Long Run*. George Allen and Unwin.

Macpherson, W. J. (1987). *The Economic Development of Japan, c.1868–1941*. Macmillan.

Manor, J. (1975). Princely Mysore Before the Storm. *Modern Asian Studies, 9*, 31–58.

Marcuzzo, M. C. (1985). *Joan Violet Robinson*. Universita Degali Studi, Dipartimento di Economia Politica. Mimeo.

Marshall, A. (1885). *The Present Position of Economics*. Macmillan.

Marshall, A. (1890). *Principles of Economics* (Vol. 1, 1st ed.). Macmillan.

Marshall, A. (1892). A Reply. *Economic Journal, 2*, 507–519.

Marshall, A. (1920). *Principles of Economics* (8th ed.). Macmillan.

Marshall, A. (1926). *Official Papers*. Macmillan.

Marshal Library. (2016). Faculty of Economics, University of Cambridge. http://marshlib.blogspot.com/2016/11/austin-robinsons-indiansojourn.html

Marshal Library. (2018). Faculty of Economics, University of Cambridge. http://marshlib.blogspot.com/2018/.

Marx, K. (1853a). The Russo-Turkish Difficulty—The East India Question. In K. Marx, & F. Engels (Eds.), (1979) *Collected Works* (Vol. 12). Lawrence and Wishart.

Marx, K. (1853b). The British Rule in India. In *Marx and Engels (1979)*.

Marx, K. (1853c). The Future Results of British Rule in India. In *Marx and Engels (1979)*.

Marx, K. (1858). Lord Canning's Proclamation and Land Tenure in India. In *Collected Works of Marx and Engels* (Vol. 15). Lawrence and Wishart, 1986.

Marx, K. (1867). *Capital* (Vol. 1). Lawrence and Wishart. Reprinted 1970.

Marx, K. (1894). *Capital* (Vol. 3). Lawrence and Wishart. Reprinted 1972.

Marx, K. (1973). *Grundrisse*. Penguin Books.

Marx, K. (1975). Draft of an article on Friedrich List's book. In K. Marx & F. Engels (Eds.), *Collected Works* (Vol. 4). Lawrence and Wishart.

Marx, K., & Engels, F. (1965). *The German Ideology*. Lawrence and Wishart.

Marx, K., & Engels, F. (1979). *Collected Works* (Vol. 12). Lawrence and Wishart.

Meier, G. M. (1984). Introduction. In G. M. Meier & D. Seers (Eds.), *Pioneers in Development*. Oxford University Press.

Meier, G. M., & Seers, D. (Eds.). (1984). *Pioneers in Development*. Oxford University Press.

Memorandum of the Indian States People. (1929). Arya Bhushan Press.

Menon, V. P. (1956). *The Story of the Integration of the Indian States*. Longmans, Green.

Mills, J. S. (1929). The Butler Report and the Indian Princes. *Asiatic Review, 25*, 413–420.

Molson, A. H. E. (1931). The Constitutional Position of the Indian States -II. *Asiatic Review, 27*, 487–495.

Morawetz, D. (1985). On the Origins of theories. Review of Meier and Seers (1984). *World Development, 13*, 1307–1309.

Morison, T. (1906). *The Industrial Organization of an Indian Province*. John Murray.

Morison, T. (1911). *Economic Transition in India*. John Murray.

Morris, M. D. (1984). The Growth of Large-scale Industry to 1947. In *Kumar (1984)*.

Mukerjee, R. (1916). *The Foundations of Indian Economics*. Longmans and Green.

Mukhia, H. (1985). Marx on Pre-colonial India: An Evaluation. In D. Banerjee (Ed.), *Marxian Theory and the Third World*. Sage.

Musgrave, R. A. (1959). *The Theory of Public Finance*. McGraw-Hill.

Musgrave, R. A. (1985). A Brief History of Fiscal Doctrine. In A. J. Auerbach & M. Feldstein (Eds.), *Handbook of Public Economics* (Vol. 1). North-Holland.

Musgrave, R. A., & Musgrave, P. B. (1984). *Public Finance in Theory and Practice*. McGraw-Hill.

Myint, H. (1958). The "Classical Theory" of International Trade and Underdeveloped Countries. *Economic Journal, 68*, 317–337.

Myrdal, G. (1968). *Asian Drama* (Vol. 1–3). Allen Lane.

Myrdal, G. (1981). Need for Reforms in Underdeveloped Countries. In S. Grassman & E. Lundberg (Eds.), *The World Economic Order: Past and Prospects*. Macmillan.

N.C.B. (1930). Review of P.L. Chudgar. *Calcutta Review, 36*, 139.

Naik, D. A. (1930). The Indian States and Mints and Coinage. *Calcutta Review, 34*, 305–309.

Naoroji, D. (1901). *Poverty and Un-British Rule in India*. Swan Sonnenschein.

Naqvi, S. (1972). Marx on Pre-British Indian Society and Economy. *Indian Economic and Social History Review, 9*, 380–412.

Narasimhan, S. (1983). Joan Robinson: In the Radical Vein a Laywoman's Homage. *Cambridge Journal of Economics, 7*, 213–219.

Near East and India. (1929). *35*, 524–5.

Nolan, P., & White, G. (1984). 'Urban Bias, Rural Bias or State Bias? Urban-Rural Relations in Post-Revolutionary China. *Journal of Development Studies, 20*, 52–81.

O'Malley, L. S. S. (1932). *Indian Caste Customs.* Cambridge University Press.

O'Rourke, V. A. (1931). The Sovereignty of the Native Indian States. *American Political Science Review, 25*, 1022–1028.

Palgrave's Dictionary of Political Economy, Vol. 1. (1925). Macmillan.

Panikkar, K. M. (1953). *Asia and the Western Dominance.* Allen and Unwin.

Panikkar, K. M. (1962). *In Defence of Liberalism.* Asia Publishing House.

Panikkar, K. M. (1979). *An Autobiography.* Oxford University Press.

Papers on Indian States Development. (1930). East and West Ltd.

Pasinetti, L. L. (1987). Robinson, Joan Violet. In J. Eatwell, M. Milgate, & P. Newman (Eds.), *The New Palgrave: A Dictionary of Economics* (Vol. 4). Macmillan.

Patiala, Maharaja of. (1928). The Indian States and the Crown. *Asiatic Review, 24*, 628–647.

Patiala, Maharaja of. (1929). Speech in the Chamber of Princes. *Asiatic Review, 25*, 353–356.

Pigou, A. C. (Ed.). (1925). *Memorials of Alfred Marshall.* Macmillan.

Premchand, K. (1929). The Economic Position in India. *Asiatic Review, 25*, 682–703.

Question Mark over Kerala. (1957) *Economic Weekly, 9*, 427–428.

Raffles, T. S. (1817). *The History of Java.* Gilbert and Rivington.

Ramaiya, A. (1929). The Point of View of the Indian States' Subjects. *Contemporary Review, 135*, 505–508.

Ramaiya, A. (1930). The Indian States and British India: Their Financial Relations. *Empire Review, 51*, 208–211.

Ranade, M. G. (1906). *Essays in Indian Economics* (2nd ed.). G.A. Natesan.

Rao Sahib, C. R. (1935). The Recent Industrial Progress of Mysore. *Journal of the Royal Society of Arts, 83*, 372–389.

Ray, R. K. (1978). Mewar. The Breakdown of the Princely Order. In *Jeffrey (1978).*

Report of Indian States Committee 1928–29. (1929). H.M.'s Stationery Office.

Robinson, A. (1977). Keynes and his Cambridge Colleagues. In D. Patinkin & J. C. Leith (Eds.), *Keynes, Cambridge and The General Theory.* Macmillan.

Robinson, A. (Ed.). (1986). *Economic Progress* (2nd ed.). Macmillan.

Robinson, E. A. G. (1931). *The Structure of Competitive Industry.* Nisbet.

Robinson, E. A. G. (1943). Review of C. Clark, *The Economics of 1960. Economic Journal, 53*, 238–242.

Robinson, E. A. J. (1929). The Indian States. *Nation and Athenaeum, 45*, 392–393.

Robinson, J. (1930). Review of H. Clay, *The Problem of Industrial Relations*. *Political Quarterly*, 1, 293–296.

Robinson, J. (1932a). *Economics is a Serious Subject*. W. Heifer and Sons.

Robinson, J. (1932b). Review of O'Malley (1932). *Cambridge Review*, 54, 138.

Robinson, J. (1933). *The Economics of Imperfect Competition*. Macmillan.

Robinson, J. (1934). Euler's Theorem and the Problem of Distribution. *Economic Journal*, 44, 398–414.

Robinson, J. (1936). Disguised Unemployment. *Economic Journal*, 46, 223–237.

Robinson, J. (1937). Review of R.H. Hall, *The Economic System in a Socialist State*. *Cambridge Review*, 58, 289–290.

Robinson, J. (1938). The Concept of Hoarding. *Economic Journal*, 48, 231–236.

Robinson, J. (1942). *An Essay on Marxian Economics*. Macmillan.

Robinson, J. (1943b). Do We Need World Markets? *Listener*, 30(490–491), 501.

Robinson, J (1946–1947). The Pure Theory of International Trade. *Review of Economic Studies*, 14, 98–112.

Robinson, J. (1948). Marx and Keynes. In *Robinson (1951a)*.

Robinson, J. (1951a). *Collected Economic Papers* (Vol. 1). Basil Blackwell.

Robinson, J. (1951b). Introduction. In *Robinson (1951a)*.

Robinson, J. (1951d). Introduction. In *Luxemberg (1913)*.

Robinson, J. (1952). *The Rate of Interest and Other Essays*. Macmillan.

Robinson, J. (1954). *Letters from a Visitor to China*. Students' Bookshops.

Robinson, J. (1955a). A Theory of Long-run Development. *Economic Review*, 6(Tokyo), 382–385.

Robinson, J. (1955b). *Marx, Marshall and Keynes*. Delhi School of Economics, Occasional Paper No. 9.

Robinson, J. (1956a). *The Accumulation of Capital* (1st. ed.). Macmillan.

Robinson, J. (1956b). Unemployment and the Second Plan. *Capital*, 7–9.

Robinson, J. (1957b). Clues to History. Letter to the Editor. *Nation* 185 (U.S.), Opposite 1.

Robinson, J. (1957c). Notes on the Theory of Economic Development. *In Robinson (1960a)*.

Robinson, J. (1957d). What Remains of Marxism. In *Robinson (1965)*.

Robinson, J. (1957e). 'The Indian Mixture,' Review of M. Zinkin, *Development for free Asia*. *New Statesman and Nation*, 54, 844–845.

Robinson, Joan (1959). Economic Possibilities of Ceylon. In *Papers by Visiting Economists*. National Planning Council.

Robinson, J. (1960). *Exercises in Economic Analysis*. Macmillan.

Robinson, J. (1962a). *Economic Philosophy*. C.A. Watts.

Robinson, J. (1962b). *Essays in the Theory of Economic Growth*. Macmillan.

Robinson, J. (1963). Review of G. Maynard, *Economic Development and the Price Level*. *Economic Journal*, 73, 299–300.

Robinson, J. (1964). Planning for Economic Development. *Trade Journal*, 5–7. (Pakistan).

Robinson, J. (1965). *Collected Economic Papers* (Vol. 3). Basil Blackwell.

Robinson, J. (1966). *Economics: An Awkward Corner*. George Allen and Unwin.

Robinson, J. (1967). Opening Remarks. In K. Martin & J. Knapp (Eds.), *The Teaching of Development Economics*. Frank Cass.

Robinson, J. (1968a). A Reply. *Journal of Economic Studies, 3,* 33.

Robinson, J. (1968b). 'The Poverty of Nations,' Review of G. Myrdal, *Asian Drama. Cambridge Quarterly, 3,* 381–389.

Robinson, J. (1968c). 'The Poverty of Nations,' Review of G. Myrdal, *Asian Drama. Listener, 80*(509–510), 17.

Robinson, J. (1973e). 'Formalistic Marxism and Ecology Without Classes,' Review of Emmanuel (1972). *Journal of Contemporary Asia, 3,* 457–461.

Robinson, J. (1973f). *Economic Management in China*. ACEI.

Robinson, J. (1973g). Ideology and Analysis. In *Robinson (1979a)*.

Robinson, J. (1974a). Introduction. In *Joan Robinson: Selected Economic Writings*. Oxford University Press.

Robinson, J. (1974b). Inflation West and East. In *Robinson (1979a)*.

Robinson, J. (1975). Introduction 1974: Comments and Explanations. In *Collected Economic Papers* (Vol. 3, 2nd ed.). Basil Blackwell.

Robinson, J. (1976). Introduction. In M. Kalecki (Ed.), *Essays on Developing Economies*. Harvester Press.

Robinson, J. (1977a). Employment and the Choice of Technique. In K. S. Krishnaswamy et al. (Eds.), *Society and Change*. Oxford University Press.

Robinson, J. (1978a). Reminiscences. In J. Robinson (Ed.), *Contributions to Modern Economics*. Basil Blackwell.

Robinson, J. (1978b). 'Formalism versus Dogma,' Review of I. Steedman, *Marx after Sraffa. Journal of Contemporary Asia, 8,* 381–384.

Robinson, J. (1979a). *Collected Economic Papers* (Vol. 5). Basil Blackwell.

Robinson, J. (1979b). Thinking About Thinking. In *Robinson (1979a)*.

Robinson, J. (1979c). *Aspects of Development and Underdevelopment*. Cambridge University Press.

Robinson, J. (1979e). 'Surplus Value and Profits: The Rectification of Names. *Development and Change, 10,* 693–695.

Robinson, J. (1980). Review of H. Chenery, *Structural Change and Development Policy. Journal of Developing Areas, 15,* 131–132.

Robinson, J., & Morison, D. (1951). Beauty and the Beast. In *Robinson (1951a)*.

Robinson, J., & Adler, S. (1958). *China: An Economic Perspective*. Fabian International Bureau, Fabian Tract No. 314.

Robinson, J., & Eatwell, J. (1973). *An Introduction to Modern Economics*. McGraw-Hill.

Rosenstein-Rodan, P. N. (1984). Natura Facit Saltum: Analysis of the Disequilibrium Growth Process. In *Meier and Seers (1984)*.

Royal Commission on Indian Currency and Finance: Minutes of Evidence Taken in India, Vol.4. (1926). H.M.'s Stationery Office.

Rushbrook-Williams, L. F. (1928). Joint Action Among the Indian Princes. *Asiatic Review, 24,* 390–396.

Salter, G. (1925). Introductory Note. In P. P. Pillai (Ed.), *Economic Conditions in India.* George Routledge.

Sarma, N. A. (1951). The Financial Implications of the Integration of States. *Indian Journal of Economics, 31,* 389–396.

Sastri, V. S. S. (1930). The Indian States Problem. *Political Quarterly, 1,* 531–544.

Saunders, A. L. (1929). Review of *The British Crown and the Indian States. Asiatic Review, 25,* 540–541.

Schumpeter, J. A. (1943). *Capitalism, Socialism and Democracy.* Allen and Unwin.

Seers, D. (1963). The Limitations of the Special Case. *Bulletin of the Oxford Institute of Economics and Statistics, 25,* 77–98.

Seers, D. (1979). 'The Birth, Life and death of Development Economics. *Development and Change, 10,* 707–719.

Sender, J., & Smith, S. (1986). *The Development of Capitalism in Africa.* Methuen.

Shackle, G. L. S. (1962). *The Years of High Theory.* Cambridge University Press.

Shah, K. T. (1927). *Sixty Years of Indian Finance.* P.S. King and Son.

Shah, K. T., & Khambata, K. J. (1924). *Wealth and Taxable Capacity of India.* P.S. King and Son.

Shoup, C. S. (1969). *Public Finance.* Weidenfeld and Nicolson.

Shove, G. F. (1933). Review of Robinson (1933a). *Economic Journal, 43,* 657–661.

Singer, H. W. (1984). The Terms of Trade Controversy and the Evolution of Soft Financing. *Meier and Seers, 1984.*

Singer, H. W. (1987). Discussion. In A. P. Thiriwall (Ed.), *Keynes and Economic Development.* Macmillan.

Smith, A. (1776). *An Inquiry into the Nature and Causes of the Wealth of Nations.* George Routledge and Sons. Reprinted 1890.

Smith, S. (1979). Colonialism in Economic Theory: The Experience of Nigeria. In S. Smith & J. Toye (Eds.), *Trade and Poor Economies.* Frank Cass.

Soffer, R. N. (1970). The Revolution in English Social Thought, 1880–1914. *American Historical Review, 75,* 1938–1964.

Sweezy, P. M. (1953). *The Present as History.* Monthly Review Press.

Symposium. (1930). Increasing Returns and the Representative Firm. *Economic Journal, 40,* 79–116.

Tahir, P. (2019a). *Making Sense of Joan Robinson on China.* Palgrave Macmillan.

Tahir, P. (2019b). Joan Robinson (1903–83). In D. Simon (Ed.), *Key Thinkers on Development* (pp. 351–356). Routledge.

Tahir, P., Harcourt, G. C., & Kerr, P. (2002). On Joan Robinson and China. In P. Kerrand & G. C. Harcourt (Eds.), *Joan Robinson. Critical Assessments of Leading Economists* (Vol. 5). Routledge.

The British Crown and the Indian States. (1929). An Outline Sketch Drawn Up on Behalf of the Standing Committee of the Chamber of Princes by the Directorate of the Chamber's Special Organisation. P.S. King and Son. Reprinted in India as Chamber of Princes (1988, 2013) *British Crown and the Indian States.* Gyan Publishing House.

The Economist. (1949). 156, 95.

'The Indian States Inquiry'. (1929) *Asiatic Review, 25,* 295–297.

The Times. (1958, September 3). Economic Advice to Ceylon: Nationalization not Advised. 9.

Thomer, D. (1966). Marx on India and the Asiatic Mode of Production. *Contributions to Indian Sociology, 9,* 33–66.

Thompson, E., & Garratt, G. T. (1934). *Rise and Fulfilment of British Rule in India.* Macmillan.

Timberg, T. A. (1978). *The Marwaris: From Traders to Industrialists.* Vikas.

Tinbergen, J. (1984). Development Cooperation as a Learning Process. In *Meier and Seers (1984).*

Timmalachar, B. (1929). Fiscal Relations between the Indian States and the Government of India. *Indian Journal of Economics, 9,* 413–440.

Tiwari, R. D. (1940). *Railway Rates Policy.* New Book Company.

Toye, J. (1981). *Public Expenditure and Indian Development Policy 1960–1970.* Cambridge University Press.

Toye, J. (1983). The Disparaging of Development Economics. *Journal of Development Studies, 20,* 87–107.

Toye, J. (1984). *A Defence of Development Economics.* University College.

Toye, J. (1987). *Dilemmas of Development: Reflections on the Counter-revolution in Development Theory and Policy.* Basil Blackwell.

Turner, M. S. (1989). *Joan Robinson and the Americans.* M.E. Sharpe.

Visvesvaraya, M. (1934). *Planned Economy for India.* Banglore Press.

Wadia, P. A., & Joshi, G. N. (1925). *The Wealth of India.* Macmillan.

Warren, B. (1980). *Imperialism: Pioneer of Capitalism.* Verso.

Watson, A. G. D. (1932). Review of Robinson (1932a). *Cambridge Review, 54,* 107–108.

Watts, M. E. (1930). Travancore-III: Economic Conditions, Trade and Commerce. *Asiatic Review, 26,* 725–740.

Willett, T. D. (1968). A Defence of Adam Smith's Deer and Beaver Model. *Journal of Economic Studies, 3,* 29–32.

Wuyts, M. (1981). The Mechanization of Present-day Mozambican Agriculture. *Development and Change, 12,* 1–27.

Young, A. A. (1928). Increasing Returns and Economic Progress. *Economic Journal, 38,* 527–542.

World Bank. (1987). *World Development Report 1987.*

Index[1]

---

[1] Note: Page numbers followed by 'n' refer to notes.

© The Author(s), under exclusive license to Springer Nature   261
Switzerland AG 2022
P. Tahir, *Joan Robinson in Princely India*, Palgrave Studies in the
History of Economic Thought,
https://doi.org/10.1007/978-3-031-10905-8

—

Printed by Printforce, United Kingdom